1996

SUBSTANCE MISUSE
IN ADOLESCENCE

ADVANCES IN ADOLESCENT DEVELOPMENT

AN ANNUAL BOOK SERIES

Series Editors:

Gerald R. Adams, *University of Guelph, Ontario, Canada*
Raymond Montemayor, *Ohio State University*
Thomas P. Gullotta, *Child and Family Agency, Connecticut*

Advances in Adolescent Development is an annual book series designed to analyze, integrate, and critique an abundance of new research and literature in the field of adolescent development. Contributors are selected from numerous disciplines based on their creative, analytic, and influential scholarship in order to provide information pertinent to professionals as well as upper-division and graduate students. The Series Editors' goals are to evaluate the current empirical and theoretical knowledge about adolescence, and to encourage the formulation (or expansion) of new directions in research and theory development.

Volumes in This Series

SUBSTANCE MISUSE
IN ADOLESCENCE

Edited by
THOMAS P. GULLOTTA
GERALD R. ADAMS
RAYMOND MONTEMAYOR

ADVANCES IN ADOLESCENT DEVELOPMENT
An Annual Book Series   Volume 7

SAGE PUBLICATIONS
International Educational and Professional Publisher
Thousand Oaks   London   New Delhi

For information address:

SAGE Publications, Inc.
2455 Teller Road
Thousand Oaks, California 91320

SAGE Publications Ltd.
6 Bonhill Street
London EC2A 4PU
United Kingdom

SAGE Publications India Pvt. Ltd.
M-32 Market
Greater Kailash I
New Delhi 110 048 India

Printed in the United States of America

Library of Congress: 90-657291

ISSN 1050-8589
ISBN 0-8039-5878-1 (cl.)
ISBN 0-8039-5879-X (pbk.)

94 95 96 97 98 10 9 8 7 6 5 4 3 2 1

Sage Production Editor: Diane S. Foster

Contents

Preface

Why title the seventh volume in this series *Substance Misuse in Adolescence?* The explanation for the choice of verb can be found in its meaning. *Misuse* has a definitional richness that *abuse* lacks. It can be understood to mean incorrect use in one context, use for a bad purpose in another, and abuse in yet a third context. We hope that after reading this volume the reader will agree with us that the richness of the verb is also found in the 11 chapters of this book.

We have attempted to provide the reader, regardless of whether that individual is a researcher, graduate student, or practitioner, with a comprehensive overview of the field as it currently exists. To accomplish this, we have constructed this volume in a way so as to lead the reader along a path of interrelated knowledge. Realizing that many edited volumes suffer from a conceptual disjointedness, we hope readers will find common threads winding through this volume that connect chapter material. This is not to say that the talented scholars the lead editor has had the opportunity to work with on this project for the past 2 years are in agreement. That often is not the case. Rather, their different worldviews add depth and meaning to material in which popular beliefs too often have concealed historical, clinical, and research evidence.

Thus, in Chapter 1, the reader is introduced to the social history of several selected substances. In Chapters 2 and 3, individual factors family variables contributing to substance misuse, and more importantly the resiliency factors that enable individuals to avoid substance misuse, are examined. Community and peer factors are investigated in Chapter 4.

From these building blocks, the volume examines in Chapters 5 and 6 adolescent substance misuse in urban and rural settings. The pharmacologic effects of selected substances are discussed in Chapter 7, and Chapter 8 explores the current approaches used to treat substance-misusing youth.

Now for the final three chapters. The current effectiveness of prevention efforts is discussed in Chapter 9; drug legalization is examined in Chapter 10; and in Chapter 11 the lead editor shares with readers the personal themes that emerged for him as this book came to fruition.

Together, these chapters urge readers to pay greater attention to the multiple harms we inflict on each other at every micro and macro psycho-socio-economic level. To illustrate, consider that the United States currently is engaged in a debate regarding the availability of national health care. Access to mental health care services, including treatment for the misuse of substances like alcohol, is part of that heated debate. The Clinton administration has already shown a willingness to compromise some mental health benefits to gain support for this badly needed legislation. To gain additional support, the Clinton administration has also retreated from earlier positions that would have significantly increased taxes on cigarettes and beer that would have been used to help pay for coverage for the uninsured. This decision not to increase taxes significantly on tobacco and beer not only will mean shifting the tax burden to other revenue centers (first harm) but unintentionally supports the continued use of these substances at higher levels than would have existed otherwise (second harm).

Now, consider these conflicting messages. Health care should be extended to presently uninsured individuals—a position the lead editor of this volume agrees with fully. Harmful substances that cost the United States' economy billions of dollars yearly should not be excessively taxed—a position the lead editor understands as politically necessary to gain needed support for health care reform but has the luxury as a bystander to disagree with strongly nevertheless. Health care for tobacco-related illnesses (cancer, respiratory diseases, etc.) will be more fully covered than diseases related to alcohol and other substances. This is because tobacco users can more easily conceal their cancer and respiratory afflictions with non-tobacco-using groups than can alcohol users whose use of detoxification and counseling services cast them with those unmentionables labeled the mentally ill (third harm).

The implications of these conflicting messages are enough to make an editor who has long worked with youth want to retire to Bedlam. In the face of these conflicting messages, zero tolerance approaches to youthful substance use are destined to fail (fourth harm). We hope that this volume will add to the understanding of adolescent behavior that is needed to enable approaches to be designed that will reduce the incidence of substance misuse in all the richness of meaning that verb possesses.

—THOMAS P. GULLOTTA
Child and Family Agency
of Southeastern Connecticut
New London, Connecticut

1. A Select Social History of the Psychoactive Drugs: Tobacco, Alcohol, Marijuana, Cocaine, and Heroin

Thomas P. Gullotta
Child and Family Agency

Gary M. Blau
Connecticut Department of Children and Families

To appreciate the struggle under way to reduce the misuse of substances among the general population and, in particular, youth, it is important to have an understanding of the origin of the issue. This chapter examines five substances that have excited varying degrees of consternation in medical and wider communities. Interestingly, two of the substances, nicotine and alcohol, are legally available despite evidence clearly detailing the negative physical consequences these substances have on the human body (Burnham, 1993; Trad, Chapter 7, this volume). Length of use in the United States, cash crop importance, and the sheer number of users help to explain the continued legality of these two harmful substances. The remaining three substances are illegal for historical reasons that include social, ethnic, and racial prejudice against immigrant or minority groups.

TOBACCO

Consider the following:

- The origins of the scientific name for tobacco, *nicotiana*, can be traced to Jean Nicot who first described the medicinal properties of the substance in 1559 (Schivelbusch, 1992).
- In the mid-1600s, two papal bulls prohibited the use of tobacco by the clergy under penalty of expulsion from the church. This ban remained in effect for roughly 100 years (Austin, 1979).

- In Russia tobacco was called "the devil's plant" in the 1600s (Austin, 1979, p. 21).
- It was the Jesuits who introduced snuff (Austin, 1979).

Tobacco (*Nicotiana tabacum*), with cocaine, was one of several "gifts" from the New World to Europe. Like every other substance described in this chapter, tobacco at one time was believed to have medicinal uses. Its principal active ingredient, nicotine, is pharmacologically related to the belladonna alkaloids (Grinspoon & Bakalar, 1979). As such, it is a nerve toxin dulling rather than stimulating the nervous system (Schivelbusch, 1992). In England from 1573 to 1625, for example, tobacco was believed to be a helpful treatment for heart pains, snake bites, fever, exhaustion, and the Black Death. It was popularized in that country by Sir Walter Raleigh for recreational use and—despite the attempts of King James I to discourage its popularity through taxation—by 1575 tobacco was quite literally worth its weight in silver (Austin, 1979).

In the American Colonies tobacco was embraced by Virginia, which used it as currency until the early 1700s, and rejected by the Puritan Massachusetts Bay Colony, which prohibited smoking in 1632. As a cash crop in colonial times, its value necessitated a 1632 Virginia law requiring, "gunsmiths, carpenters, joiners, brickmakers, and other craftsmen" to remain in their occupations (Lee & Lee, 1987, cited in Rogalski, 1993, p. 6). The salaries of clergy and the fines of those who would bear children without benefit of marriage were paid for in pounds of tobacco (Boorstin, 1958). During the 1700s tobacco played an important role in the war the colonies waged against England. Trading tobacco with the French provided badly needed revenue to finance the American revolution (Austin, 1979).

The first modern efforts to limit tobacco usage coincided with the fledgling temperance movement. The linking of tobacco and alcohol achieved temporary success at the turn of the 20th century when 14 states prohibited cigarettes. With the introduction of the first "mild" cigarette (Camels), this movement faltered and failed by the end of the 1920s. As an interesting side note, cigarettes were not developed in the United States. Rather, American travelers in the 1850s returning home from England introduced the cigarette to America. By 1885, cigarette production in the United States had reached one billion cigarettes a year. It grew rapidly to more than 80 billion by the 1920s and to almost 400 billion by 1949. The first serious medical evidence of the harmful effects of cigarette smoking and lung disease appeared in 1939. A quarter of a century later the 1964 Surgeon General's Report established that relationship permanently. Even so, the tobacco industry that same year was able to gain the support of the American Newspapers Publishers Association and the National Association of Broadcasters in opposing warnings in tobacco advertising. Currently an estimated 51 million Americans continue to use tobacco products (Austin, 1979; Burnham, 1993; Schivelbusch, 1992; Slade, 1989).

ALCOHOL

A stroll through recorded history would reveal:

- Prior to the 17th century, beer and wine consumption in Europe was commonplace. Even children consumed, on average, three liters of beer a day (Schivelbusch, 1992).
- During the 13th century, the process of distillation became known in Europe. Distilled beverages were treated as medicines called "aqua vitae," meaning water of life (Austin, 1979).
- By the 1500s aqua vitae in Elizabethan England was associated with growing criminal activity (Schivelbusch, 1992).
- In the mid-1600s gin was developed in Holland by distilling grain with juniper berries (Austin, 1979).

Since the beginning of time, humans have consumed beverages made by fermenting grains or the juices of vine-ripened fruits. The "healthy," portly appearance of Western Europeans, often associated with engravings from the time of Charles Dickens's England and before, can be attributed to the heavy consumption of beer and wine by the populace. Beer, in particular, found its way into nearly every meal as either a beverage or ingredient added liberally to soups and porridge (Schivelbusch, 1992). It should be understood that this pattern of consumption not only provided food in the form of carbohydrates and calories to an often impoverished diet but also afforded a much safer beverage to consume than the septic water of the day. Indeed, at the time of the U.S. Civil War beer was often referred to as "liquid bread" (Burnham, 1993).

Accompanying this behavior, however, were warnings that over-indulgence might have disastrous effects. No clearer example of this tension to restrict but not prohibit use can be found than in the laws of the Massachusetts Bay Colony, which sought to control drunken behavior but required inns to provide beer for guests (Austin, 1979). Indeed, the records of the Mayflower passengers reported that provisions upon landing in the new colony were nearly exhausted, "especially our beer" (Rogalski, 1993, p. 6). This was a fact that the Massachusetts Bay Colony's Governor William Bradford found quite distressing.

In America the earliest prohibition efforts occurred in Georgia in the mid-1700s. This first effort to control alcohol failed within 10 years of its passage. It would not be until the end of the 18th century that the American temperance movement would again begin to take root. Congressional attempts at the taxation of distilled spirits resulting in the Whiskey Rebellion in 1794 aside, by the mid-1850s the temperance movement had begun to drift away from voluntary abstinence to prohibiting consumption through legislative efforts. Gaining strength as America's Protestants reacted worriedly to new immigrant waves flooding coastline cities with foreign-speaking Europeans, the temperance movement succeeded in 1919 in enacting the 18th Amendment, prohibiting the sale of alcohol. Interestingly, possession of alcohol for personal use was still allowed. By 1932, the "nobel" experiment, ignored by many and the source of income for a newly organized criminal element, was judged a failure.

But was it really a failure? Burnham (1993), in his book *Bad Habits*, suggests that prohibition was not a failure. Saloons were closed and medical illnesses related to excessive alcoholic intake dropped significantly. Furthermore, per capita consumption of gallons of ethanol declined from two gallons in 1920 to less than one gallon per person by 1933. Often ignored is the fact that alcohol usage remained below two gallons per person for more than a decade after the repeal of prohibition (Burnham, 1993; Institute for Health Policy, 1993). What, then, explains the perception that prohibition failed? Burnham argues that a coalition of brewers and publishers actively worked to overturn the 18th Amendment. The loss of income to these individuals provided the necessary motivation to create the myth that prohibition was unsuccessful. Repeal occurred in 1933 (Adams, Gullotta, & Markstrom-Adams, 1994).

Until recently, attitudes toward alcohol have been relatively benign. It was the subject for comedy rather than condemnation throughout most of society from the 1930s through the 1960s. Those generations were able to ignore medical evidence that linked alcohol abuse to a number of debilitating illnesses. Americans in the 1970s and since have not been able to ignore as easily new temperance groups such as Mothers Against Drunk Driving (MADD). This newest movement, emerging from the heartache of the loss of a loved one at the hands of an intoxicated individual, has focused new and critical attention on this substance once again.

MARIJUANA

From George Washington to Reefer Madness, were you aware that:

- In 1991, 13% of the nation's young adults between the ages of 18 and 25 admitted using marijuana within the past month (U.S. Bureau of the Census, 1992, p. 127).
- Marijuana use (defined as use within the past month) among youth between the ages of 12 and 17 has declined from 12% in 1974 to 4.3% in 1991 (U.S. Bureau of the Census, 1992, p. 127).
- In 1977 President Carter stated that, although "we can and should discourage the use of marijuana . . . [I support] legislation amending Federal law to eliminate all Federal criminal penalties for the possession of up to one ounce of marijuana" ("President Carter's Address," 1977, p. 6).

The history of marijuana (*Cannabis sativa*) in North America is a curious one involving a king, an American president, ethnic prejudice, and the Great Depression. To start at the beginning, the earliest English settlements in America raised marijuana (then called "hemp") as a cash crop. The hemp plant was extremely useful. Its fibers could be turned into sails, linens, blankets, clothing, flags, and most important of all, rope. Its seeds could be used as feed or pressed for oil used to make paint. So important was this commodity to England that King James I ordered the settlers of Virginia to produce hemp for the mother country (Austin, 1979; Drug Enforcement Administration [DEA], n.d.; Grinspoon, 1971; Grinspoon & Bakalar, 1993; Sloman, 1979).

Production of marijuana continued after the revolution of 1776 without concern for its intoxicating qualities. In fact, George Washington cultivated the plant. Like many other gentlemen of the day, he raised hemp to be sold for making cloth and rope. At the time of the Civil War, the growing of marijuana as a cash crop declined. Other parts of the world, notably Russia and the Philippines, produced a superior product to what could be grown in North America.

Like many presently illegal substances, marijuana was used during the 1800s and up to the 1930s for medicinal purposes. It never captured the support other drugs were able to attract, however. The lack of medical enthusiasm for marijuana was due to the variable quality of the psychoactive substance THC (tetrahydrocannabinol), found in the plant.

Recent social histories of marijuana suggest that the events that moved marijuana from being considered a relatively harmless plant that Margaret Mead once described as "less toxic than tobacco and milder than liquor," to the status of "killer weed" began with the Great Depression (Schivelbusch, 1992, p. 225). Prior to that time the substance was, relatively speaking, ignored. For example, it was not regulated by the Harrison Narcotics Act of 1914. Indeed, in 1920 the U.S. Department of Agriculture published a booklet encouraging its production as a cash crop. The circumstances surrounding marijuana's decline from relative obscurity to infamy involve the migration of Mexicans into the United States during the Great Depression and the scarcity of work. It appears that in the late 1920s and early 1930s the largest group of users of marijuana for recreational purposes was Mexican Americans. Ethnic prejudices against this immigrant group in Texas and nearby states, fueled by the high unemployment of the Great Depression, evidently encouraged federal authorities to label marijuana a narcotic in 1937 (Austin, 1979; Grinspoon, 1971; Morgan, 1981; Musto, 1991; Sloman, 1979).

Since that episode marijuana has been understood at various times in North American society to offer one moment of bliss and a lifetime of regret or to provide a mildly intoxicating, sensory altering view of the cosmos. Some have suggested the substance possesses no legitimate medicinal uses. Others, including President Clinton's Surgeon General Joycelyn Elders, believe marijuana (more accurately the active ingredient in marijuana, THC) does have medicinal value—in the reduction of side effects in the treatment of cancer, for example (Grinspoon & Bakalar, 1993; Treaster, 1993). In recent decades, most notably just prior to and during the Carter presidency, unsuccessful attempts were made to legalize marijuana usage in the United States. These efforts to loosen tight regulatory control of the drug continue with the objective of enabling physicians to prescribe the substance for those suffering from cancer, AIDS, and other diseases.

COCAINE

A gift from the New World, were you aware that:

- In 1991, 2% of the nation's young adults between the ages of 18 and 25 admitted using cocaine within the past month (U.S. Bureau of the Census, 1992, p. 127).
- Cocaine use among youth between the ages of 12 and 17 declined from 6.5% in 1982 to 2.4% in 1991 (U.S. Bureau of the Census, 1992, p. 127).
- Notables such as Ulysses Grant and Thomas Edison were, perhaps unknowingly, consumers of products containing coca (Grinspoon & Bakalar, 1976).

Since cocaine's reappearance in the 1960s, a day does not pass in which cocaine or one of its derivatives is not linked with some crime or associated with the decline and fall of a professional athlete, actor, or rock musician. For this generation, cocaine has replaced heroin as the drug of enslavement. It has acquired notoriety as the cash drug for crime syndicates, the drug for temporary personal pleasure and unimaginable individual psychological craving. Of all the substances described in this chapter, cocaine has a history that is particularly interesting, for it involves the New World, a soft-drink company, the father of the psychoanalytic movement, and the greatest literary detective of all time.

Cocaine is found in the leaves of a South American plant, the coca shrub (*Erythroxlon coca*). Possessing religious significance for the Incas, coca was controlled directly by the Incan emperor, and its use was limited to the privileged nobility of that society. This practice ceased with the arrival of the Spanish Conquistadors and their conquest of the native population. Enslaving the local people, the Conquistadors discovered that (slave) work productivity rose and slave food rations could be reduced by freely distributing and encouraging the chewing of coca leaves (Inglis, 1975).

Coca did not become popular in Europe until the mid-1850s, when it was introduced into a number of products ranging from patent medicines to wine. The wine, in particular a product called Vin Mariani's Wine, won a number of endorsements, including one from Pope Leo XIII who in awarding it a gold medal described the beverage as a "benefactor of humanity." The popularity of coca spread back to North America, where an Atlanta druggist, John Syth Pemberton, in 1886 introduced a patent medicine based on coca and caffeine whose slogan, "the pause that refreshes," would eventually carry multiple meanings for drinkers of Coca-Cola (Austin, 1979; Grinspoon & Bakalar, 1976).

Cocaine, the "kick" in coca, was chemically isolated in Germany, where it was used as a stimulant and as an anesthetic in eye surgery. The medical popularity of cocaine as an anesthetic, a reliever of depression, and a substitute for morphine in treating morphine addiction spread quickly. This miracle drug attracted the attention of one ambitious young physician, Sigmund Freud, who described it as a "magical drug" and prescribed it for himself, friends, and family (Brecher, 1972).

Not only Freud but other notables of the time used the substance. For example, the writer Robert Louis Stevenson was reported to have written *The Strange Case of Dr. Jekyll and Mr. Hyde* under the influence of cocaine. Family members reported that Stevenson, then a sickly weak man, wrote the first draft of this manuscript in three sleepless days and then destroyed it. He then rewrote the story in another three sleepless days. The motivation for this tale of a physician who, through a powerful elixir, struggled unsuccessfully with his drug-transformed alter ego aptly describes the psychological torment others experience today.

The same might be said for another fictional literary figure who, while leading a productive life, nevertheless remained remote, aloof, and strangely removed from his surroundings. That fictional character was Sherlock Holmes, who in *The Sign of Four* concludes the story with the following conversation with Dr. Watson:

> "The division seems rather unfair," [Watson] remarked. "You have done all the work in this business. I get a wife out of it, Jones gets the credit, pray what remains for you?"
>
> "For me," said Sherlock Holmes, "there still remains the cocaine-bottle." And he stretched his long white hand up for it. (Doyle, 1930, p. 158)

Indeed, during the late 1800s, when the drug was still at the height of its popularity, the Parke-Davis Company, McKesson & Robbins Pharmaceuticals, and other companies marketed a variety of cocaine-based products ranging from pocket cocaine cases to coca cigarettes (Morgan, 1981; Musto, 1991). Interest in cocaine began to wane at the turn of the century when growing reports of its psychologically addictive qualities emerged. Indeed, Freud's support of the substance ceased with the emotional breakdown of a close friend, Dr. Ernst von Fleischl-Marxow. Fleischl-Marxow was addicted to morphine, and Freud had prescribed cocaine as a replacement drug for him only to watch him descend into a deeper personal drug-driven hell. This incident had a profound effect on Freud, who forswore the personal use of cocaine and other drugs from that time forward (Grinspoon & Bakalar, 1976; Petersen, 1977).

The movement to prohibit the availability of cocaine in the United States grew between 1910 and the First World War. Given the present concern over this substance, it is an interesting historical side note that President William Howard Taft reported to Congress in 1910, "that cocaine was the most serious drug problem America had ever faced" (Musto, 1991, p. 45). The origins of this movement to reduce access to cocaine, like the one for marijuana, can be traced in part to racial and ethnic issues—in this instance, reports that black men under the influence of cocaine were committing violent crimes, particularly rape. We suspect that at a time in American history when violent behavior against blacks was not uncommon, fear of drug-induced black reprisals hastened the decision to restrict the usage of cocaine. By 1932 the sale of the substance was prohibited (Austin, 1979; Morgan, 1981).

HEROIN

From classic black and white television shows like *The Naked City* to films like *The French Connection*, heroin's white powder brings a special meaning to these facts:

- During the 1700s and 1800s white middle-class Americans consumed opium by mixing it with alcohol. The resulting mixture was called laudanum, a drug readily available from the corner drugstore and used by none other than Benjamin Franklin (Adams et al., 1994; Musto, 1991).

- The cause of the Chinese Opium Wars was the Chinese Emperor's refusal to continue to permit the English to sell opium to the Chinese populace (Schivelbusch, 1992).
- Opiate users included such literary figures as Byron, Shelley, Coleridge, Dickens, Poe, and De Quincey (Austin, 1979; Schivelbusch, 1992).

The opium poppy (*Papaver somniferum*) grows throughout much of the world. Its use as a medicine to ease pain and to treat dysentery, malaria, and other illnesses predates the birth of Christ. Perceived to be a helpful medicinal substance, it was readily combined with a number of products and in the case of laudanum was priced below the cost of beer, opening a huge market to the poor. In China, the British fought two separate wars in the 19th century to maintain access to that nation's people in order to market "Chinese whiskey." Their victory ensured that China would enter the 20th century with an enormous drug addiction problem. The subject of this section, heroin, was first synthesized from morphine, which is derived from opium, in 1874. Commercial production of the drug began in 1898 by the German company Bayer as a pain remedy (Austin, 1979; DEA, n.d.; Schivelbusch, 1992).

Concern for the potential to abuse these substances grew gradually with the isolation of the alkaloidal extract morphine (1803), the development of the hypodermic needle, which permitted morphine to be injected (1853), and later the development of heroin (1874). Ironically, the development of morphine was heralded as a nonaddictive alternative to opium, and heroin was similarly heralded as a nonaddictive alternative to morphine. In the United States the use of morphine during the Civil War as a surgical pain killer and its later abuse by war veterans led some to observe that morphine had become the "army disease." Despite this observation, the two decades following the Civil War saw the proliferation of patent medicines containing opium-based products. Among these was one popular product of the day labeled "Mrs. Winslow's Soothing Syrup." Liberally laced with laudanum, it was advertised as having a most calming effect on children. With dutiful parents spooning a daily prescribed dose down the throats of their ever-cooperative children, little wonder that today's youth are seen as rambunctious in comparison (Adams et al., 1994; Austin, 1979; Schivelbusch, 1992).

The availability of all three drugs in the United States was not limited until the Harrison Narcotics Act of 1914. Even so, 2 years later the U.S. Supreme Court still upheld the right of a physician to continue to prescribe opiates to an addict. It was not until 1919 that the act was strengthened and the Court in another decision later that year denied physicians the right to prescribe narcotics to addicts. In 1924 the importation to and manufacture of heroin in the United States was prohibited (Austin, 1979; DEA, n.d.).

CONCLUSION

Although the desire to alter states of consciousness is not uniquely human, human beings are unique in their attempt to develop, consume, and regulate the chemical and organic substances known as drugs. Current estimates indicate that nearly every American has used a "mind altering" substance. How many of you reading this chapter have not smoked a cigarette, enjoyed a glass of wine, or wandered bleary-eyed into the kitchen for a cup of either coffee or hot chocolate? Over the years, attitudes regarding substances have changed. What is commonplace and legal at one point in time is unacceptable and illegal at another. In reality, the legality of substance use is based largely on sociopolitical standards. The historical information indicates that no relationship can be established between the harmfulness of a substance and its legality. If harmfulness were the criterion for illegality, then cigarettes and alcohol would obviously be taboo (see Trad, Chapter 7, this volume).

Clearly there are other factors that influence the legality of substance use. One factor, from our perspective, is that locally produced and therefore "cash crop" substances have been favored for legalization over imported substances. The federal government has supported tobacco growers in the United States; this same government has assisted in sending troops to South America to spray the defoliant paraquat on marijuana fields or assisted in the raiding of suspected illegal drug factories. From a historical perspective, it is cynically amusing to observe that the United States and other Western nations are today fighting their own version of the Chinese Opium Wars against third-world nations in an attempt to keep profitable illicit drugs from apparently all-too-willing Western consumers. This last point, in particular, may help to explain why substances having an ethnic or minority following are much more likely to be targeted for restriction. We offer as further evidence for this hypothesis the number of African American and Hispanic males who are currently incarcerated for drug offenses.

It is an arguable point to conclude that previous attempts to control substance use have proven to be less than successful. Imposing drug restrictions on the population has resulted in the growth of a highly successful and profitable underground economy and has not significantly decreased the problems of substance abuse. In fact, despite an estimated $35 billion dollars spent between 1986 and 1991 on the War on Drugs, there has been only a slight reduction in the recreational use of drugs, a modest increase in conservatism toward drugs, and no reduction in drug-related crimes (Duncan, 1992). In turn, billions of dollars are funneled out of the economy to support nefarious criminals and encourage the gang warfare that currently plagues America's central cities.

Duncan (1992) suggests numerous reasons why current approaches have failed to minimize the impact of drug and alcohol abuse. First, because the majority of human beings have historically sought altered states of consciousness, the emphasis on abstinence is too weak an argument to deter most users. In addition, drug use is a personal health decision, and law enforcement strategies—which have been the primary tool to combat drug use—are virtually impossible to enforce on a national level. Furthermore, with prevention and treatment programs inadequately funded, the most at-risk members of the population receive a "double whammy." The first whammy comes from the personal consequences of untreated drug use (e.g., medical and psychological problems, along with lost economic life opportunities). The second whammy comes from any legal difficulties that drug use might create. Minority and poor populations incur the greatest impact of the legal system, a direct consequence of current law enforcement strategies.

This is not to say that all drugs should be legal or that there should be no consequences or penalties for substance involvement. Current laws are inconsistently applied, however, and current public policy does not differentiate between what constitutes responsible substance use and what constitutes irresponsible substance use (instead of the War on Drugs, it should be the "war on which drugs").

We suggest that what is needed is a more reasoned approach to reducing the impact of drugs on our society. We must address the artificial dichotomy (legal vs. illegal) that remains inconsistent and continues to be based on a sociopolitical history of oppression and insensitivity. We must identify and ameliorate contributing variables (e.g., peer, family, community) that increase the probability of substance involvement. And we must take a pragmatic approach to prevention and the minimization of drug use by U.S. citizens, especially our youth.

Finally, we are reminded of the old Broadway hit tune from *Bye Bye Birdie*, "Kids." As that tune speculated, how might we understand what has gone wrong with today's youth? In many cases, today's adolescents are literally and figuratively foreigners to the communities in which they live. Their rap music, hip-hop dress, bilingual ability, and street values appear as strange to us as our hippie antics appeared to an earlier generation of parents. What is unfamiliar is often perceived as threatening. Thus their use of substances either unknown to our generation or familiar to the bell-bottom wearers of the past is worrisome. From this worry, we urge readers to let motivation generate knowledge that can be used to design meaningful interventions to minimize drug use among youth and to enfranchise them. Let not that anxiety be used to sentence these youth to marginal roles in society. For as surely as we condemn them, so too do we condemn this nation in 50 years to an unprecedented violent upheaval.

REFERENCES

Adams, G. R., Gullotta, T. P., & Markstrom-Adams, C. (1994). *Adolescent life experiences* (3rd ed.). Pacific Grove, CA: Brooks/Cole.

Austin, G. (1979). *Research issues 24: Perspectives on the history of psychoactive substance abuse*. Washington, DC: National Institute on Drug Abuse.

Boorstin, D. J. (1958). *The Americans: The colonial experience.* New York: Random House.

Brecher, E. (1972). *Licit and illicit drugs.* Boston: Little, Brown.

Burnham, J. C. (1993). *Bad habits.* New York: New York University Press.

Doyle, A. C. (1930). *The complete Sherlock Holmes.* Garden City, NY: Doubleday.

Drug Enforcement Administration. (n.d.). *Drugs of abuse.* Washington, DC: Department of Justice.

Duncan, D. F. (1992). Drug abuse prevention in postlegalization America: What could it be like? *Journal of Primary Prevention, 12,* 317-322.

Grinspoon, L. (1971). *Marijuana reconsidered.* Cambridge, MA: Harvard University Press.

Grinspoon, L., & Bakalar, J. B. (1976). *Cocaine: A drug and its social evolution.* New York: Basic Books.

Grinspoon, L., & Bakalar, J. B. (1979). *Psychedelic drugs reconsidered*. New York: Basic Books.

Grinspoon, L., & Bakalar, J. B. (1993). *Marihuana: The forbidden medicine*. New Haven, CT: Yale University Press.

Inglis, B. (1975). *The forbidden game: A social history of drugs*. New York: Scribner.

Institute for Health Policy. (1993). *Substance abuse: The nation's number one health problem*. Waltham, MA: Brandeis University.

Lee, H. G., & Lee, A. E. (1987). *Virginia wine country*. White Hall, VA: Betterway Publications.

Morgan, W. H. (1981). *Drugs in America: A social history, 1800-1980*. Syracuse, NY: Syracuse University Press.

Musto, D. (1991). Opium, cocaine, and marijuana in American history. *Scientific American, 236*, 40-47.

Petersen, R. C. (1977). History of cocaine. In R. C. Petersen & R. C. Stillman (Eds.), *Research 13: Cocaine* (pp. 17-35). Washington, DC: National Institute on Drug Abuse.

President Carter's address to the U.S. Congress on drug use. (1977, September-October). *Drug Survival News*, p. 6.

Rogalski, C. J. (1993). The political process and its relationship to the psychotherapy of substance misusers: A historical perspective. *The International Journal of the Addictions, 28*, 1-46.

Schivelbusch, W. (1992). *Tastes of paradise: A social history of spices, stimulants, and intoxicants*. New York: Vintage.

Slade, J. (1989). The tobacco epidemic: Lessons from history. *Journal of Psychoactive Drugs, 21*, 281-291.

Sloman, L. (1979). *The history of marijuana in America: Reefer madness*. Indianapolis: Bobbs-Merrill.

Treaster, J. B. (1993, November 14). Healing herb or narcotic? Marijuana as medication. *The New York Times*, pp. 37, 44.

U.S. Bureau of the Census. (1992). Statistical abstract of the United States (112th ed.). Washington, DC: Government Printing Office.

2. Personal Factors Related to Substance Misuse: Risk Abatement and/or Resiliency Enhancement?

Elaine Norman
Fordham University

Given the limitations of present resources, a debate seems to be forming in the area of adolescent substance-abuse prevention about whether or not public policy and service interventions should target risk factors or resiliency factors. The former attempts to prevent alcohol and other drug abuse by eliminating, reducing, or mitigating those factors that have been shown to be associated with, or to be precursors of, that abuse (Hawkins, Catalano, & Miller, 1992). The latter would attempt to prevent substance abuse by enhancing factors that protect against vulnerability and "enable sustained competent functioning" even in the presence of major life stressors (Masten, Best, & Garmezy, 1990).

Risk factor interventions try to stem the tide of negative stressors in a youngster's life. Resiliency factor interventions focus on strengthening the remarkable capacity of individuals to withstand considerable hardship, to bounce back in the face of great adversity, and to go on to live relatively normal lives.

A great deal of research has accumulated with regard to risk factors; this chapter will summarize the major findings. Much present-day adolescent prevention programming is based on that risk research. Several streams of scholarship have recently met to form a new focus on resiliency. The major part of this chapter will attempt to summarize the resiliency research literature. Few adolescent prevention programs that integrate resiliency findings have as yet been developed. It is hoped that will be the work of the near future.

Whether we are talking about risk or resiliency, it is crucial to explore at least three integrated systems: (a) the characteristics of

AUTHOR'S NOTE: The work for this chapter was supported by a contract from the New York State Office of Alcohol and Substance Abuse Services.

the individual adolescent associated with greater risk or greater resiliency; (b) the family interaction system in which that adolescent is absorbed; and (c) the school and community milieu in which the youngster is embedded. This chapter will deal only with the first. Other chapters in this book have the task of exploring the others.

PERSONAL ATTRIBUTES RELATED TO RISK

Past research has been most fruitful in delineating risk factors related to family interaction patterns, but a short list of characteristics of individuals that are predictive of subsequent alcohol or other drug-taking behavior can be developed.

Physiological, and possibly genetically based, factors lead the list. Possessing a difficult childhood temperament with irritable, anxious mood states; temper tantrums; and social withdrawal is predictive of substance use in adolescence (Brook, Brook, Whiteman, & Cohen, 1990; Shedler & Block, 1990). Continuing behavior problems, most usually hyperactive, aggressive, and seemingly rebellious activity that reflects poor impulse control; an inability to delay gratification; sensation seeking; and low harm avoidance are predictive as well (Block, Block, & Keyes, 1988; Cloninger, Sigvardsson, & Bohman, 1988; Penning & Barnes, 1982; Shedler & Block, 1990). Other antisocial behavior not necessarily physiologically based, such as theft and chronic fighting in childhood (Kandel, Simcha-Fagan, & Davis, 1986), add to the list.

Psychological factors such as childhood distress, often manifested as depression, may signal later substance misuse (Brook et al., 1990; Shedler & Block, 1990). School failure (Jessor, 1976; Jessor & Jessor, 1977; Kandel, Kessler, & Margulies, 1978), lack of attachment to school, and a low degree of commitment to education in general (Fleming, Kellam, & Brown, 1982; Penning & Barnes, 1982) also increase the risk of adolescent substance use.

Choosing to associate with drug-using peers and having attitudes favorable to use are additional risk factors for any adolescent (Brook et al., 1990; Kandel et al., 1986). Finally, alienation from, nonacceptance of, or outright rejection of the dominant values of the society have been shown to be associated with greater risk of alcohol and other drug-use problems (Jessor & Jessor, 1977; Penning & Barnes, 1982).

TABLE 2.1   Personal Attributes Related to Risk for Substance Misuse

Risk Factor	Study
Difficult childhood temperament	
negative mood states	
temper tantrums	Brook et al., 1990
irritability	
withdrawal	
Childhood emotional distress	
depression	Shedler & Block, 1990
high anxiety	
Behavior problems	
hyperactivity	
aggression and rebellion	Block et al., 1988
poor impulse control	Cloninger et al., 1988
sensation seeking	Penning & Barnes, 1982
low harm avoidance	Shedler & Block, 1990
inability to delay gratification	
Antisocial behavior	
theft	Kandel et al., 1986
chronic fighting	
School failure	Jessor, 1976; Jessor & Jessor, 1977; Kandel et al., 1978
Lack of attachment or low commitment to school	Fleming et al., 1982; Penning & Barnes, 1982
Associating with drug-using peers	Brook et al., 1990
Having attitudes favorable to use	Kandel et al., 1986
Alienation from dominant societal values, including low religiosity	Jessor & Jessor, 1977; Kandel, 1982; Penning & Barnes, 1982

This might include rejection of religious beliefs and values as well (Kandel et al., 1986). Table 2.1 summarizes the most salient personal attributes found to be related to risk for substance misuse.

This risk-focused research has produced a number of functional results for prevention practitioners. One of these is the enhancement of good diagnostic checklists that help pinpoint at-risk youngsters (Zunz, Turner, & Norman, 1993). Another is school-based prevention programming that includes attempts to change student norms and to supply adolescents with resistance strategies to counter peer pressure to use (Norman & Turner, 1993). Generally, however, the results of risk-focused research seem to leave practitioners feeling overwhelmed and hopeless because of its concern with breakdown and deficit, pathology, and fatalism.

EXPLORING RESILIENCY

The recognition of both the assets and the limits of the risk perspective has led some in the prevention field to explore the recently accumulated body of work on resiliency and protective factors. Two strands of scholarship seem to have met in this new focus. First, the growing research literature on coping and stress moved scholars away from an emphasis on risk factors and rotated the spotlight onto the coping skills that individuals utilize to meet environmental challenges. The focus on coping was in marked contrast to that on risk. The risk research enumerated a multitude of factors impinging upon individuals that, in a seemingly fatalistic manner, put them at greater risk for behavioral deviance including alcohol and other drug abuse (Hawkins et al., 1992; Wyman, Work, Hightower, & Kerley, 1993). Emphasis on coping rather than risk shifted the perspective from fatalism to opportunity.

Second, many clinicians grew disillusioned with the efficacy of the traditional clinical disease model, which emphasized pathology and injury, victimization, and learned helplessness. One of the pioneers in the field of resiliency, Michael Rutter (1987), noted that scholars began to feel a need to find hope in the midst of an excess of stress and adversity. Momentum developed to move away from the pervasive clinical bias of problems and maladjustment, to a focus on wellness and self-repair (Wolin & Wolin, 1993).

Researchers began to frame different questions. Rather than asking what puts individuals at greater *risk* of behavioral deviance such as alcohol and other drug abuse, the question became, "Given similar high-risk environments, why do people who *do not* abuse alcohol or other drugs, *not* do so?" (Kumpfer, 1993). The overwhelming research question became, "How can we understand the process by which young people make it, despite the adversity they face?" (Jessor, 1993). And the search to identify the factors and processes underlying the development of resiliency gained momentum.

COMPONENTS OF
THE RESILIENCY PROCESS

Resilience is seen as the factors and processes enabling *sustained competent functioning* even in the presence of major life stressors (Masten et al., 1990). Other major figures in the field have variously defined it as: "competence and strength despite the presence of [considerable] adversities" (Garmezy, 1987, p. 164); "successful adaptation following exposure to stressful life events" (Werner & Smith, 1982, p. 3); and "successful adaptation under adverse conditions" (Luthar & Ziegler, 1991, p. 8).

Although models of the resiliency process differ to some extent, they all imply the interaction of two components (Jessor, 1993; Kumpfer, 1993; Masten et al., 1990; Rutter, 1987):

1. The presence of biological, psychological, and environmental *risk factors* (adverse conditions or stressful life events) that can increase the vulnerability of the individual, *and*
2. The presence of *protective factors* (social, personal, familial, and institutional buffers) that moderate the effects of individual vulnerabilities and environmental hazards.

Anthony (1987) attempted to clarify the differences between *risk, vulnerability,* and *resilience* with the following story. Three dolls, one made of glass, one of plastic, and one of steel, are exposed to the same risk, a heavy hammer blow. The glass doll shatters totally. The plastic one sustains a permanent dent. The steel doll responds only with a loud metallic sound.

Embedded in Anthony's analogy are several important ideas:

1. Individuals have differing capacities to withstand "blows" (i.e., differing *vulnerabilities*).
2. Persons have differing abilities to recover rapidly from a "temporary collapse" and bounce back to normal or even greater than normal functioning (i.e., differing *resiliency*).
3. If the environments of the three dolls had been different, if they had buffered the blow by offering different *protective* factors, then the outcomes for the dolls might have been different.

Because of the fragmented manner in which the field has grown, researchers from different specialties and perspectives frequently called the same or similar ideas by different names, resulting in inconsistency of definitions. In an attempt to clarify matters, Karol Kumpfer (1993) has proposed a consolidated definitional framework. She separates qualities of the environment from characteristics of the individual and calls: (a) negative characteristics of the environment *risk factors*, (b) positive characteristics of the environment *protective factors*, (c) negative characteristics of the individual *vulnerability factors*, and (d) positive characteristics of the individual *resiliency factors*. All of these *interact* to result cumulatively in adaptation or maladaptation of the individual. She notes that:

> This conceptualization separates protective factors from resiliency factors in hopes of removing the current confusion about the differences between these two concepts. . . . According to this definition, resiliency factors are characteristics of the person, and protective factors are characteristics of the environment. (Kumpfer, 1993, p. 4)

Of all attempts to date, Kumpfer's model seems to come closest to definitional clarity.

INDIVIDUAL ATTRIBUTES ASSOCIATED WITH RESILIENCY

In the past few decades researchers in the United States and in England have conducted studies of particular aspects of resiliency. Each study focused on those variables of most interest to the researcher. The best known of these research efforts include: Norman Garmezy and associates' Project Competence at the University of Minnesota, which studied resiliency in children of mentally ill parents (Garmezy, Masten, & Tellegan, 1984); Michael Rutter's British study of resilience in children at risk because of substantial family dysfunction (Rutter, 1985); and Emmy Werner and Ruth Smith's 30-year longitudinal study of the entire multiracial cohort of children born on the island of Kauai, Hawaii, in 1955 (Werner & Smith, 1982). Other important efforts include: The University of Rochester's Child Resilience Project, which studied stress-resistant and stress-affected 9- to 12-year-olds (Cowen, Wyman, Work, & Parker, 1990;

Wyman et al., 1993); the St. Louis Risk Research Project and other studies of its kind, which researched resilience in children of mentally ill parents (Beardsley & Podorefsky, 1988; Worland, Weeks, & Janes, 1987); and numerous other studies of resilience in stressed individuals such as concentration camp survivors (Moskowitz, 1983), youngsters coping with diabetes (Hauser, Vieyra, Jacobson, & Wertlieb, 1989; Schwartz, Jacobson, Hauser, & Dornbush, 1989), inner-city youngsters living in poverty (Clark, 1991; Garmezy, 1991; Luthar, 1991), survivors of cancer (Beardsley, 1989), children from alcoholic families (Berlin & Davis, 1989), and street children from Colombia, South America (Felsman, 1989).

A body of results has accumulated that begins to describe a common core of personality characteristics and dispositions that enable highly stressed children to maintain a sense of competence and control in their lives. The accumulated research suggests the following characteristics are associated with resilience.

Genetic and Biological Factors

Two factors have consistently emerged as associated with resiliency that are most likely genetically based and, as such, not likely to be responsive to intervention.

Easy Temperament and/or Disposition

Numerous studies have found easy temperament and/or disposition from birth to be associated with resiliency (Block et al., 1988; Garmezy, 1985; Rutter, 1979; Werner, 1990; Wyman et al., 1993). Werner and Smith (1982) explain the relationship by suggesting that pleasant, easygoing, responsive individuals tend to elicit more positive responses from others and possibly receive greater support from them as a result.

Intellectual Capabilities

Intellectual capabilities, particularly verbal and communication skills, have emerged in several studies as resiliency-related (Garmezy, 1985; Masten et al., 1990; Worland et al., 1987). Because such capabilities are generally an index of academic aptitude, they likely function to protect children, particularly disadvantaged children, because of the benefits of academic achievement (Masten et al., 1990).

The relationship between intelligence and resiliency is not a simple one, however. A few studies have indicated that high intelligence sometimes operates as a vulnerability rather than a resiliency factor, because high intelligence is frequently coupled with greater sensitivity to the environment (Luthar & Ziegler, 1991; Masten, 1982).

Personality Factors

Self-Efficacy

The personality characteristic most consistently associated with resilient outcome is a sense of self-efficacy. Bandura (1977) defined self-efficacy as a positive *perception* of one's competence to perform certain tasks. Rutter (1984) considers self-efficacy to be a feeling that one has worth, that one can deal with things that come up and have at least some control over important events. Werner (1984) refers to the concept as a "sense of coherence" and describes it as the confidence that one's external and internal worlds are predictable and hopeful, that life makes sense, and that one has some control over one's fate—that things will work out and odds can be surmounted.

Rutter's and Werner's descriptions of self-efficacy are closely allied to the concept of *internal locus of control*—that is, the belief that even in the face of adversity one can exert considerable control over one's fate (Werner & Smith, 1982). It is the perception that one has some influence over the current environment and one's future destiny (Kumpfer, 1993). Rather than being a separate resiliency factor, internal locus of control seems to be an important integral dimension of self-efficacy. Both refer to a *sense* of mastery, or to the *feeling* that one possesses the potential for mastery of one's self and one's external environment.

A large number of studies have demonstrated the link between resiliency and self-efficacy. Werner and Smith (1982) found that their resilient Hawaiian youngsters had a greater faith in their ability to control their environment positively. Both Michael Rutter's (1984) study of high-risk children in England and Norman Garmezy's (1985) study of children of mentally ill parents found that the more resilient children felt a greater degree of control over their environment and were more likely to hold the belief that effort pays off. In the Rochester studies, 9- to 12-year-old stress-resistant youngsters were found to have greater self-esteem and a greater sense of competence than their stress-vulnerable age-mates (Cowen et al., 1990). Those with a greater global sense of self-worth and high internal locus of control were also less likely to use alcohol or other drugs (Wyman et al., 1993). Resilient adolescents with diabetes researched by Schwartz and his colleagues (1989) had high self-esteem, a positive self-concept, and a sense of personal power (Schwartz et al., 1989).

Some studies suggest that belief and action go hand in hand. Hays and Ellickson (1990) found that adolescents who felt they were *able* to resist drugs were more likely *to do so*. They called this "resistance self-efficacy." The most resilient of the institutionalized females in Rutter's 1984 study were those who attempted some type of mastery over their circumstances and took active steps toward changing their environment (Rutter, 1984). The successful 7- to 12-year-old street children in Columbia, South America, studied by Felsman (1989), constantly corroborated their sense of self-efficacy through repeated and effective daily behavior aimed at obtaining a livelihood in the streets.

One can see that self-efficacy contrasts sharply with Seligman's (1975) "learned helplessness," in the throes of which the external environment is seen as random and immutable, not within one's personal influence (Kumpfer, 1993; Luthar & Ziegler, 1991).

Self-efficacy, then, involves several related things: a sense of self-esteem and self-confidence, and a belief in one's own ability to have some influence upon one's internal and external environment. It is reinforced by two other resiliency factors, the ability to appraise the environment realistically and a repertoire of social problem-solving skills that positively reinforce a continuing sense of confidence and mastery.

Realistic Appraisal of the Environment

Resilient persons have the ability to differentiate between the possible and the impossible. They are better able to appraise their own abilities realistically and to know what they can and cannot do, and can and cannot change. In addition, they are better able to appraise the consequences of their actions realistically. In their study of civil rights workers, survivors of cancer, and children of parents with affective disorder, Beardsley and Podorefsky (1988) found resiliency to be associated with this personality attribute. The better adapted individuals were characterized by their ability to make accurate cognitive appraisals of the stress to be dealt with and to assess realistically their capacity to act and affect the situation. Cowen and his Rochester colleagues also found stress-resilient preteens to have greater realistic control attributions than their stress-vulnerable agemates (Cowen et al., 1990). Similar study findings are cited by Garmezy and Masten (1986) and Werner (1986).

Social Problem-Solving Skills

Possessing a variety of social problem-solving skills that reinforce one's sense of competency and self-esteem is also a component of resiliency. This has been demonstrated in several studies, including the Kauai longitudinal effort (Werner & Smith, 1982), the Project Competence studies at the University of Minnesota of children of schizophrenic parents (Masten et al., 1990), and Rutter's British study of children from dysfunctional families (Rutter, 1979). Many successful school-based alcohol and other drug-abuse prevention programs recognize the value of social problem-solving skills and include them in their student training (Botvin, Baker, Renick, & Filazzola, 1984; Ellickson, 1984; Pentz et al., 1989).

Sense of Direction or Mission

Many of the children in Moskowitz's sample of concentration camp survivors had been designated by parents or others to take care of their younger siblings. Most reported that through their single-minded focus on seeing that their younger sibs survived, they survived too (Moskowitz, 1983). Similarly, Beardsley learned that civil rights workers in the South found personal strength in saving others (Beardsley, 1989). Werner and Smith found their resilient Hawaiian youngsters to have a strong sense of responsibility for helping and taking care of others (Werner & Smith, 1982). Through acts of "required helpfulness" their lives took on meaning (Garmezy, 1985). Stressful life events need not have an abnormal outcome, notes the psychiatrist Bleuler (1978), if the child develops some sense of purpose or life task through them.

Some special talent, passion, faith, or strong interest can also spark a sense of mission, a sense of purpose, a sense of meaning, or a sense of a compelling future in an individual, thereby strengthening his or her resiliency (Cameron-Bandler, 1986; Danziger & Farber, 1990; Richardson, Neiger, Jensen, & Kumpfer, 1990).

Empathy

Empathy, the capacity to understand and respond to another's feelings, has been identified as a resiliency skill in a number of studies.

Resilient Hawaiian adolescents of both sexes possessed greater amounts of what Werner called "traditional feminine characteristics," otherwise known as empathy. That is, they were more appreciative, gentle, nurturing, and socially perceptive, reflecting a caring and responsible attitude toward others (Werner, 1985, 1987). Schwartz et al. (1989) found resilient adolescents with diabetes to have greater interpersonal sensitivity and responsiveness. Preteen stress-resilient youngsters studied by Cowen and his fellow researchers (1990) had greater empathy than similarly aged stress-vulnerable children.

As with intellectual capacity, the relationship between empathy and resilience is not completely straightforward. Wyman and colleagues at the University of Rochester studied the relationship between the degree of empathy in 9- to 12-year-olds and their risk of taking drugs. Low-stressed youngsters with high empathy had a low risk for drug taking, but highly stressed children with high empathy had a sharply increased risk of taking drugs. Apparently, high empathy may act as a vulnerability factor under high-stress conditions, at least for drug-taking risk (Wyman et al., 1993).

Humor

Studies from the University of Minnesota Project Competence clearly demonstrate the relationship between resiliency and humor. Garmezy and colleagues (1984) demonstrated that highly stressed but competent children had higher humor generation scores than their highly stressed but less competent counterparts. And Masten (1982, 1986) revealed in a study of 10- to 14-year-olds that the highly stressed youngsters with greater competence had greater ability to use humor, appreciated humor more, were more readily able to find the comic in the tragic, and to use humor to reduce tension and restore perspective. Such abilities served the added function of maintaining social relationships (Kumpfer, 1993).

Adaptive Distancing

Faced with mentally ill, alcoholic, or drug addicted parents, and family dysfunction in other guises, resilient children fare well through the mechanism of adaptive distancing. Studies of offspring of parents with severe psychiatric disorders found that the resilient children had adopted a healthy separation from their parents' maladaptive patterns. They did not identify with the dysfunctional parent(s) and found successful role models elsewhere. The resilient children had the ability to think and act separately from the troubled adults, to see themselves as separate from their parents' illness system and not responsible for it. They could distinguish between their own experience and their parents' illness. They were saddened by their parents' problems but not overwhelmed by them. Their approach to a mentally ill parent was compassionate but detached (Anthony, 1987; Beardsley, 1989; Beardsley & Podorefsky, 1988).

Berlin and her colleagues, and others as well, have found adaptive distancing to be an important mechanism for children of alcoholics. Those who could psychologically step back from their dysfunctional environment fared best (Berlin & Davis, 1989; Berlin, Davis, & Orenstein, 1988; Chess, 1989; Wallerstein, 1983).

Adaptive distancing is clearly not "reactive distancing," which is marked by fight, flight, and isolation. It is rather a condition in which self-understanding and separateness prevail. The adaptively distant individual sees him- or herself as separate from the ill parent, not the cause of the illness, and not to blame for it (Kumpfer, 1993).

There is, however, inherent danger in this mode of adaptation. The rationalization and intellectualization involved may rescue the child from mental illness but may make it hard for the child to maintain other relationships with adequate levels of intimacy and generativity (Worland et al., 1987).

Gender

Gender differences have been found to be associated with resiliency, particularly concerning (a) the timing of, (b) the family context of, and (c) the sex-role behavior related to vulnerability versus resiliency.

Gender and Age

Both Werner and Smith's Hawaiian study and Rutter's children of dysfunctional families study found boys to be less resilient than girls in early childhood (Rutter, 1987; Werner & Smith, 1982). At that time girls have more competent same-sex role models, such as teachers and caretakers, after whom to pattern themselves (Masten et al., 1990). In the first decade of life, cultural sex-role expectations and a paucity of time spent with same-sex role exemplars put boys at a disadvantage psychologically, socially, and academically. Their vulnerability is often manifested by greater behavioral problems and poorer academic achievement than girls. Boys of that age live in a predominantly female world both at home and at school. Control of expression, especially of aggressive behavior, is often a major issue in such environments. Werner and Smith have concluded that "the physical immaturity of boys, the expectations of sex-role behavior, and the feminine environment in which they live . . . increase the amount of stress experienced by [boys] in childhood," and result in their being less resilient than girls of the same age (Werner & Smith, 1982, p. 44). This changes substantially in adolescence.

In the second decade it is girls who become more vulnerable. They often start to do poorly in school and to lose considerable self-esteem (Gilligan, Lyons, & Hanmer, 1990). Adolescent girls are now subject to a great deal of pressure to adopt traditional feminine sex-role behavior, to be "ladylike" and *not* to compete with boys in their school and social worlds. In adolescence, girls go through the same process that boys were subjected to earlier. That is, they are "trying to cope with a set of sex-role expectations that may limit their behavior and the expression of their competence" (Werner & Smith, 1982, p. 44). Societal expectations, sexual pressures, and biological changes turn the tables on the girls (Masten et al., 1990). Autonomy and mastery are no longer expected of girls; dependency is what is expected (Benard, 1991).

The mechanism by which this probably occurs is described by Rutter (1981, 1984). Adolescent girls are often disadvantaged by traditional gender stereotyped responses to them by the adults in their lives. This tradition-based response is antimotivational and subduing. A gender-traditional response to adolescent girls, on the part of the adults in their lives, often limits and undermines their motivation. This dampening feedback from adults contributes to girls' feeling unsuccessful and not capable. Learned helplessness defeats them early. Girls now tend to believe that their fate depends on the actions of others rather than on their own control. "Just as *aggressiveness* tended to get boys in trouble in childhood, *dependency* may become a major problem for girls in adolescence" (Werner & Smith, 1982, p. 45).

Gender and Sex-Role Behavior and Resiliency

In the Werner and Smith (1982) study, resilient youngsters, both male and female, appeared to have adopted an androgynous personality. That is, they blended both masculine and feminine characteristics and acted in a flexible non-sex-typed manner, being both yielding and assertive, expressive and instrumental, able to care about themselves and about relationships with others. Resilient girls tended to be more autonomous and independent than nonresilient girls. Resilient boys tended to be more emotionally expressive, socially perceptive, and nurturant than nonresilient boys. Their families aided and abetted this androgynous adaptation.

Gender and the Family Context

Boys and girls seem to thrive in somewhat different types of households. Werner and Smith (1982) found their Hawaiian resilient *females* most likely come from households that contained:

1. An absence of parental overprotection
2. An emphasis on risk-taking and independence
3. Reliable support from the primary caretaker
4. Mother's long-term employment
5. A home in which the father was permanently absent, because he was dead, their mother had never married, or their parents had separated during their childhood

Resilient *males* were more likely to come from households characterized by:

1. Greater structure, rules, and parental supervision
2. Encouragement of emotional responsiveness
3. A male present who serves as a positive model for identification

The family context of resiliency will be further explored in Chapter 3.

RESILIENCY ENHANCEMENT PROJECTS

A number of programs across the country are attempting to incorporate resiliency theory and research findings into adolescent substance-abuse prevention programs. These efforts are aimed at a variety of populations and settings and are in different stages of development, implementation, and evaluation. Just a few examples will be noted here.

The University of Rochester Child Resilience Project—Project Competence—grew out of the findings of research efforts conducted with high-risk youngsters in the Rochester Public Schools. A curriculum is being developed to enhance those factors found to be protective against life stress. The curriculum includes developing peer support, understanding and expressing feelings including empathy, enhancing social problem-solving skills, and cultivating a realistic locus of control (Cowan et al., 1990; Wyman et al., 1993).

Roger Mills and his associates have developed an intervention program in the Modello/Homestead Gardens Public Housing Project in Dade County, Florida. They use a "wellness" model that views resiliency as the "natural state" of every person. The model emphasizes the inherent capacity of individuals to function at a very high level, use common sense in problem solving, and enhance their own self-esteem. Participants are helped to uncondition their usually negativistic thinking and develop a more positive belief system about their own ability to change their lives (Mills, 1991, 1992).

The Rockville, Maryland, Office of Substance Abuse has sponsored the "Athletes Coaching Teens" prevention program. Targeting health classes in middle schools in Richmond, Virginia, where students are primarily African Americans from disadvantaged backgrounds, this project uses specially selected athletes as coaches to deliver a seven-session curriculum. The curriculum attempts to enhance resiliency by encouraging the students to turn their "dreams" into personal goals, identify obstacles in the way of reaching those goals, and develop strategies to overcome the obstacles (Farrell et al., 1992).

Judge Baker Children's Center in Boston has developed a program for children of families with chronic affective disorders (some of whom have substance abuse as a dual diagnosis). Among other things, techniques are being explored that promote "adaptive distancing." That is, they are helping the children to see themselves as separate from their mentally ill and/or substance-abusing parents, and are assisting them to plan independent action strategies that permit them to cope with the family illness system (Steinbaum, 1993).

A number of other resiliency-related substance-abuse prevention programs are beginning across the country. Still to be developed are programs addressing resiliency differences between boys and girls and the positive outcome associated with androgynous character structure.

CONCLUSION

Authors such as Hawkins et al. (1992) and Kandel et al. (1986) see a risk-focused approach as the most promising route to effective adolescent alcohol and other substance-abuse prevention. This approach, although useful in many ways, is reactive in nature, responding to negative personal and environmental circumstances already in place. It reminds me of the metaphor of an 8-ounce glass with 4 ounces of water in it described as "half-empty."

The second approach, that of a resiliency focus, seems to be considerably more proactive and optimistic, indeed a "half-full" glass. Its emphasis on factors that encourage competence in the face of adversity offers substantial promise.

This chapter has attempted to describe the multitude of personal characteristics and dispositions that recent research has indicated *enable* environmentally stressed youngsters to cope adequately with adversity. In other words, the focus has been on the "half-full" perspective. We have found such "resiliency" factors to include:

- An easy temperament and/or disposition
- Intellectual capability
- A sense of self-efficacy, which includes
  a sense of self-esteem and self-confidence, and
  a belief in one's own ability to influence one's internal and external environment
- An ability to appraise the environment realistically

- Social problem-solving skills
- A sense of direction or mission
- Empathy
- Humor
- Adaptive distancing abilities when faced with a dysfunctional environment

Gender differences were also found to be associated with resiliency. Societal sex-role expectations help girls to be more resilient in early childhood and boys to be more resilient in adolescence. Those youngsters, both male and female, who acted in a flexible non-sex-typed, androgynous manner were the most resilient of all. Boys and girls thrive in different kinds of households as well. The most resilient girls come from households that encouraged risk-taking and independence. Resilient boys come from households characterized by structure and rules and by encouragement of emotional responsiveness.

A number of programs throughout the country are attempting to incorporate resiliency ideas into adolescent substance-abuse prevention programs. All attempt to amplify one or more of the resiliency characteristics noted in this chapter. Each focuses on strength-building and empowerment rather than pathology and risk. Both need to be taken into account in program planning, but the former has been underemphasized for too long.

The challenge we all face now is to learn how to *accentuate the positive,* to find further ways to move away from the problem-oriented, damage control perspective with which we have become all too familiar and to move toward the inclusion of more resiliency enhancement components in our substance-abuse prevention programs.

REFERENCES

Anthony, E. J. (1987). Children at high risk for psychosis growing up successfully. In E. J. Anthony & B. J. Cohler (Eds.), *The invulnerable child* (pp. 147-184). New York: Guilford.

Bandura, A. (1977). *Social learning theory.* Englewood Cliffs, NJ: Prentice Hall.

Beardsley, W. R. (1989). The role of self-understanding in resilient individuals: The development of a perspective. *The American Journal of Orthopsychiatry, 59*(2), 266-278.

Beardsley, W. R., & Podorefsky, D. (1988). Resilient adolescents whose parents have serious affective and other psychiatric disorders: Importance of self-understanding and relationships. *American Journal of Psychiatry, 145,* 63-69.

Benard, B. (1991). *Fostering resiliency in kids: Protective factors in the family, school and community.* Unpublished manuscript, Western Regional Center for Drug-Free Schools and Communities, Far West Laboratory, San Francisco.

Berlin, R., & Davis, R. (1989). Children from alcoholic families: Vulnerability and resilience. In T. Dugan & R. Coles (Eds.), *The child in our times: Studies in the development of resiliency* (pp. 81-105). New York: Brunner/Mazel.

Berlin, R., Davis, R., & Orenstein (1988). Adaptive and reactive distancing among adolescents from alcoholic families. *Adolescence, 23*(91), 577-584.

Bleuler, M. (1978). *The schizophrenic disorders.* New Haven, CT: Yale University Press.

Block, J., Block, J. H., & Keyes, S. (1988). Longitudinally foretelling drug usage in adolescence: Early childhood personality and environmental precursors. *Child Development, 59,* 336-355.

Botvin, G. J., Baker, E., Renick, N., & Filazzola, A. (1984). A cognitive-behavioral approach to substance abuse prevention. *Addictive Behaviors, 9,* 137-147.

Brook, J. S., Brook, D. W., Whiteman, M., & Cohen, P. (1990). The psychosocial etiology of adolescent drug use. A family interaction model [Special issue]. *Genetic, Social and General Psychology Monographs, 116*(2).

Cameron-Bandler, L. (1986, July/August). Strategies for creating a compelling future. *Focus on Family and Chemical Dependency,* pp. 6-7.

Chess, S. (1989). Defying the voice of doom. In T. Dugan & R. Coles (Eds.), *The child in our times: Studies in the development of resiliency* (pp. 179-199). New York: Brunner/Mazel.

Clark, M. (1991). Social identity, peer relations and academic competence of African-American adolescents. *Education and Urban Society, 24*(1), 41-52.

Cloninger, C. R., Sigvardsson, S., & Bohman, M. (1988). Childhood personality predicts alcohol abuse in young adults. *Alcoholism, 12,* 494-503.

Cowen, E., Wyman, P., Work, W., & Parker, G. (1990). The Rochester Child Resilience Project: Overview and summary of first year findings. *Development and Psychopathology, 2,* 193-212.

Danziger, S. K., & Farber, N. B. (1990). Keeping inner-city youth in school: Critical experiences of young black women. *Social Work Research and Abstracts, 26*(4), 32-39.

Ellickson, P. L. (1984). *Project ALERT: A smoking and drug prevention experiment* (Rand Corporation, N-2184—CHF). Santa Monica, CA: Rand Corporation.

Farrell, A., Howard, C., Danish, S., Smith, A., Mash, J., & Stovall, K. (1992). Athletes coaching teens for substance abuse prevention: Alcohol and other drug use and risk factor in urban middle school students. In C. Marcus & J. Swisher (Eds.), *Working with youth in high-risk environments: Experiences in prevention. OSAP prevention monograph-12.* Rockville, MD.

Felsman, J. K. (1989). Risk and resilience in childhood: The lives of street children. In T. Dugan & R. Coles (Eds.), *The child in our times: Studies in the development of resiliency* (pp. 56-79). New York: Brunner/Mazel.

Fleming, J. P., Kellam, S. G., & Brown, C. H. (1982). Early predictors of age at first use of alcohol, marijuana and cigarettes. *Drug and Alcohol Dependence, 9,* 285-303.

Garmezy, N. (1985). Stress-resistant children: The search for protective factors. In J. E. Stevenson (Ed.), *Recent research in developmental psychopathology. Journal of Child Psychology and Psychiatry (Book Suppl. No. 4)* (pp. 213-233). Oxford: Pergamon.

Garmezy, N. (1987). Stress, competence and development: Continuities in the study of schizophrenic adults, children vulnerable to psychopathology and the search for stress resistant children. *American Journal of Orthopsychiatry, 57*(2), 159-174.

Garmezy, N. (1991). Resiliency and vulnerability to adverse developmental outcomes associated with poverty. *American Behavioral Scientist, 34*(4), 416-430.

Garmezy, N., & Masten, A. S. (1986). Stress, competence, and resilience: Common frontiers for therapist and psychopathologist. *Behavior Therapy, 57*(2), 159-174.

Garmezy, N., Masten, A. S., & Tellegan, A. (1984). The study of stress and competence in children: A building block for developmental psychopathology. *Child Development, 55,* 97-111.

Gilligan, C., Lyons, N. P., & Hanmer, T. J. (Eds.). (1990). *Making connections: The relational worlds of adolescent girls at Emma Willard School.* Cambridge, MA: Harvard University Press.

Hauser, S. T., Vieyra, M. A., Jacobson, A., & Wertlieb, D. (1989). Family aspects of vulnerability and resilience in adolescence: A theoretical perspective. In T. Dugan & R. Coles (Eds.), *The child in our times: Studies in the development of resiliency* (pp. 109-133). New York: Brunner/Mazel.

Hawkins, J. D., Catalano, R. F., & Miller, J. Y. (1992). Risk and protective factors for alcohol and other drug problems in adolescence and early adulthood: Implications for substance abuse prevention. *Psychological Bulletin, 112*(1), 64-105.

Hays, R. D., & Ellickson, P. L. (1990). How generalizable are adolescent beliefs about pro-drug pressures and resistance self-efficacy. *Journal of Applied Social Psychology, 20*(4), 321-340.

Jessor, R. (1976). Predicting time of onset of marijuana use: A developmental study of high school youth. *Journal of Consulting and Clinical Psychology, 44,* 125-134.

Jessor, R. (1993). Successful adolescent development among youth in high-risk settings. *American Psychologist, 48*(2), 117-126.

Jessor, R., & Jessor, S. L. (1977). *Problem behavior and psychosocial development: A longitudinal study of youth.* San Diego, CA: Academic Press.

Kandel, D. B., Kessler, R. C., & Margulies, R. S. (1978). Antecedents of adolescent initiation into stages of drug use: A developmental analysis. *Journal of Youth and Adolescence, 7,* 13-40.

Kandel, D., Simcha-Fagan, O., & Davis, M. (1986). Risk factors for delinquency and illicit drug use from adolescence to young adulthood. *Journal of Drug Issues, 60,* 67-90.

Kumpfer, K. (1993). *Resiliency and AOD use prevention in high risk youth.* Unpublished manuscript. [Available from School of Social Work, University of Utah, Salt Lake City, UT, 84112]

Luthar, S. (1991). Vulnerability and resilience: A study of high risk adolescence. *Child Development, 62*(3), 600-616.

Luthar, S., & Ziegler, E. (1991). Vulnerability and competence: A review of research on resilience in childhood. *American Journal of Orthopsychiatry, 61*(1), 7-22.

Masten, A. S. (1982). *Humor and creative thinking in stress-resistant children.* Unpublished doctoral dissertation, University of Minnesota.

Masten, A. S. (1986). Humor and competence in school aged children. *Child Development, 57,* 461-473.

Masten, A. S., Best, K. M., and Garmezy, N. (1990). Resilience and development: Contributions from the study of children who overcome adversity. *Development and Psychopathology, 2,* 425-444.

Mills, R. (1991). A new understanding of self: The role of affect, state of mind, self-understanding and intrinsic motivation. *Journal of Experimental Education, 60*(19), 67-81.

Mills, R. (1992). *Toward a comprehensive model for prevention: A new foundation for understanding the root causes of drug abuse.* From reports presented at the Annual Meeting of the Office for Treatment Improvement—Special Initiative Branch, New Orleans, LA, on March 31, 1992, and the State of Florida Department of Health and Rehabilitative Services Alcohol and Drug Abuse Program, Tallahassee, FL (1991-1992).

Moskowitz, S. (1983). *Love despite hate.* New York: Schocken.

Norman, E., & Turner, S. (1993). Adolescent substance abuse prevention programs in the encouraging 80's. *Journal of Primary Prevention, 14*(1), 3-24.

Penning, M., & Barnes, G. E. (1982). Adolescent marijuana use review. *International Journal of the Addictions, 17,* 749-791.

Pentz, M. A., Dwyer, J., MacKinnon, D., Flay, B. R., et al. (1989). A multicommunity trial for primary prevention of adolescent drug abuse. *Journal of the American Medical Association, 261*(2), 3259-3266.

Richardson, G., Neiger, B., Jensen, S., & Kumpfer, K. (1990). The resiliency model. *Health Education, 21*(6), 33-39.

Rutter, M. (1979). Protective factors in children's responses to stress and disadvantage. In M. W. Kent & J. Rolf (Eds.), *Primary prevention of psychopathology: Vol. 3. Social competence in children* (pp. 49-74). Hanover, NH: University Press of New England.

Rutter, M. (1981). Stress, coping and development: Some issues and some questions. *Journal of Child Psychology and Psychiatry, 22*(4), 323-356.

Rutter, M. (1984, March). Resilient children. *Psychology Today,* pp. 57-65.

Rutter, M. (1985). Resilience in the face of adversity: Protective factors and resistance to psychiatric disorder. *British Journal of Psychiatry, 147,* 598-611.

Rutter, M. (1987). Psychosocial resilience and protective mechanisms. *American Journal of Orthopsychiatry, 57*(3), 316-331.

Schwartz, J., Jacobson, A., Hauser, S., & Dornbush, B. (1989). Explorations of vulnerability and resilience: Case studies of diabetic adolescents and their families. In T. Dugan & R. Coles (Eds.), *The child in our times: Studies in the development of resiliency* (pp. 134-144). New York: Brunner/Mazel.

Seligman, M. (1975). *Helplessness: On depression, development and death.* San Francisco: Freeman.

Shedler, J., & Block, J. (1990). Adolescent drug use and psychological health: A longitudinal inquiry. *American Psychologist, 45,* 612-630.

Steinbaum, E. (1993, April 25). The resilient ones. *Boston Globe* [magazine section], pp. 10-36.

Wallerstein, J. (1983). Children of divorce: Preliminary report of a ten-year follow-up of older children and adolescents. *Journal of the American Academy of Child Psychiatry, 24,* 545-553.

Werner, E. E. (1984, November). Resilient children. *Young Children*, pp. 68-72.

Werner, E. E. (1985). Stress and protective factors in children's lives. In A. R. Nicol (Ed.), *Longitudinal studies in child psychology and psychiatry* (pp. 335-355). New York: John Wiley.

Werner, E. E. (1986). Resilient offspring of alcoholics: A longitudinal study from birth to age 18. *American Journal of Orthopsychiatry, 59*, 72-81.

Werner, E. E. (1987). Vulnerability and resiliency in children at risk for delinquency: A longitudinal study from birth to young adulthood. In J. Burchard & S. Burchard (Eds.), *Prevention of delinquent behavior* (pp. 16-43). Newbury Park, CA: Sage.

Werner, E. E. (1990). High risk children in young adulthood: A longitudinal study from birth to 32 years. *American Journal of Orthopsychiatry, 59*(1), 72-81.

Werner, E. E., & Smith, R. S. (1982). *Vulnerable but invincible*. New York: McGraw-Hill.

Wolin, S. J., & Wolin, S. (1993). *The resilient self: How survivors of troubled families rise above adversity*. New York: Villard Books.

Worland, J., Weeks, D., & Janes, C. (1987). Predicting mental health in children at risk. In E. J. Anthony & B. J. Cohler (Eds.), *The invulnerable child* (pp. 185-210). New York: Guilford Press.

Wyman, P., Work, W., Hightower, A., & Kerley, J. (1993). *Relationships among childhood competencies, psychological stress, and substance use risk behaviors in early adolescence*. Unpublished manuscript, University of Rochester, NY.

Zunz, S., Turner, S., & Norman, E. (1993). Accentuating the positive: Stressing resiliency in school-based substance abuse programs. *Social Work in Education, 15*(3), 169-178.

3. Family Variables Related to Adolescent Substance Misuse: Risk and Resiliency Factors

Sandra Turner

Fordham University

INTRODUCTION

Just as the strategies in the field of prevention programming have moved from an "information only" approach to a comprehensive model that incorporates several strategies at once, so has the target group moved from the individual to a larger system that includes the family, the school, and the community (Gullotta, 1987). This chapter will focus on the family.

First *risk* and *resiliency* will be defined, and the theoretical underpinnings of the new work in resiliency will be discussed. Resiliency is very much related to risk; indeed, it can be considered the other side of the coin, and it is important to consider the factors that put families at great risk for substance misuse. These risk factors will be highlighted. However, emphasizing the scores of risk factors that can be found in all too many families in the 1990s can be overwhelming. It was out of frustration at focusing on the negative that several researchers and practitioners embraced the concept of resiliency (Zunz, Turner, & Norman, 1993).

Recent research in the field of resiliency as it relates to substance-abuse prevention examines the differences between a resiliency-based approach and a risk-based approach, then concentrates on how to enhance and protect resiliency in both individuals and families. There are some generally agreed upon family protective factors that help to create and maintain resilient family members, and these will be examined.

AUTHOR'S NOTE: The work for this chapter was supported by a grant from the New York State Office of Alcohol and Substance Abuse Services.

Definitions

Risk factors can be considered the predictors of substance misuse. They obviously exist before alcohol and other drug misuse begins, and those who subscribe to a risk-focused approach seek to eliminate or lessen risk factors as the chief means of prevention of drug misuse. A risk-focused approach looks at what is wrong and seeks to "fix" it before it becomes a serious problem (Hawkins, Catalano, & Miller, 1992).

A resiliency-focused approach, on the other hand, looks at what is right and tries to protect or enhance that. *Resiliency* can be defined simply as the ability to bounce back or cope well in the face of adversity. Risk-focused and resiliency-focused approaches to prevention are not diametrically opposed to each other; they both seek to accomplish similar goals. But whether one targets problems or strengths is an important difference in perspective—it represents a paradigm shift whose effect is to generate optimism and hope as opposed to frustration and despair (Benard, 1993).

THEORETICAL UNDERPINNINGS OF WORK IN RESILIENCY

Most of the prevention approaches of the late 1980s were rooted in problem behavior theory (Jessor & Jessor, 1977) and social learning theory (Bandura, 1977). The model of resiliency builds on social learning theory and incorporates cognitive behavioral theory (Beck, 1976) as well as health realization theory, recently developed by Roger Mills (1991), which contains aspects of the first two theories.

Social learning theory sees human behavior as the product of continuous reciprocal interaction between cognitive, behavioral, and environmental factors (Bandura, 1977). It posits that the interaction of inner forces and environmental stimuli determines how people will behave; that is, that one's behavior is learned and molded by watching others' behavior and by integrating how people respond to one's own behavior. Social learning theory predicts that adolescents are more likely to use alcohol and other drugs to relax or cope with stress if these behaviors are modeled by their parents, peers, or the culture in general. Some adolescents learn to use drugs after repeated exposure to highly influential role models (parents, older siblings) who use drugs.

One prominent feature of social learning theory is its emphasis on an individual's self-regulating capacities. People have the capacity to anticipate the consequences of their own actions as well as other people's responses to these actions (Norman & Turner, 1993). Unlike some of the traditional psychological theories, social learning theory contends that people can learn by *observing* other people's behavior as well as from direct experience. Bandura sees people as neither totally free agents nor powerless objects controlled by external forces. Sometimes personal factors exercise more control over behavior; at other times environmental factors maintain dominance.

Cognitive behavioral theory, as formulated by Aaron Beck (1976), asserts that affect and behavior are primarily determined by the way a person cognitively views the world. In cognitive behavioral theory, how we think about ourselves is of utmost importance: "We are what we think." Cognitions are based on attitudes or assumptions (schemas), which develop from previous experiences. If a person has a certain mind-set or schema, according to which she interprets all her experiences, her thinking about herself will be virtually predetermined. If she thinks only in terms of perfection, then all experiences will be dominated by the presumption that she must do everything perfectly. Anything not done perfectly will result in a self-evaluation of total incompetence. The pronoun *she* is deliberately chosen in this example, as recent evidence has shown that whereas boys who make a mistake or do poorly on a task tend to externalize the experience and say "I made a mistake" or "That was a terrible test," starting in adolescence, girls who make mistakes or fail tests internalize this and say "I am a failure" (Gilligan, Lyons, & Hanmer, 1990). Practitioners who work in a cognitive behavioral mode use both cognitive and behavioral strategies and techniques to do the following:

1. Learn to recognize negative thoughts and behavior and then challenge them.
2. Substitute more reality-oriented interpretations of behavior.
3. Use techniques to achieve behavior goals that will further help change negative thoughts (Beck, Rush, & Shaw, 1979).

The philosophical roots of cognitive behavioral theory go back to the Stoic philosophers, Zeno, Cicero, Seneca, and Epictitus, the latter of whom wrote, "Men are disturbed not by things but by the views which they take of them" (Beck et al., 1979, p. 8).

Mills's health realization theory resembles both cognitive behavioral theory and social learning theory in that it recognizes the importance of perceptions. Mills's primary tenet is that everyone has the innate capacity to function with self-esteem and good judgment. Mills believes it is essential to recognize and understand one's own mood because it is from having easier access to good moods that a higher level of mental health emerges. Secure feelings that can emerge from learning how to access good moods engage an innate capacity for common sense and self-esteem.

Mills (1991) outlines a process in which the first step is to recognize a feeling and then see how this feeling influences actions and behaviors. The next step is to change negative behaviors. Once behaviors have changed, self-perceptions will be more positive. In other words, if one can readily differentiate one's good and bad moods and develop a sense of how to get into a good mood before taking an action, then more competent and successful behaviors will be developed. Thus if a mother, coming home exhausted at the end of a working day, can tell the children who are demanding her attention that she needs to rest and put her feet up for 10 minutes before she starts making dinner and attending to their needs, she will be much better able to take care of them. This will make her feel more like a competent and successful parent. Mills describes a family he worked with in a housing project in Florida: The exhausted mother returning home from work used to scream at her kids to leave her alone. Mills's team helped her to take time for herself when she got home; her children learned to line up quietly outside her door to wait to tell her about their day.

Health realization theory is not unlike Seligman's "learned helplessness" model of depression. Seligman contends that if one learns early in life that one has no control over events or outcomes in life, then feelings of effectiveness or self-efficacy will not develop. People who do not see any relationship between their own actions and outcomes tend to feel depressed, according to Seligman (1975). Those who subscribe to this model see the major therapeutic task as that of helping people regain an internal or realistic locus of control. According to both Mills and Seligman, people who have been beaten down by life have to learn how to get their hope back. Hope is the foundation of resiliency. Werner and Smith discovered this in their study of the resilient children of Kauai, Hawaii. They quote from Lillian Smith's, *The Journey* (1954):

> And hope? What is this stubborn thing in man that keeps him forever picking the lock of time? The odds are against him, the odds have always been against him, and he knows it, but he has never believed it. (Werner & Smith, 1982, p. 1)

FAMILY PREDICTORS
OF MISUSE (RISK FACTORS)

As previously stated, a risk-focused approach to family predictors of misuse involves eliminating, lessening, or offsetting the precursors of drug abuse. There is, to date, no conclusive evidence about which risk factors are specific to drug abuse and which are associated with other adolescent problems, such as dropping out of school, pregnancy, poor academic performance, and so forth, nor is it yet clear which risk factors are the most serious and which are the most amenable to intervention or prevention efforts (Hawkins et al., 1992).

Stress might be considered a universal or comprehensive risk factor, and it plays a large part in creating distress and vulnerability, but it is difficult to predict how much stress and what kind of stress is most harmful. In illustrating this point, one researcher quotes Charles Bukowski: "It's not the large things that send a man to the madhouse. . . . No, it's the continuing series of small tragedies that send a man to the madhouse . . . not the death of his love but a shoelace that snaps with no time left" (Lazarus & Launier, 1978, p. 290).

Although it might be something minor, like a broken shoelace, that finally causes a crisis or a descent into dysfunctionality, it has been documented that generally the more risk factors or stressors that a child is exposed to, the more vulnerable he or she becomes, and the more likely it is that the shoelace will break (Cowen et al., 1991; Rutter, 1987). Pryor-Brown and Cowen (1989) found that children who experienced many stressful events were less competent (more vulnerable), and Rutter (1987) found that there were not significant differences in terms of vulnerability between those who experienced no stressful events and those who experienced up to two stressful life events, but after two the harmful effects were compounded geometrically.

What exactly are these risk factors that can lead to vulnerability and maladjustment? Some of the most serious ones are:

- Being born into poverty (Garmezy, 1991; Hawkins et al., 1992).
- Living with chronic familial tension and discord. Some studies have found that family conflict is a more serious risk factor and therefore a stronger predictor of substance misuse than is divorce or separation per se (Rutter & Giller, 1983).
- Having a parent or sibling who abuses alcohol or other drugs. As social learning theory predicts, adolescents growing up in families where drug use is the behavior that is modeled will have a tendency to adopt that behavior.
- In general, any kind of parental nondirectiveness and permissiveness are risk factors for adolescent drug misuse. Lewis (1991), however, found that parents who simply used powerful control techniques often feel they have no control over their children's behavior, and their children were not as resilient.
- Membership in a family where there is little warmth, acceptance, and understanding and much devaluing and indifference is related to impairment in adolescent ego development (Hauser, Powers, Noam, & Jacobson, 1984).
- Living in a family where one or both parents or caretakers are seriously disturbed or dysfunctional, especially if this results in the inability of the primary caretaker to bond and become involved in a major way in the child's life, can have a strong impact (Hawkins et al., 1992).
- The death of a significant adult in a child's life, particularly before the child has reached age 11, is a serious risk factor (Werner & Smith, 1992).
- Living with a serious or chronic illness (their own or that of their primary caretaker) can cause vulnerability in a youngster of any age (Hauser et al., 1984).
- The birth of a sibling, especially less than 2 years after their own birth (Cowen et al., 1991).
- Living in a neighborhood where there is a great deal of turmoil and violence can have a negative influence (Rutter, 1979).
- Divorce or separation of parents, especially if it involves a loss of a loved parent, is a significant risk factor (Hauser, Vieyra, Jacobson, & Wertlieb, 1989).
- Experiencing physical or sexual abuse as a child or adolescent is a major risk factor for substance abuse and many other problem behaviors (Hauser et al., 1989). The younger the age at which a child experiences stress in the family (especially sexual or physical abuse, or death or

life-threatening illness), the more pernicious are the effects (Gomes-Schwartz, Horowitz, & Cardarell, 1990).

Kumpfer (1993) cautions that we cannot assume that children growing up in what could be considered risky environments will experience risk identically. Eleanor Roosevelt was an extraordinarily resilient person who grew up in a family environment full of stress and dysfunction. On the surface it appears that the death of her mother when Eleanor was only 8 years old would have put her in a very vulnerable state. This, however, seems not to have been the case, according to her most recent biography (Cook, 1992). Her mother had always been very cold and critical of Eleanor, and it was her father whom she adored and who made her feel most loved, although he had been banished from the house due to his alcoholic drinking and rampages. Right after learning of her mother's death Eleanor wrote in her journal, "Death meant nothing to me, and one fact wiped out everything else—my father was back and I would see him very soon" (Cook, 1992, p. 78). Her much loved father was allowed back in the house after her mother died, and this was what Eleanor longed for.

It later proved to be Eleanor's loving and responsible teacher who exerted the most protective influence on her life. First her father made her feel loved, then her teacher helped her to feel secure, confident, and competent. She drew upon this resilient foundation throughout her life. Researchers and preventionists have found that positive role models and mentors or coaches who serve as forms of social support can have a powerful restorative influence on a youngster or adolescent, and these relationships can help to promote social competence and a sense of internal locus of control (Gullotta, 1987; Mitchell, Billings, & Moos, 1982).

GENDER AND ETHNIC CONSIDERATIONS OF STRESSORS AND RISK FACTORS

It is important to note that just as all stressors do not affect children and adolescents uniformly, some important differences characterize gender and ethnicity. In Chapter 2, Norman discussed gender differences in terms of individual risk and protective factors. As we turn now to family variables, boys are more affected than girls by separation and loss of parents or primary caregivers in early and middle childhood, whereas girls are more vulnerable than boys to chronic familial discord and disturbed interpersonal relationships in adolescence (Werner & Smith, 1992).

DIFFERENT PROTECTIVE
FACTORS FOR BOYS AND GIRLS

For both boys and girls, the level of education of their parents can serve as an important element in the building of resiliency. Girls whose mothers work outside the home, particularly in jobs they find fulfilling, tend to be more resilient, whereas boys who have a male mentor and who are the firstborn son tend to be more resilient (Werner & Smith, 1982, 1992).

There have been few studies that have looked at family risk factors in terms of race, although Garmezy (1991) discussed the role of poverty in the development of risk factors and family stress, and a study done by the Children's Defense Fund found that "America's black children were twice as likely as white children to (a) die in the first year, (b) be born prematurely, (c) suffer low birth weight, (d) have mothers who received little or no prenatal care, and (e) have no employed parent" (Garmezy, 1991, p. 415). Almost 50% of black children and two fifths of Hispanic children in America live in poverty (Garmezy, 1991).

Nettles (1993) has investigated the effect of race in terms of risk and protection and found that, for adolescent blacks, growing up and going to school with whites serves as a protective factor, just as families and schools that promote raceless values and norms serve as protective factors for black and Hispanic children.

FAMILY PROTECTIVE FACTORS

As discussed earlier, resiliency is the ability to bounce back in the face of adversity. According to many who espouse the resiliency model, it is the falling apart or disruption caused by stressors that impels a person to look inward and adapt—to learn new skills that will enhance his or her ability to adapt and to hurdle life events (Richardson, Neiger, Jensen, & Kumpfer, 1990). Werner conceptualizes resilience as the capacity to cope effectively with internal vulnerabilities and environmental stress (Hauser et al., 1989). Werner and Smith (1992) found that the more stressors a person was exposed to, the more protective factors were needed to offset these stressors to help enhance resiliency.

Of all the potential risk and protective factors available, the family is still the most powerful and exerts the most influence over the child's emotional, social, psychological, and physical environment. This is true whether one grows up in a two-parent or a single-parent family or is raised by other kin or foster parents. *Family* can be defined as two or more people who consider themselves a family (Hartman & Laird, 1983). Chapter 2 identified what the most important protective factors are that help to build a sense of resiliency in the individual—the significant protective factors within the family will now be discussed.

Biological or Genetic

The building of family protective factors begins before the birth of the child with the provision of quality prenatal care for the mother (Werner & Smith, 1982, 1992). We are becoming more and more aware of the effects of prenatal care on temperament. Babies who have a heavier birth weight and who have not suffered prenatal stress are more likely to be calmer, to sleep more regularly, and to have a greater ability to self-soothe (Werner & Smith, 1992). Research in the substance-abuse field has demonstrated that babies exposed to alcohol and other drugs in the womb are more likely to suffer birth defects and other problems: mental retardation, hyperactivity and agitation, withdrawal symptoms, low birth weight, and difficulty in self-soothing. And these needy babies are least likely to get the love they need so desperately. As discussed earlier, poverty is a major risk factor, and poor women often have difficulty obtaining good prenatal care, a problem compounded if they are also drug abusers (Chavkin, 1990). Benard (1993) talks about creating a continuum of caring as we work to build resiliency. Provision of good prenatal care to those who are most in need of it is an essential first step in the development of family protective factors.

Warm, Positive Relationship
With a Caring Adult

At a conference in Oakland, California, in 1991, Dr. Barbara Staggers reported on a study that she had done on the adolescents with whom she works in her family practice clinic. She had asked the youngsters what was most important to them in their day-to-day lives. She expected answers such as boyfriends, hanging out, music, sports, and so forth. Surprisingly, the overwhelming majority of the adolescents responded that the single most important thing for them was to spend time with an adult who cared about them. Although Dr. Staggers was not specifically working on a resiliency project, her findings are supported by several researchers in the field who have concluded that having a warm, positive, long-term relationship with an adult caretaker may be the single most important family protective factor for young children and adolescents (Kumpfer, 1993; Rutter, 1979; Werner, 1987). Rutter (1979) also found that having a warm and supportive relationship with one parent can offset the negative influence of a dysfunctional parent or of living in a family with a great deal of discord and tension. Others have recently found that the positive relationship does not even have to be with a primary caretaker. It can be with a friend, a coach, or the parent of a friend (Wolin & Wolin, 1993). Nettles (1993) has found the coaching relationship to be a powerful one. Coaches, not only in athletics but in all types of activities such as exercise, outdoor activities, music, drama, and so forth, can provide a structured learning environment for the development of competence, training in giving feedback, and instruction in a positive environment. Gullotta (1987) stresses the importance and wealth of resources of natural caregivers and urges preventionists to encourage youth to turn to the nonprofessionals in their environment for guidance and support. Programs that use peer tutors and cross-age tutors are building social supports by training these natural caregivers.

Positive Family Environment and Bonding

Cohesive, supportive families offer protection even when there is also dysfunction, such as substance abuse, by the parents (Kumpfer & DeMarsh, 1985). Brook, Gordon, Whiteman, and Cohen (1986) found that children who are attached to their parents and involved in family activities, whatever they may be, are less likely to initiate substance use and less likely to associate with drug users. If parents are also involved in their adolescents' lives in ways such as influencing peer choice and fostering prosocial activities, they create a strong positive bond. On the other hand, one recent study has found that if youngsters feel an attachment to a parent or parents and the parent does not spend time with them, this attachment actually becomes a risk factor. For example, a loved parent who moves out of the home after a divorce or separation and then does not spend a lot of time with the child (or children) left behind will cause the child to feel rejected and unlovable. This youngster would be more protected by being able to distance adaptively from the parents who are not eager to spend time with her or him (Richardson et al., 1989).

High Parental Expectations

Parents are all too often unaware of the degree to which children respond to parental expectations. Regardless of their own substance use, a parent who expects his or her child not to drink or take other drugs and makes this expectation known can have a tremendous influence on the child's decision not to use substances (Benard, 1990; Brook et al., 1986). Also, parents who have high but realistic expectations for their children's performance can help to create a protective environment, whereas parents who have expectations beyond what their children are developmentally capable of achieving may instill a self-perception of failure in their youngsters, because it is highly unlikely that such parents will praise their children enough for what they do achieve (Kumpfer & DeMarsh, 1985). The child who continuously hears a parental message of "You can do it!" will have a better chance of internalizing an optimistic attitude about his or her own ability (Mills, 1991).

Family Responsibilities

"You must do it!" is also an important message for parents to convey. Werner substantiated the importance of youth being given responsibilities in the household. Specifically, she found that being given chores to do on a regular basis, with the parental expectation that they will be done, was an important protective factor for high-risk youth (Werner & Smith, 1982, 1992). Her findings in this area were similar to those of Bleuler (1978), who realized that youth whose families need them to do tasks will feel that they have something to contribute and will feel valued and empowered. Youth who are given responsibility for taking care of some aspect of family life will internalize a feeling of competence, a sense that they can be counted on to contribute (Benard, 1990). A child who knows she can be counted on to care for younger siblings and to assume other family responsibilities, such as cleaning and taking charge of pets, will internalize a feeling of being able to rely on herself as well as a sense of being valued as a family member.

Positive Parental Modeling

Social learning theory (Bandura, 1977) stresses the importance of modeling behavior, and several researchers have found parental modeling to be a critical protective factor. It is very likely that parents who model resilient characteristics will exert influence in a positive way. Parents who are able to cope well in the face of adversity convey the message to their children that they can learn to do the same thing. An example of the direct effect of parental ability to cope with stress is how parents reacted to the closing of a New York City elementary school the day after it opened in fall 1992 due to a "lead paint crisis." Levels of lead paint were unacceptably high throughout the school. Some parents panicked and withdrew their children from the school; some brought their youngsters every day to be bused to a museum at the other end of the city and were visibly overwrought by the situation. Many were able to rise to the occasion and convey their sense of excitement that their kids were able to spend hot fall days in the Planetarium and Museum of Natural History. In general, the young students whose parents coped well with this lead crisis also coped well.

Good Parenting Skills and Supervision

Many prevention programs have been teaching parenting skills or family effectiveness training skills and have found positive results, particularly in combination with resistance skills training and parental involvement in school policy (Johnson et al., 1989). Kumpfer and DeMarsh (1985) found that even parents who were dysfunctional themselves, in terms of personal behaviors such as substance use, could be coached and assisted in developing more effective parenting styles. If these parents can be helped to establish good communication patterns and firm family boundaries and to provide consistent supervision and discipline, they will lay a protective foundation for their children. Mills (1993) describes a mother, often called to the school principal's office because of her adolescent son's bad behavior, who would immediately start yelling and swearing at her boy before she even found out what happened. When the housing project team suggested another way for her to respond she was able to do it. The next time she was called to school she did not yell or swear at her son but waited until they were home and quietly asked him what happened. He felt so supported by her that he soon stopped his disruptive behavior.

Werner and Smith (1982) emphasized the importance of firm parental discipline and monitoring the behavior of their children. They found this to be particularly important for adolescents. Hauser et al. (1989) also found that families tended to produce more resilient youth where there were consistently enforced rules in an atmosphere of praise and support. Baumrind's (1991) study of parenting styles found that authoritative but democratic parents who developed coherent and consistent family policies generate secure attachment and tend to produce the most competent resilient youth. Those who encouraged a verbal give-and-take, used reason and negotiation, and were willing to comply with some of their children's requests seemed to be fostering a sense of competence (Lewis, 1991).

Family Traditions and Rituals

Wolin and Wolin (1993) have studied the children of alcoholics extensively and have consistently found that firm rituals and traditions serve as powerful protective factors, even in the face of family dysfunction and chaos. If the family always has Sunday dinner together, celebrates holidays and birthdays, and honors achievements of the children such as graduations and sports events, the family will most likely see itself as cohesive and enduring. Families that have firm routines and rituals can actually foster a sense of independence in their children that will serve as a protective factor.

If adolescents can consistently rely on the fact that, no matter what else is going on, everyone will be home for dinner in the evening or they always will go to Grandma's on Sundays, they can feel freer to come and go, because they will have internalized a routine around which they can build a sense of personal freedom (Wolin & Wolin, 1993). An adolescent who never knows if or when the family will have dinner may become anxious and too watchful of family members' behavior and thus not feel free to establish a sense of independence or be able to separate from the family in an appropriate way. Wolin and Wolin (1993) state that children who grow up in families where there are rituals and traditions that are pleasant feel part of a unit larger than themselves. Children who grow up in families where traditions are absent tend to see themselves as alone.

The encouragement of religiosity is another family ritual that can serve as protection for adolescents. Developing a sense of spirituality, which may be achieved through membership in a religious institution as well as in other ways such as meditation or belonging to a positive larger community, can nurture a sense of belonging as well as competence. Researchers have found that adolescents who consider themselves spiritual or religious tend to be socially competent, a trait that is "defined by such characteristics as self-esteem, academic achievement, intellectual development, creativity, moral behavior, and/or an internal locus of control" (Thomas & Carver, 1990, p. 195). It is not so much the *doctrine* of the religious institution that helps to foster prosocial values and behavior, but rather the social and emotional support that religious affiliation can provide, as well as the nourishment of values that then help the adolescent to plan in a realistic way for his or her future (Thomas & Carver, 1990).

Werner (1987) affirms that it is essential to the development of effective coping strategies that children believe their environment to be reasonably predictable and that they can make realistic plans for their lives.

SUPPORTIVENESS OF YOUTH'S COMPETENCIES AND LIFE GOALS

Parents help build resiliency if they are involved in and supportive of a child's developing talents, competencies, and life choices (school, friends, career, mate), and if at critical turning points in a child's life they influence his or her choice of prosocial peers and instill prosocial norms (Brook, Nomura, & Cohen, 1989; Kumpfer & Turner, 1991). According to Rutter (1987), a family involved in a positive way in a child's decision-making processes, especially at key turning points in his or her life, will help build self-esteem and self-efficacy in that youngster. Perhaps this kind of interest on the part of the family helps to shape children who become what Garmezy (1981) has called "keepers of a dream."

Extended Family Support Networks

Garmezy (1993) relates how important a supportive extended family can be in times of crisis. He describes a woman in New York City who was in crisis: Her husband had died, she was being evicted, she had no money, no job, and three young children. She called her sister in Minneapolis who said, "Come to Minnesota." When the desperate sister arrived with her children, her sister helped her find public housing, enroll the children in school, and get on welfare until she could find a job. The support of her sister—and the state of Minnesota—enabled her to "bounce back in the face of adversity" and teach her children how to do the same. Obviously, if she had not had a sister in Minneapolis she would probably not have fared so well. Building and being able to rely on extended family and friend support networks has become almost "un-American" in this century, but resilient families are aware of the protective nature of this extended support system (Garmezy, 1993).

Werner (1979), too, underscores the importance of the extended family, and also friends who become like family, as sources of support and protection. Grandparents, particularly if they are not assuming primary responsibility for the supervision and discipline of their grandchildren, can provide a tremendous source of nurturance and warmth. It has also been found that a mother who has other adults living in the house or close by to help her with parenting is more able to maintain emotional stability and feelings of warmth toward her children (Werner & Smith, 1982). This argues for the development of support systems of uncles, aunts, roommates, close friends, and so forth, for the benefit of both the primary caretaker and her or his children.

SUMMING UP

In summation, this chapter presented the major risk and resiliency factors in the family that are associated with adolescent substance misuse as well as the theoretical underpinnings of the work in resiliency. The most significant family risk factors are:

- Being born into poverty and living with chronic familial tension and discord
- Having dysfunctional parents who are physically or sexually abusive, who abuse substances, and who suffer from serious mental illnesses
- Membership in a family where there is little warmth, support, or positive bonding, and there is parental nondirectiveness and permissiveness and not adequate supervision
- Experiencing the death of a significant adult before a child has reached the age of 11
- Living in a neighborhood where there is a great deal of turmoil and violence

There are numerous family attributes that can offer support and protection and thus serve to enhance resiliency.

- The most important family protective factor may be having an ongoing warm, positive relationship with a caring adult.
- Other critical family attributes are a home environment that is cohesive and supportive and parental expectations that are both realistically high and include non-drug-use values.
- Having to assume family responsibilities or chores serves as a protective factor because this gives the message to youngsters that they can be counted on to contribute to family life.
- Positive parental modeling, particularly in the areas of coping skills and educational level and job satisfaction, has a great influence on building and maintaining resiliency.
- Good parenting skills and supervision, supportiveness of youths' competencies and life goals, maintaining family traditions, and having extended family support networks are all significant family protective factors.

CONCLUSION

The shift in focus from risk to resiliency in the field of substance misuse prevention may have resounding significance. In many cases the strategies that prevention specialists choose to work with may be quite similar, whether they are proceeding from a risk-focused approach or a resiliency-focused approach. Efforts to strengthen family communication patterns and training in parenting skills are strategies that proponents of both approaches employ. Even though the strategies and practical implications may be similar, the shift in perspective is formidable. Developmental psychology has shown the importance of building self-efficacy and a sense of competence, of praising children for their accomplishments and achievements— their strengths (Baumrind, 1983, 1991; Masten, 1991). Whether one looks at what is wrong and tries to mitigate or correct it or looks at what is right and tries to enhance or strengthen it constitutes the fundamental difference between a focus on risk or resiliency.

REFERENCES

Bandura, A. (1977). *Social learning theory*. Englewood Cliffs, NJ: Prentice Hall.

Baumrind, D. (1983, October). *Why adolescents take chances—And why they don't*. Paper presented at the National Institute for Child Health and Human Development, Bethesda, M.D.

Baumrind, D. (1991). The influence of parenting style on adolescent competence and substance use. *Journal of Early Adolescence, 11*(1), 56-95.

Beck, A. T. (1976). *Cognitive therapy and the emotional disorders*. New York: International Universities Press.

Beck, A. T., Rush, A., & Shaw, E. (1979). *Cognitive therapy of depression*. New York: Guilford.

Benard, B. (1990). *The case for peers*. Portland, OR: Western Center for Drug-Free School and Communities.

Benard, B. (1993, April). [Discussion during conference on "Putting Resiliency into Substance Abuse Prevention for Adolescents."] Unpublished presentation, New York.

Bleuler, M. (1978). *The schizophrenic disorders*. New Haven, CT: Yale University Press.

Brook, J., Gordon, A. S., Whiteman, M., & Cohen, P. (1986). Some models and mechanisms for explaining the impact of maternal and adolescent characteristics on adolescent stage of drug use. *Developmental Psychology, 22*, 460-467.

Brook, J., Nomura, C., & Cohen, P. (1989). A network of influences on adolescent drug involvement: Neighborhood, school, peer and family. *Genetic, Social and General Psychology Monographs, 115*, 125-145.

Chavkin, W. (1990, July 10). Help, don't fail addicted mothers. *Village Voice*, p. 11.

Cook, B. W. (1992). *Eleanor Roosevelt*. New York: Viking.

Cowen, E., Work, W. C., Hightower, A. D., Wyman, P. A., Parker, J. R., & Lotyczewski, B. (1991). Toward the development of a measure of perceived self-efficacy in children. *Journal of Clinical Child Psychology, 20*(2), 169-178.

Garmezy, N. (1981). Children under stress: Perspectives on antecedents and correlates of vulnerability and resistance to psychopathology. In A. I. Rabin, J. Aronoff, A. N. Barclay, & R. A. Zucker (Eds.), *Further explorations in personality* (pp. 196-269). New York: John Wiley.

Garmezy, N. (1991). Resiliency and vulnerability to adverse developmental outcomes associated with poverty. *The American Behavioral Scientist, 34*(4), 416-430.

Garmezy, N. (1993, April). [Discussion during conference on "Putting Resiliency into Substance Abuse Prevention for Adolescents."] Unpublished presentation, New York.

Gilligan, C., Lyons, N. P., & Hanmer, T. J. (Eds.). (1990). *Making connections: The relational worlds of adolescent girls at Emma Willard School*. Cambridge, MA: Harvard University Press.

Gomes-Schwartz, B., Horowitz, J., & Cardarell, A. (1990). *Child sexual abuse: The initial effects*. Newbury Park, CA: Sage.

Gullotta, T. (1987). Prevention's technology. *Journal of Primary Prevention, 8*(1 & 2), 4-23.

Hartman, A., & Laird, J. (1983). *Family centered social work practice*. New York: Free Press.

Hauser, S. T., Powers, S. I., Noam, G. G., Jacobson, A. (1984). Familial contexts of adolescent ego development. *Child Development, 55*, 195-213.

Hauser, S. T., Vieyra, M. A., Jacobson, A., & Wertlieb, D. (1989). Family aspects of vulnerability and resilience in adolescence: A theoretical perspective. In T. Dugan & R. Coles (Eds.), *The child in our times: Studies in the development of resiliency* (pp. 109-133). New York: Brunner/Mazel.

Hawkins, J. D., Catalano, R. F., & Miller, J. Y. (1992). Risk and protective factors for alcohol and other drug problems in adolescence and early adulthood: Implications for substance abuse prevention. *Psychological Bulletin, 112*(1), 64-105.

Jessor, R., & Jessor, S. (1977). *Problem behavior and psychosocial development*. New York: Academic Press.

Johnson, C. A., Pentz, M. A., Weber, M. D., Dwyer, J. H., MacKinnon, D. P., Flay, B., Baer, N. A., & Hansen, W. B. (1989). The relative effectiveness of comprehensive community programming for drug abuse with high-risk and low risk adolescents. *Journal of Consulting and Clinical Psychology, 58*(4), 447-456.

Kumpfer, K. (1993). *Resiliency and AOD use prevention in high risk youth*. Unpublished manuscript. [Available from School of Social Work, University of Utah, Salt Lake City, UT 84112]

Kumpfer, K., & DeMarsh, J. (1985). Family environmental and genetic influences on children's future chemical dependency. *Journal of Children in Contemporary Society: Advances in Theory and Applied Research, 18*, 49-92.

Kumpfer, K., & Turner, C. (1991). The social ecology model of adolescent substance abuse: Implications for prevention. *The International Journal of the Addictions, 25*(4A), 435-463.

Lazarus, R. S., & Launier, R. (1978). Stress-related transactions between person and environment. In L. A. Pervin & M. Lewis (Eds.), *Perspectives in international psychology* (pp. 287-327). New York: Plenum.

Lewis, C. S. (1991). The effects of parental firm control: A reinterpretation of findings. *Psychological Bulletin, 90*(3), 547-563.

Masten, A. (1991, November). *Risk and resilience in children.* Paper presented at the Protecting Vulnerable Children Project, Children of Alcoholics Foundation, Inc., Princeton University, Princeton, New Jersey.

Mills, R. (1991). A new understanding of self: The role of affect, state of mind, self-understanding and intrinsic motivation. *Journal of Experimental Education, 60*(10), 67-81.

Mills, R. (1993, April). [Discussion during conference on "Putting Resiliency into Substance Abuse Prevention for Adolescents."] Unpublished presentation, New York.

Mitchell, R. E., Billings, A. G., & Moos, R. H. (1982). Social support and well-being: Implications for prevention programs. *Journal of Primary Prevention, 3*(2), 77-98.

Nettles, S. M. (1993, April). [Discussion during conference on "Putting Resiliency into Substance Abuse Prevention for Adolescents."] Unpublished presentation, New York.

Norman, E., & Turner, S. (1993). Adolescent substance abuse prevention programs in the encouraging 80's. *Journal of Primary Prevention, 14*(1), 3-24.

Pryor-Brown, L., & Cowen, E. (1989). Stressful life events, support and children's school adjustment. *Journal of Clinical Child Psychology, 18*(3), 214-220.

Richardson, J., Dwyer, K., McGuigan, R., Hansen, W. B., Dent, C., Johnson, C. A., Sussman, S. Y., Brannon, B., & Flay, B. (1989). Substance use among eighth-grade students who take care of themselves after school. *Pediatrics, 84*(3), 556-566.

Richardson, G. E., Neiger, B. L., Jensen, S., & Kumpfer, K. (1990). The resiliency model. *Health Education, 21*(6), 33-39.

Rutter, M. (1979). Protective factors in children's responses to stress and disadvantage. In M. W. Kent & J. Rolf (Eds.), *Primary prevention of psychopathology: Vol. 3. Social competence in children* (pp. 49-74). Hanover, NH: University Press of New England.

Rutter, M. (1987, July). Psychosocial resilience and protective mechanisms. *American Journal of Orthopsychiatry, 57*(3), 316-331.

Rutter, M., & Giller, H. (1983). *Juvenile delinquency: Trends and perspectives.* New York: Penguin.

Seligman, M. (1975). *Helplessness: On depression, development and death.* San Francisco: Freeman.

Smith, L. (1954). *The journey.* New York: Norton.

Staggers, B. (1991, November). [Discussion during Conference for Prevention Specialists, Oakland, CA.] Unpublished presentation.

Thomas, D. L., & Carver, C. (1990). Religion and adolescent social competence. In T. Gullotta, G. Adams, & R. Montemayor (Eds.), *Developing social competency in adolescence* (pp. 195-213). Newbury Park, CA: Sage.

Werner, E. (1979). *The transactional model: Application to the longitudinal study of the high risk child on the Island of Kauai, Hawaii.* Paper presented at the Biannual Meeting of the Society for Research on Child Development, San Francisco.

Werner, E. (1987). Vulnerability and resiliency in children at risk for delinquency: A longitudinal study from birth to young adulthood. In J. Burchard and S. Burchard (Eds.), *Prevention of delinquent behavior* (pp. 16-43). Newbury Park, CA: Sage.

Werner, E., & Smith, R. S. (1982). *Vulnerable but invincible.* New York: McGraw-Hill.

Werner, E., & Smith, R. S. (1992). *Overcoming the odds: High risk children from birth to adulthood.* Ithaca, NY: Cornell University Press.

Wolin, S., & Wolin, S. (1993). *The resilient self.* New York: Villard Books.

Zunz, S., Turner, S., & Norman, E. (1993). Accentuating the positive: Stressing resiliency in school-based substance abuse prevention programs. *Social Work in Education, 15*(3), 169-176.

4. Social and Community Factors Associated With Drug Use and Abuse Among Adolescents

David F. Duncan
Brown University

Rick Petosa
The Ohio State University

Standards of acceptable drug use are a function of cultural and societal norms. In the United States, public concern and political response have produced a public policy of "War" on drugs. Yet at the same time, Americans continue to consume huge quantities of alcohol, tobacco, caffeine, over-the-counter (OTC) remedies, and medical prescriptions. Despite the documented social, health, and economic costs of misuse, these drugs continue to be subsidized by the government, produced and promoted by manufacturers, and overused by consumers. In this climate it is not surprising that adolescents in the United States have the highest levels of illicit drug use of any industrialized nation in the world (Johnston, O'Malley, & Bachman, 1991). Nearly all young people (93%) have tried alcohol by the time they graduate from high school, and 41% report occasional binge drinking (five or more drinks at one time). Although rates have declined, 63% of adolescents experiment with an illicit psychoactive drug other than alcohol before they finish high school. Clearly, experimentation with drugs is normative for adolescents, but drug abuse is not.

The purpose of this chapter is to examine three distinctive transitions in drug use among adolescents. The first is the transition from nonuse to drug use characteristic of most adolescents. The second is the less frequent but potentially more harmful transition from use to drug abuse. The third transition is from abuse back to use or nonuse. These transitions are, by definition, sequenced but not inevitable. An adolescent cannot become a drug abuser without first beginning to use drugs—but the initiation of drug use does not inevitably, or even usually, lead to drug abuse. A host of peer, family, and community factors can either inhibit or facilitate these transitions. These factors serve as the foundation for effective drug-abuse prevention efforts.

These transitions are one aspect of adolescent development and can best be understood in the contexts of normal and abnormal development. The transition from nonuse to use of some drugs is a normative part of adolescent development in American culture. Initial drug use is socially learned, developmentally functional behavior. The transition from use to abuse, on the other hand, is a maladaptive response pattern marked by a failure to achieve successfully developmental tasks characteristic of adolescence.

The analysis of drug use presented in this chapter focuses on the dynamic interaction between drugs, adolescents, and their environment. The patterns of interaction-producing transitions to drug use and drug abuse are best described in behavioral, developmental, and social terms. Common legal and moral definitions of drug abuse are inconsistent with this approach. Drug abuse is indicated when a pattern of consistent drug use is maintained despite of negative social and health consequences. Drug taking assumes an increasingly central role in the abuser's life. Other daily activities become subordinate to drug use. Considerable time and effort is spent raising money for, buying, and using drugs. This investment of effort in drug use supports the development of a drug-centered social network and the emergence of the addict role-identity. Concurrently, adolescent social role function becomes impaired. Effectiveness in family, school, work, and peer roles becomes compromised. The transition from drug user to drug abuser is complex, gradual, and rarely a cognizant choice made by individuals. Critical to our purposes is an understanding of the factors that increase adolescent susceptibility to the drug-abuse process.

THE TRANSITION FROM NONUSE TO USE

In an overview of the literature on risk factors for drug abuse, Glantz and Pickens (1991) conclude that "In general, drug use appears to be more a function of social and peer factors, whereas abuse appears to be more a function of biological and psychological processes" (p. 9). One example of research on risk factors for use and abuse is the three-wave study of drinking behavior among seventh graders conducted by Ellickson and Hays (1991). They surveyed

1,966 students at 30 schools—20 where a smoking and drug prevention program had been conducted and 10 control schools. Students were surveyed at baseline and 3-month and 12-month intervals afterward. At the beginning of the study, 23% of the students reported that they had never tried alcohol. The only significant predictors of alcohol use at Wave 2 were marijuana use by peers and alcohol use by peers and adults; at Wave 3 the most powerful predictor was use at Wave 2. Future heavy drinking among the initial nonusers was best predicted by exposure to marijuana and cigarettes and by expectations of future drug use, but parental drinking and peer approval of cigarettes were also significant if less powerful. Beliefs about the danger of alcohol were not strong enough to prevent heavy drinking. The results of this study make clear that the paths to alcohol use and abuse are complex. Programs that target a single risk factor, such as self-esteem or poor school achievement, are unlikely to have a significant impact.

Kandel and Davies (1991) identified risk factors for the onset of marijuana use. The risk factors identified for both genders were: low attendance at religious services, high educational expectations, participation in delinquent activities, and parental use of psychoactive drugs such as minor tranquilizers. Risk factors for females were: use of marijuana in their peer group, high level of family education, and lack of closeness to their parents. Male risk factors were: low level of parent education and strong peer orientation. Summarizing their results, Kandel and Davies (1991) concluded that:

> In general, young people at risk for marijuana initiation are more deviant than their peers and come from families where the parents appear to experience some form of psychological problems. . . . Conventionality is a restraining factor for involvement in marijuana, although high levels of educational aspirations increase the risk. (p. 231)

These and similar studies indicate that a complex web of social factors influence decisions to use drugs. Figure 4.1 illustrates these factors in a model. Peer and parental use appears to provide: models of use, access to drugs, and the motivation and support to initiate use. An adolescent's transition from nonuse to use of any drug may be conceived of as resulting from a combination of three factors: First, the drug must be sufficiently available to the adolescent.

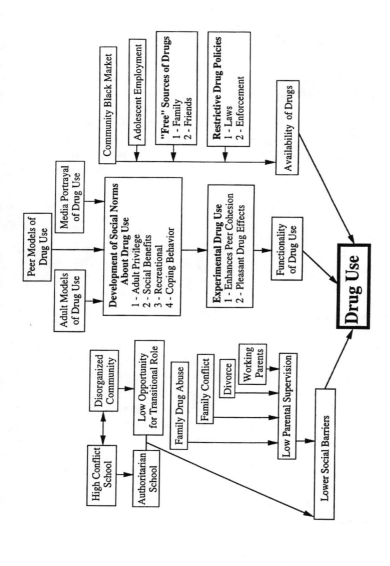

Figure 4.1. Web of Causation for Drug Use

Second, the adolescent must perceive some functional value in using the drug. Third, restraints against use must be eliminated, reduced, or neutralized.

AVAILABILITY OF DRUGS

Availability means that the drug must be obtainable within the community where the adolescent lives. Drugs are most often acquired from adults and peers in the immediate social environment. The drug must be obtainable at a cost the adolescent can afford. Furthermore, the adolescent must know how to obtain the drug in a relatively risk-free manner. Risk assessments are based primarily on perceived ability to avoid negative legal or social consequences.

Community Factors in Availability

Specific psychoactive drugs are more available in some communities than in others. Alcohol, tobacco, and marijuana are available, to some degree, in virtually every American community. The quality, cost, and ease of availability, however, may vary widely. Other drugs, including cocaine, crack, coca paste, heroin, and LSD, are available in some communities and unavailable in others. Obviously an adolescent must have access to a drug before becoming a user of it. The more available the drug is, the easier it is for an adolescent to become a user. Kaplan and Johnson (1991) note the role of opportunities in which "a supply of drugs is available and there is an occasion for use" (p. 301) in increasing the likelihood of drug use.

Alcohol availability has been manipulated through various public policy interventions in an effort to moderate drinking on a community-wide basis. This has included such measures as:

1. restricting sales of alcohol to a limited number of state-owned liquor stores
2. forbidding sales in pharmacy, grocery, and "convenience" stores
3. restricting the days and hours on which alcohol can be sold
4. restricted numbers of liquor licenses
5. restrictions on advertising of alcohol

Whether or not such policies have any impact on adult alcohol consumption, Coate and Grossman (1985) found that they had no influence on adolescent drinking.

The failure of availability restriction policies to reduce adolescent drinking may be related to the means by which adolescents obtain alcohol. Teenagers, for the most part, do not buy alcohol in stores (whether convenience stores or state-monopoly liquor stores). Nor do they get most of their alcohol in bars. Their sources are more often friends and older associates as well as thefts from their parents' liquor supplies. These sources are little affected by public policy restrictions on availability.

One public policy that is aimed particularly at restricting the availability of alcohol to adolescents is the minimum drinking age. Minimum drinking age laws are a direct attempt to keep teens from drinking by force of law. In 1984, the U.S. Congress passed the Uniform Minimum Drinking Age Act (Public Law 98-363). Under this law, a percentage of federal highway funds would be withheld from states that did not make the legal drinking age 21. In response, all 50 states and the District of Columbia have a drinking age of 21. Most studies have failed to show any impact of drinking age laws on adolescent drinking. In a review conducted during the early 1970s, Smart and Goodstadt (1977) concluded that raising the minimum drinking age produced a small reduction in alcohol consumption. Later studies, however, did not support this effect. Coate and Grossman's (1985) analysis of data from the second National Health Examination Survey revealed that a lower minimum legal drinking age was associated with lower rates of adolescent beer drinking. It is possible that minimum drinking age laws have a small effect when first adopted, but effects on availability fade after a few years.

Furthermore, recent initiatives to raise the drinking age from 18 to 21 in many states have been urged, in part, on the grounds that 18- to 20-year-olds often act as suppliers of alcohol to younger adolescents. Raising the drinking age, it has been argued, would restrict early adolescents' access to alcohol by creating a greater age gap between them and legal alcohol purchasers. Evidence suggests that these measures have reduced availability of alcohol to teenagers but appear to have done so at the cost of increasingly deviant drinking behavior in the 18- to 20-year age group: more drinking of distilled liquor, obtaining alcohol in larger quantities, and more drinking in cars (Hughes, Power, & Francis, 1992; O'Hare, 1990).

Prohibition is intended as the ultimate restriction on availability. Outlawing a drug is supposed to make it unavailable to everyone. In reality, however, outlawing a popular drug only drives it into a black market economy. It is in the nature of black markets that they are unregulated. There are no age limits or other regulatory restrictions in a black market. Anyone who has the cash can buy drugs from black market dealers, who seldom have any hesitation about selling drugs to adolescents.

When prohibition reduces drug availability it tends to inflate the price of the drugs. This may limit adolescent access to drugs to some extent. Less expensive drugs, such as marijuana and crack, are likely to be the first illicit drugs used by adolescents because of their greater affordability. It is relevant to this point that high school students with after-school jobs are more likely to become illicit drug users (O'Malley, Johnston, & Bachman, 1985). Robins and Regier (1991) suggest in this light that "drug use may be promoted by a relative abundance of disposable income" (p. 139). In relation to alcohol, Coate and Grossman (1985) found that adolescent consumption of wine and liquor, but not of beer, was reduced by higher prices. They hypothesized that beer was so cheap that variations in its price did not limit adolescents' access to it. Another way to increase the price of drugs is to increase excise taxes. On the basis of simulations conducted for NIAAA, Grossman (1989) concluded that substantial increases in excise taxes for beer would reduce motor vehicle fatalities among 18- to 20-year-olds by 21%. Grossman asserts that the tax would have greater effect than increases in minimum drinking age because the restrictions on drinking age are commonly circumvented. It is important to note that Grossman's simulations have not been tested empirically.

Skager and Fisher (1989) found—contrary to popular expectations —in a representative survey of 11th-grade students in California public high schools, that the highest rates of drug abuse occurred in rural or small town schools with the highest proportions of white students. Next highest levels were reported by students in large, predominantly white high schools in urban or suburban settings. Lowest levels of drug use were reported in urban, heavily minority schools. One reasonable interpretation of these results is that drug use is highest in the population of adolescents who are best able to afford drugs.

Social Factors in Availability

Popular media mythology depicts the drug pusher hanging around the schoolyard, trying to entice schoolchildren into trying his illicit wares. Real drug dealers, of course, do not behave this way. Most have a ready market for their drugs and no need to develop new clientele, especially among schoolchildren who have too little disposable income to be an attractive market.

Instead of the pusher, it is usually a friend, older sibling, or parent who introduces adolescents to drug use. Numerous studies show that most illicit drug users received their first dose as a gift from a close friend. As they continue to use, their earliest purchases are likely to be from friends who sell the drug to them at little or no profit. Eventually they learn where and who the drug dealers are, and this, too, they learn from their peers.

Parents can also be a source of drugs for adolescents. In an extensive review of the literature, Blane and Hewitt (1977) found that parents were the most commonly reported source of alcohol for teenagers. Parent supplies appear common in rural areas (Globetti, Alsikafi, & Morse, 1977). Some parents claim they have more control of their child's drug of choice and subsequent risk behavior (i.e., drinking and driving) if they provide the alcohol (McKechnie, 1976). Often parents are not aware that their children are secretly accessing their stores of alcohol or drugs. Baumrind (1985) found that children of illicit drug users are much more likely to be directly exposed to these drugs and even be supplied by their parents.

COMMUNITY FACTORS
IN THE FUNCTIONALITY OF DRUG USE

It is a common observation that ours is a drug-using culture. In one sense this is a meaningless observation. All human cultures are drug-using cultures. The only drug-free people, since the Stone Age, were those whom whites called "Eskimos." Their culture remained drug free only as long as their environment contained no available drugs. Once trade with whites made alcohol and tobacco available, the prevalence of addiction to both drugs rapidly approached 100%. Some archaeologists have suggested that human culture had its beginnings in drug use, with primitive hunter-gatherers first settling down and adopting agriculture in order to raise grapes for wine and/or barley for beer.

In a sense, though, the United States' drug culture may be relevant. Gerbner (1990) suggests that U.S. society promotes the idea that drugs can provide any easy answer to any problem. Berger (1974) calls this the "pain-pill-pleasure" model, in which people with a problem (upset stomach, headache, general stress) take a pill and obtain relief. It is not much of a leap from the notion that small problems can be "fixed" by taking drugs to drugs as a response to most problems. We are exposed to the pain-pill-pleasure model so often that it is probably ingrained in our psyches. Johnson (1974) goes so far as to describe television as a pusher of drugs through the effects of drug advertising. Choate and Debevoise (1976) contend that "children who see over 1,000 OTC commercials each year are picking up a pro-drug message and can be expected to act upon those messages sometime in the subsequent months and years" (p. 91).

Testing this hypothesis, Hulbert (1974) surveyed 990 college students regarding their television viewing and drug use. He found a positive association between the number of nonprescription drug ads the subjects could recall and marijuana use. He also found a negative association between the number of hours of weekend television viewing and use of marijuana, barbiturates, LSD, and cocaine. Weekday television viewing showed no associations with drug use.

A later study by Milavsky, Pekowsky, and Stipp (1976) found a weak positive relationship between drug advertising and use of nonprescription drugs but no association with illicit drug use. Studies by Robertson, Rossiter, and Gleason (1979) and by Martin and Duncan (1984) found no link between exposure to drug advertisements and illicit drug use. The evidence thus remains mixed as to whether drug advertising and the pain-pill-pleasure model are a factor in promoting drug use.

Some concern has been raised about the effectiveness of alcohol and cigarette advertising in promoting use among young people. A larger concern is the impact of all media portrayals of drug use on the attitudes of youth. Young adolescents are preoccupied with the need to enhance personal attractiveness and social value (Elkind, 1978). As a consequence, it is hypothesized that they are extremely susceptible to the glamorous images of alcohol and cigarette users portrayed in the media. Over time these images may support attitudes toward drug use as a sign of autonomy, competence, attractiveness, maturity, or "toughness." Research on the impact of mass media on children's behavior has focused on preadolescents' retention of commercials and impact on aggressive behavior (Esserman, 1981). Cigarettes and hard liquor are not advertised on television or radio but can be in magazines and on billboards. Beer and wine can be advertised in any medium. Goodstadt and Mitchell (1990) concluded that studies of the impact of alcohol advertising have demonstrated little or no effect on alcohol consumption. This supports the alcohol industries' claim that their advertising focuses on brand selection and not on promoting use among youth. This claim should be viewed tentatively, however, because studies of the advertising/consumption link have not been specific to adolescents.

PEER FACTORS AND LEARNING FUNCTIONALITY OF DRUG USE

As social beings, adolescents are heavily influenced by values, beliefs, and social norms acquired through relationships with others. Adults and the peer group play an important role in teaching adolescents to use drugs. Social cognitive theory (Bandura, 1986) provides a useful framework for describing the basic processes involved in learning drug-use behavior. Experimentation with drug use originates from exposure to models in the adolescent's social environment. Influential models tend to hold some desirable status or valued attributes to the observing adolescent. Observed consequences of modeled actions promote the development of outcome expectations. Maturity, independence, attractiveness, and social acceptance are just a few of the personal needs adolescents may associate with drug use. These outcome expectations serve as powerful motivations for experimentation with drug use. Actual drug use is then reinforced through processes of personal attribution, peer response, and parental reactions. For example, if a parent has a strong negative emotional response upon discovering his or her child's drug use, it may serve directly to reinforce beliefs of drug use as rebellion and challenge to adult authority.

Popular conceptions of peer pressure to use drugs imply direct, coercive ploys designed to force adolescents to comply with group norms. In most cases, however, peer pressure to use drugs appears to be a subtle, indirect process of influence. In a prospective longitudinal study, Newman (1984) found that peer groups influence the social meaning of drug use by associating it with images of social recognition, independence, maturity, fun, and a variety of desirable outcomes. Thus drug use often occurs in peer groups because adolescents reinforce each other's beliefs in these images. Peer mutual reinforcement of beliefs regarding the payoffs for drug use provides a powerful social basis for drug use.

LOWER SOCIAL BARRIERS

Our society sets many restraints in the path of becoming a user of illicit drugs. Far more important than the external barriers placed in the path of availability are those internal restraints that society seeks to ingrain in each citizen. In order to become a drug user an adolescent must overcome these internalized restraints to some degree. Internalized barriers often become situational as adolescents discover social and physical environments that are supportive of drug use.

Community Factors
That Neutralize Restraints

In every society the use of certain drugs is accepted as normative but the use of other drugs is taboo. Norms also dictate acceptable situations, purposes, and participants. Use of alcohol by adults is widespread and widely accepted in most elements of American society. Tobacco use was widely accepted in the past but is increasingly becoming a taboo practice. "It is noteworthy that the caffeine in coffee is the one remaining psychoactive drug whose regular use is acceptable and encouraged at work in our society" (Lewis, 1993). Gitlin (1990) raises the possibility that "glamorous representations of drugs may well have an added effect of rendering drugs legitimate for some portion of the audience" (p. 47), and "in American society, the likelihood is that the direct and specific images of drugs, whether positive or negative, play an independent part in accelerating drug use, and that the impact of these images, although limited, is not negligible" (p. 49).

The news media play an important role in shaping youth's ideas about drugs—both establishing restraints and neutralizing them. In Canada, for instance, Fejer, Smart, Whitehead, and Laforest (1971) found that nearly 6 out of 10 high school students reported that the news media were their primary sources of information about drugs; next most common (but far behind) were friends. The same is probably true for American adolescents. This is important because news media reports and antidrug messages in the mass media are frequently distorted and could have a negative impact on rational decision making regarding drugs (Gerbner, 1977, 1990).

Both antidrug messages and news reports are dominated by "pro-phylactic lies"—false or distorted reports of the dangers of illicit drug use. A good example is the famous television spot that shows an egg, declaring, "This is your brain," then the egg being fried in a skillet, to the words, "This is your brain on drugs." Of course, none of the illicit drugs has an effect on the human brain that remotely resembles being fried, nor have any abusable drugs other than alcohol and tobacco been demonstrated to be associated with clinically signifi-cant brain damage. Petosa (1992), in a review of drug-use preven-tion approaches, found that many programs also use exaggerated and obscure dangers as a motivational basis. When adolescents learn through association with drug-using peers that these distortions are lies, they come to mistrust these prevention programs. Thus scare tactics aimed at protecting adolescents from drug use may actually help tear down the restraints against such use.

The school environment plays a major role in the process of developing adolescent drug use. Schools that are rigid and authori-tarian in their disciplinary policies tend to promote disrespect for authority. When students are subject to rules that exist purely by the fiat of some authority figure, without need for any rational basis, they can come to doubt the rationality of all of society's rules—in-cluding those regarding drugs. The negative attitudes fostered by authoritarian school systems make students more susceptible to drug use. Low perceived peer affect toward school, low academic performance, low perception of freedom in school, and negative attitude toward school have been identified—along with few friend-ships and low affiliation with children—by Scheier and Newcomb (1991) as risk factors for experimentation with drug use.

Lack of church involvement also appears to be a factor in the in-itiation of drug use. Fors and Rojek (1983), for instance, found in a survey of 6th- through 12th-grade students that the greater the regu-larity of church attendance, the lower the use of alcohol, tobacco, and marijuana.

Peer Factors That Neutralize Restraints

Association with drug-using peers is a powerful influence promoting adolescent drug use (Kaplan & Johnson, 1991). The importance of peer pressure urging the adolescent to use drugs may well have been generally overestimated. Although direct pressures to use drugs may be substantial in some cases, this is probably less often the case. Drug use may be a condition for acceptance as a member of some peer groups, but many drug-using peer groups contain nonusing members who are well accepted into the group. Homogeneity of drug use in peer groups is often motivated by pressures or support toward conformity to expectations, but it is also common for members of a peer group to be chosen on the basis of possessing similar attitudes and behaviors. The extent to which each of these two forces explains shared drug-use patterns is not clear.

Far more important than direct pressure is the effect association with drug-using peers has on social restraints against drug use. As mentioned above, the adolescent learns from these associations that much of what school and media have taught the adolescent about drugs is false. The drug-using peer group teaches the adolescent that drug users as a group are no more sick or evil or weak or dependent than the rest of their peers.

Perceived drug use by peers may be as important as actual peer drug use. Adolescents who believe that drug use is common among their peer group are likely to accept the idea that drug use is normative behavior. Drug users tend to overestimate the proportion of their peers who also use drugs (Bowker, 1974; Duryea & Martin, 1981). This distortion in perceived norms may influence students' motivations to use drugs. The adolescent inclination to think in exaggerated terms (i.e., "everybody does it") contributes to this tendency.

Sheppard (1989), however, has challenged this view. He found, in a study of 2,319 elementary and secondary school students in Ontario, that there was no significant association between perceived drug use, either at their own school or generally among Ontario students, and students' self-reported intentions to use cannabis in the next 2 years. The weakness of this study is its use of behavioral intentions that may or may not be closely related to actual future use.

Peer influence on the neutralization of restraints is not limited to drug-using peers. Association with peers who are socially deviant reduces the impact of social restraints on adolescent behavior. Cadoret (1991), for instance, identified "bad friends"—friends not approved of by the adolescent's parent—as a risk factor for initiation of drug use. Downs and Rose (1991) likewise found that identification with delinquent peers was associated with the highest levels of alcohol and drug use, the most positive attitudes toward such use, the lowest levels of perceived harm due to such use, and the highest levels of other psychosocial problems such as depression, low self-esteem, and alienation. Brook, Cohen, Whiteman, and Gordon (1991) found that adolescents who associated with deviant peers were 2.66 times as likely to use drugs; peer drug use showed a positive but nonsignificant association with adolescent drug use in their study.

THE BENEFITS OF
EXPERIMENTAL DRUG USE

It is often assumed that psychoactive drug use among adolescents is always negative. Newcomb and Bentler (1989) suggest that "infrequent, intermittent, or occasional use of drugs by a basically healthy teenager probably has few short-term and no long-term negative or adverse consequences" (p. 246). Baumrind (1985) perceives adolescent experimentation of various types as being more "health-enhancing" than are risk avoidant behaviors that are phobic or sedentary. As evidence, Baumrind points to studies that show that experimental use of marijuana in nondelinquent populations is associated with positive attributes including independence, friendliness, self-confidence, and intelligence. Newcomb and Bentler (1989) found that in the quantities typically used by normal adolescents, cigarettes were more harmful to health than alcohol, marijuana, or most other drugs used over a 4-year period.

It is apparent that for most healthy adolescents there are clear social benefits and minimal perceived negative health consequences of experimental drug use. The social milieu of American adolescence clearly defines social benefits of the experimental use of psychoactive drugs. Simultaneously, adolescents have difficulty estimating drug-use risk or accepting personal susceptibility to negative outcomes. In addition, most adolescents will use drugs with little or immediate health consequences. These experiences simultaneously increase the functional role of drugs and reduce social barriers to drug use.

THE TRANSITION FROM USE TO ABUSE

Glantz and Pickens (1991) state that "In general, drug use appears to be more a function of social and peer factors, whereas abuse appears to be more a function of biological and psychological processes" (p. 9). Although we agree in part, we believe that peer and community influences do play an important role in the transition from use to abuse. An adolescent's transition from use to abuse of any drug may be conceived of as resulting from an interaction among three factors: First, genetic or biological predisposition; second, use of drugs becomes a central element in the user's life; third, the user's identification with the addict role and fear of withdrawal (see Figure 4.2).

The genetic or biological predisposition is outside the scope of this chapter. Excellent reviews of the literature on genetic predisposition to alcoholism are to be found in Sher (1991) and Anthenelli and Schuckit (1992). A genetic predisposition to alcoholism does seem to exist, but it appears to be much less important than nonbiological factors in the etiology of alcoholism. There is far less evidence to tell us whether such predispositions exist for any other drug of abuse.

CENTRALITY OF DRUG TAKING IN THE ABUSER'S LIFE

One reason why the abuser persists in drug taking despite negative consequences is that the drug has come to hold a central place in the abuser's life. Drug taking has entered into a great many arenas of the abuser's life. The adolescent abuser goes to school under the influence of drugs, plays sports under the influence, socializes under the influence, works under the influence, and so forth. Discontinuing drug taking would disrupt the abuser's entire life. Drug taking becomes one of the major life activities of the abuser. For the dependent abuser, or addict, drug taking has become a major end in itself and much of the adolescent's life comes to be organized around the need to obtain and use his or her drug of choice. At this stage it

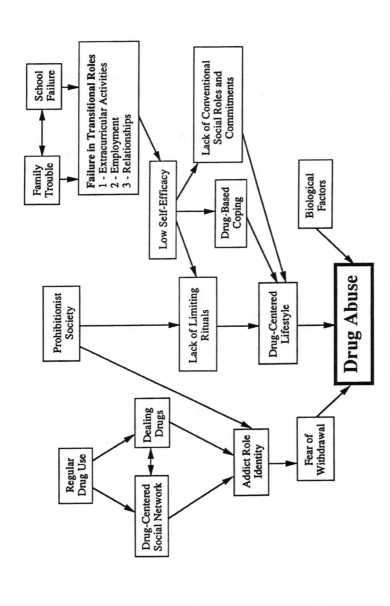

Figure 4.2. Web of Causation for Drug Abuse

71

is obvious that the centrality of drug taking to the abuser's life has become more symptomatic of abuse than causal of it. This state, however, is only gradually achieved.

The way that drugs come to occupy such a central role in the abuser's life is largely a result of the principle of learning known as negative reinforcement. Although the drug user typically takes drugs in order to achieve a pleasant state of mind, the drug abuser is more likely to take drugs in order to escape from an unpleasant state of mind. When any behavior, such as taking a drug, is followed by relief from an ongoing unpleasant condition, such as anxiety or depression, the frequency of that behavior in the future is increased. This process is known as negative reinforcement (Holland & Skinner, 1961; Skinner, 1953), a concept often confused with, but actually more nearly the opposite of, punishment. The result of negative reinforcement is a habit that is likely to occur very frequently and is highly resistant to change.

Alcohol, marijuana, and other sedative-hypnotic drugs are highly effective in relieving anxiety and loosening inhibitions. The oblivion resulting from using these drugs to the point of loosing consciousness provides an escape from any negative affect. Heroin and other narcotics are particularly effective in the suppression of sexual or aggressive impulses. They also provide relief from feelings of alienation, depersonalization, or fragmentation. Both heroin and LSD have been used in some cases to suppress psychotic symptoms or to give them a more acceptable attribution—"I'm only 'seeing things' because I took a drug, not because I'm crazy." In any of these instances, drug use becomes negatively reinforced. The adolescent will feel a need for the drug whenever there is a possibility of experiencing the negative emotions. A negatively reinforced behavior is likely to become a part of every aspect of a person's life. If drugs are being taken to avoid a negative emotional state, such as depression, then they will be taken whenever the adolescent wishes to avoid depression. Because depression is not something anyone ever wants to experience, drug taking soon becomes an everyday activity.

Cocaine abuse seems to be the major exception to the abuse pattern described above. A significant minority of cocaine abusers do seek escape from depression or feelings of inferiority through this drug of choice. A far more common pattern, however, is the abuser whose cocaine taking is a means of coping with high-pressure demands for performance—at school, in athletics, or on the job—that the abuser has difficulty in meeting. For reasons that are primarily a function of price structures, the first pattern is more often found in crack users, and the second pattern is more common in users of cocaine powder (cocaine hydrochloride).

Another principle of learning that plays a part in the growing centrality of drug taking in the lives of some abusers is that of *state dependent learning*. State dependent learning takes place under the influence of a psychoactive drug and is only fully remembered when the learner is again under the influence of the same drug. Through this process, drug taking may become inseparably linked with other aspects of the adolescent's life. For the abusing adolescent in particular, having fun may become a state dependent behavior, with the adolescent actually finding difficulty performing in the drug-free state certain behaviors, such as dancing, socializing with the opposite sex, or playing pool, that have habitually been done under the influence of drugs.

Peer Factors in the Growing Centrality of Drugs

The transition from drug use to abuse is partly due to the lack of internalized rules and rituals that make the controlled use of potentially abusive drugs a possibility (Duncan & Gold, 1985; Zinberg, Harding, & Winkeller, 1977). For the controlled user these rules define how, when, and where the drug is to be taken. The controlled user has learned to use the drug in a minimally hazardous fashion, to recognize a safe level of intoxication and not exceed it, and to take the drug only at times and places where it will be safe. Perhaps the most common such rules are time limits—not drinking alcohol before noon (or some later hour); using marijuana only on the weekend; or not using drugs during school hours or before driving. Abusers lack such limits, using drugs indiscriminately at nearly any time, place, or circumstance.

Keeping drug use within limits is also partially made possible by drug-use rituals. Rituals are stylized and predictable ways of doing something that are characteristic of a group. Always eating food with alcohol or mixing distilled spirits with soda or fruit juices are rituals that help keep alcohol use within bounds. The custom of passing a "joint" around a circle of friends serves a similar role in limiting marijuana intoxication. The drug-using peer group is the main source of the rules and rituals that help the controlled user to avoid abuse. Young (1971) was among the first to note that drug-users' lore provides prescriptions for keeping drug use in check as well as prescribing informal sanctions against going beyond those bounds. The drug-using peer group brings sanctions such as rejection or ridicule to bear on the adolescent who takes too much or indulges under the wrong circumstances or too often. These sanctions help prevent a transition from use to abuse.

One way that the abuser may have failed to learn such rules is because of isolation from a drug-using peer group. This may be a major factor in the high risk of alcoholism in children of nondrinking parents and members of churches that forbid alcohol use. Such persons have had less opportunity to learn rules and rituals for safe alcohol use.

Alternately, the abuser may have learned abusive patterns of drug taking through association with a peer group of abusers. Association with abusers results in learning norms that are antithetical to the rules and rituals that sustain controlled use. By criminalizing drugs and driving their users underground, our society increases the likelihood that the novice user will be thrown into association with abusers and may come to learn abuse-promoting rules rather than use-promoting rules.

Involvement in a delinquent peer group is another peer factor that can contribute to a lack of conventional commitments. As Duncan and Gold (1985) have said, "The usual concern in our society is with drug abuse leading to crime, but there is reason to believe that crime leads to drug abuse" (p. 182). Of course, any use of illicit drugs is criminal behavior in itself and use of alcohol by adolescents is also a crime, but we are talking about criminal involvement that precedes that. Likewise, we are referring to delinquent activity that precedes any crimes committed in order to obtain money for the purchase of drugs.

A number of studies have shown that antisocial behavior beginning in childhood is highly predictive of later abuse of drugs (Robins & Ratcliff, 1978; cf. Robins & Wish, 1977). One such study, by Lukoff (1974), found that the younger the age at which the delinquency began, the more intense and committed the addictive career that followed. Surveys of two samples of heroin addicts revealed that 36.6% of a group of imprisoned addicts and 21.0% of a group of methadone patients had their first experience of illicit drug use while in a jail or detention home (Duncan, 1975). The same study found that more than 75% of the methadone patients reported having been arrested at least once before their first illicit drug use.

The stigma of being labeled a delinquent cuts an adolescent off from many legitimate opportunities (Duncan, 1969). For instance, expulsion from school or loss of job may result from being labeled a delinquent. Social isolation may also result—even if the adolescent's peers are not unwilling to associate with a "delinquent," their parents may forbid such associations.

The delinquent label not only may cut the adolescent off from nondelinquent peers, but it increases involvement with antisocial peers. The jail or detention home provides a meeting place in which the first-time offender is introduced to a new peer group of delinquents (Duncan, 1969; Gold & Williams, 1969). With increasing rejection by prosocial peers, the adolescent becomes more intensely involved with antisocial peers.

Yet another peer-related factor, identified by Jacobson and Zinberg (1975), is that serious dealing in drugs is a major factor in moving some drug takers toward abuse. Nearly all drug users engage in occasional dealing for little or no profit, but serious dealing is associated with a greatly increased risk of abuse. Professional dealers have made dealing their work, so work can no longer be a factor mitigating against abuse. Drugs necessarily become a central factor in the life of a dealer. Furthermore, dealing is a stressful occupation with high risks of being cheated, robbed, or arrested. Such stress can contribute to negative affect states and the dealer-user has a ready supply of drugs with which to medicate that negative affect.

Community Factors in the Growing Centrality of Drugs

The failure to learn limiting rules and rituals is not just a matter of which peer group the user associates with. It also involves, in part, the larger society. Waldorf, Reinarman, and Murphy (1991) have pointed out that in American society, "such controlled use norms and other informal social controls remain anemic; they have not been allowed to become part of public discourse and culture" (p. 276). Waldorf et al. make the point that criminalizing drugs makes it less likely that such rules and rituals will be developed and disseminated. What one user, or group of users, has learned to do in order to minimize drug-related risks cannot readily be passed on to others when use must be surreptitious.

Societal rejection and scapegoating of illicit drug users contributes to the transition to abuse by cutting the identified user off from competing conventional involvements. When a student is expelled from school for using drugs or alcohol, he or she is closed off from a conventional involvement and potential route to achievement. The same thing happens when a user is fired for taking drugs. When parents, frightened at learning their child is a drug user, react with rejection or "tough love" they too contribute to the transition to abuse by reducing their child's participation in family activities and values.

ADDICT ROLE AND FEAR OF WITHDRAWAL

Another major factor is the acceptance of the role of abuser. Our society has developed certain shared images of what a drug abuser is like. If the user comes to accept those images as elements of self-identity, then the role prescribed by those images will increasingly come to shape the user's life. The addict lifestyle is a role that is learned in the course of the transition from user to abuser. Fear of withdrawal illness is another influence that can keep the abuser taking a drug despite negative consequences.

Community Contributions to Addict Role Adoption

Where the illicit drugs are concerned, our society recognizes only two possibilities—abstinence or addiction. Under these circumstances, "the idea that one can and should exercise control can atrophy" (Waldorf et al., 1991, p. 277).

Some years ago a drug education slogan in use on the West Coast was "Heroin, it's so good, don't even try it once." Just consider the implications of that message. How many of us could resist anything that was made to sound that good? In fact, wasn't this antidrug slogan remarkably similar to the old potato chip advertising slogan declaring, "I bet you can't eat just one." Did the one sell as much heroin as the other did chips? The worst part of this message was that anyone who believed it and yet did try heroin was convinced that they could not stop.

The myth of instant addiction is less common than it once was. We no longer see movies and television dramas in which a character is given, unknowingly or against their will, an injection of heroin and as a result becomes an addict. Such plots were once common in the media. Not too long ago drug educators and law enforcement officials seriously warned of drug pushers putting marijuana in tobacco cigarettes or tea to recruit marijuana addicts. More recently there have been claims that drug pushers were putting heroin or cocaine in marijuana to turn marijuana users into cocaine or heroin addicts. Ridiculous though such stories are, they contribute to a belief in the overwhelming power of addiction. Belief in that power makes the abuser feel powerless to stop or limit drug use.

Although the instant addiction myth may be less widely promoted than in the past, our mass media and much of our drug education still exaggerate the power of drugs to control, rather than be controlled by, the user. The stereotypical image of drug withdrawal illness has been presented in innumerable movies and television shows. Such media images may make for good drama, but they are grossly exaggerated portrayals of a real phenomenon. Persons addicted to heroin or other opiates do suffer physical illness when they are unable to take their usual dose, but the illness is nothing like the famous performance by Frank Sinatra in *The Man With the Golden Arm*. The severity of withdrawal symptoms experienced by a narcotics addict varies greatly but at their worst they are no worse than a fairly severe case of influenza and are not life threatening. Withdrawal from addiction to alcohol or sedative hypnotics such as Seconal or methaqualone can be much more severe and potentially life threatening, but because these drugs are legal little attention is paid to their withdrawal effects. Controversy still exists over whether or not cocaine or the amphetamines produce a withdrawal illness, which shows that any withdrawal illness produced is too minor to be unequivocally identified.

By teaching adolescents that addiction follows inevitably on the use of illicit drugs and that once addicted the user must continue taking the drug or suffer severe illness, our society promotes abuse. Such exaggerations may scare some adolescents away from drug use, but they can also make those who have tried using drugs believe that they cannot stop.

The "Just Say No" approach to drug education also contributes to the transition from use to abuse. This approach not only confounds use with abuse but implies that all that is necessary to prevent drug abuse is a simple act of will. That being the case, then anyone who uses drugs must simply be weak willed. If adolescents are given this message and then do try drugs, their self-esteem is likely to suffer. In the words of one middle school student: "You say to yourself when you're younger, 'I would never use drugs.' And so, then if you do, some part of you always hates yourself" (quoted by Nora L. Ishibashi, personal communication, April 14, 1993).

Many of our society's efforts to prevent drug use and abuse seem to contribute, instead, to the transition from use to abuse. Outlawing drugs may have such an abuse-promoting effect. The impact on alcohol use of Prohibition from 1920 until 1933 is still debated. Per capita consumption appears to have decreased, but this may only be due to the difficulties in estimating the size of an illicit market. Drunkenness may have increased or it may only have become more notable due to the illegality of alcohol.

McCord (1991) examined the effects of Prohibition on alcohol use and abuse through a study of two cohorts of men. One cohort was composed of men who were over 21 at the time Prohibition began. The second cohort experienced Prohibition during their adolescence. McCord found that the second cohort experienced significantly higher rates of alcohol problems and nontraffic criminal offenses. The reasons for such an effect are open to debate, but it does appear that living through Prohibition as an adolescent raised the risk of alcoholism and crime.

Another abuse-promoting factor related to societal prohibition of certain drugs or of adolescent use of others (such as alcohol) is the impact of negative consequences. A number of studies have shown that severe punishment or harsh rejection by parents after being caught using drugs increases the chances of an adolescent becoming a drug abuser (cf. Kaplan & Johnson, 1991). This is particularly true if the negative consequences occur early in the adolescent's drug-use experience.

Peer Contributions to Addict Role Adoption

Although the community gives broad shape to the addict role, it is in the addict peer group that the role is refined and learned in detail. Just as a peer group of controlled users may teach limiting rules and rituals, an abuser peer group may teach norms that contribute to abuse.

Participant observation research by Eckert (1983) reveals that adolescents often draw very sharp distinctions in social role affiliation. A typical high school will have three or four clearly identified groups.

In this context drug use is part of a complex symbolic process of social stratification. For some adolescents, group affiliation becomes a fundamental aspect of personal identity. For the adolescent drug abuser the reciprocal reinforcement of group affiliation and personal identity tends to reduce behavioral options. This situation makes it more difficult for the abuser to disassociate from the addict role.

THE TRANSITION BACK
FROM ABUSE TO USE OR NONUSE

A third transition that may be seen in adolescents is a transition back from drug abuse to drug use or nonuse. Data from the National Institute of Mental Health's Epidemiologic Catchment Area (ECA) Study (Helzer, Burnham, & McEvoy, 1991) indicate that alcoholism has a mean duration of 9 years, with a majority (54%) of cases running their course in 5 years or less. The ECA data for illicit drug abuse (Anthony & Helzer, 1991) show a mean duration of 2.6 years, with 75% of all cases ending within 4 years.

In some cases this transition is a result of treatment for drug abuse, but Regier et al. (1993) have found that less than one of every four persons with an addictive disorder receives treatment for that disorder. In a majority of cases the transition takes place without formal treatment (Davies, 1992; Hammersley, Morrison, Davies, & Forsyth, 1990; Stimson & Oppenheimer, 1982). On the basis of the ECA data, Helzer et al. (1991) conclude that, "Many [alcoholics] appear to be able to reduce their drinking sufficiently to terminate their difficulties quite early in the course of their disorder. It is those who try and fail that appear for treatment" (p. 98).

In his study of treated and untreated ex-addicts, Biernacki (1986) found that the experience of recovery from heroin addiction varied by level of immersion and identification with the addict lifestyle. Street addicts had a very hard time kicking the habit because so much of their lives hinged on the addict lifestyle and because they were excluded from conventional society. They usually had to hit "rock bottom" or some existential crisis before quitting. They remained stigmatized and had a hard time finding a new social identity or place in society after quitting. Addicts whose immersion and commitment to the junkie lifestyle was tenuous or fleeting found it easy to quit; some just walked away from heroin and simply resumed their conventional lives.

MOTIVATIONS FOR QUITTING

A 1982 research conference sponsored by the National Institute on Drug Abuse concluded that studies of the motivations of youth who stopped using marijuana should be given high priority because of their potential value in guiding future interventions (Cohen, 1982). Despite this recommendation's focus on young abusers, the few studies that have examined motives for quitting drug abuse have all dealt with adults. How far these results can be applied to adolescents is uncertain.

The earliest such study, by Martin, Duncan, and Zunich (1983), surveyed college students who had quit abusing any of a variety of illicit or prescription drugs. Health reasons were the most frequently reported reason for quitting. Mental and emotional problems related to the drug was the second most frequent reason. This was followed by a dislike for effects produced by the drug—a category that often overlapped with the preceding two. Fourth was a simple loss of interest in the drug and its effects.

A survey of 61 Central European athletes who had quit using hashish produced similar results (Duncan, 1988). The most frequently reported reason for quitting in this group was a dislike for the drug's effects. The second most common reason in this group of athletes was that quitting was necessitated by their training regimen. Health reasons and mental/emotional problems were tied for third most common reason.

Brooke, Fudala, and Johnson (1992) surveyed 20 subjects from the subject pool of two treatment studies and found that the most frequently reported reasons for seeking treatment were related to what might be called the hassles of being addicted—"being out of control . . . needing drugs every day and suffering from a longstanding problem" (p. 40). Next came mental and physical problems related to drug use, inability to afford the drug, and difficulty in obtaining the drug.

Fears that had discouraged the subjects from seeking treatment were also examined in the Brooke et al. study. The most frequently reported fear was that of failing in treatment or that their problem was incurable. Fear of their drug use becoming known to friends, family, and so forth was the second most common fear discouraging treatment seeking. A third fear, expressed by a minority of subjects, was that the police would learn about their drug associations if they sought treatment.

Waldorf et al. (1991) found that the most common reason for quitting among adult cocaine addicts was health problems, given as a reason by nearly half (47.2%) of their subjects. The next most frequent was financial problems (40.6%). This was followed by work-related problems (35.8%), pressure from spouse or lover (33%), decision to stop selling (29.2%), fear of arrest (28.3%), pressure from friends (27.3%), and pressure from family (26.4%).

They found differences in reasons for quitting between 30 subjects who quit after receiving treatment and 76 who quit on their own. For the untreated quitters, health problems remained the most common reason (reported by 46.1%), followed by financial problems (31.6%), pressure from spouse or lover (25%), and work problems (23.7%). For the treated group the same reasons were in the top four but their order and frequency were different. For these subjects the most common reason was work problems (66.7%), followed by financial problems (63.3%), pressure from spouse or lover (53.3%), and health problems (50.0%).

Waldorf et al. (1991) found that few of the quitters in their study had experienced a state of despair or had hit rock bottom. Shaffer and Jones (1989), who also studied recovery from cocaine abuse, identified two types of quitters: Those they called "rock bottom quitters" had become increasingly immersed in cocaine use until virtually all aspects of normal life disintegrated and they were moved to quit. "Structure builders," on the other hand, were people who did not necessarily experience dislocation because of their cocaine use but who set about finding activities to take its place. The former were more likely to require formal treatment, whereas the latter seem to be candidates for natural recovery.

NATURAL RECOVERY

The term *natural recovery* has come to be used for any transition back from abuse to nonuse or controlled use that occurs without treatment. As the ECA data (Anthony & Helzer, 1991; Helzer et al.,

1991) have indicated, most drug abusers experience recovery after relatively few years and most do so without treatment. Furthermore, as Waldorf et al. (1991) observe, "Those who underwent natural recovery processes were as likely to succeed as those who went through formal treatment" (p. 216).

Shaffer and Jones (1989) found three ideal-typical phases of natural recovery: first, "turning points," when addicts begin consciously to experience negative effects; second, "active quitting," when they take steps to stop using; and third, "maintaining abstinence" or "relapse prevention." Klingemann (1991, 1992) reached very similar conclusions, describing the three stages of natural recovery as being a motivational stage, a stage of decision implementation, and a struggle for maintenance characterized by the negotiation of a new identity or meaning in life.

Recovery always involves some degree of abstinence from drug taking, but it does not necessarily mean total abstinence. Describing both natural recovery and recovery with treatment, Waldorf et al. (1991) state that "rigid abstinence from all consciousness-altering substances is not a prerequisite for recovery. Among both our groups of quitters, occasional drug use (sometimes called 'slips') was common, but for most this did not appear to be particularly consequential" (p. 217).

In fact, recovery can mean the return to controlled use of the drug in question. Ever since Davies (1962, 1969) reported cases of alcoholics whose drinking had returned to normal levels, the idea of controlled drinking as a successful outcome for recovered alcoholics has been a subject of controversy. Despite widespread opposition to the idea by treatment professionals and by Alcoholics Anonymous, the accumulating evidence clearly shows that such outcomes not only do occur but occur frequently. Vaillant's (1983) longitudinal study, for instance, showed social drinking and abstinence to be about equally common outcomes of recovery from alcoholism.

Controlled use of illicit drugs as a positive outcome has been less frequently discussed. Davies (1992) suggests that this is because our society labels all use of illicit drugs as abuse, regardless of the consequences (or lack of them) for the drug user.

> All use of illicit drugs is illegal and therefore "abnormal," and public perceptions cannot at the present time entertain concepts such as "normal heroin use" or "normal cocaine use." Consequently, the idea of

returning to normal levels of drug use from levels that are abnormal cannot be demonstrated, primarily on account of the linguistic and moral contexts surrounding the words "drugs" and "normal." (p. 42)

Natural recovery seems largely to involve two processes: (a) displacing drugs from their central place in the abuser's life, (b) learning different ways to deal with stress and other underlying problems.

Community Factors in Natural Recovery

An important element in the recovery process is what Duncan (1975) called "environmental restructuring," removing the abuser from the sources of the problem and the environments associated with drug taking. In its most extreme form this would include what were once called "geographic cures"—moving to another city or traveling to another country. This effectively removed abusers from their usual sources of drugs and the places in which they were accustomed to taking drugs, as well as the peers they were used to taking drugs with.

Obviously such geographic cures are not generally practical for adolescents. They can, however, avoid the specific places where they bought and used drugs in the past. Shaffer and Jones (1989) found that "energetic attempts" to avoid drug users and places where the drug was being sold or used played a key part in the success of cocaine users who quit without treatment.

Waldorf et al. (1991) found that "the most frequently used strategies for quitting cocaine were what we call social avoidance strategies" (p. 205). More than two thirds of the quitters reported that they had stopped going to specific places—parties, bars, and so forth—where they knew cocaine was likely to be used.

Peer Factors in Natural Recovery

As mentioned above, the avoidance of drug-taking friends was also a part of a typical natural recovery. In the Waldorf et al. (1991) study, 62.3% of the cocaine quitters reported making conscious efforts to avoid cocaine using friends, and 41.5% reported seeking new, non-drug-using friends.

Finding a new peer group is often a major part of natural recovery for adolescents. This may be a conscious choice by the adolescent.

On the other hand, the adolescent's parents may have arranged this change by sending the adolescent away to a boarding school or by moving the family to a new neighborhood. In either case, a new peer group is often a vital part of an adolescent's natural recovery.

RECOVERY THROUGH TREATMENT

It appears that treatment is necessary for those abusers who have become most deeply involved with drugs. In the Waldorf et al. (1991) study the treated group reported a higher frequency of drug-related problems in general. This could be interpreted as indicating a more serious drug-abuse problem. That in turn could explain the need for treatment in order to quit cocaine. Of the treated quitters in that study, 80% had tried to stop at least once prior to their last successful attempt. One abuser estimated that he had tried to stop at least 40 times. Only 32.9% of the untreated quitters had experienced a previous attempt to quit. Although some users, especially those who wound up undergoing formal treatment, found it very difficult to quit using cocaine, roughly half of the untreated quitters had no difficulty quitting.

Community Factors in Recovery Through Treatment

Historically, treatment programs have often made use of the principle of the geographic cure by taking the addict out of the community in which drugs had been obtained and used in the past. The "drying out farms" of the 1920s and 1930s (along with dubious treatments) mainly kept the patients away from their usual community and peers. The same principle continues to be used by many therapeutic communities. Patients applying for admission to the Cenicor Community through their center in Houston, Texas, would be admitted to treatment at their center in Denver, Colorado, and vice versa.

Relapse following treatment is often the result of exposure to environmental stimuli of persons and places with whom drug use was associated in the past. Such stimuli that have been repeatedly associated with drug use may become discriminative stimuli tending to elicit further drug use. They may even become conditioned stimuli eliciting conditioned responses that mimic the drug effects themselves. Wallace (1989) found that such environmental stimuli were causal factors in more that one third of the relapses in her study of crack cocaine relapses.

The therapeutic community attempts to be literally a community—a group of persons who are drug free and committed to a common set of values. Those values typically include an emphasis on openness and honesty. The adolescent is subjected to intense group pressure for conformity to the community's values in a process that attempts to break down the abuser personality and to rebuild a healthy personality through a process of resocialization.

The larger community may also impact in important ways on the adolescent in treatment. For one thing, many treatment services rely on public funding for their continued existence. Political factors may determine whether services are even available for the adolescent.

If the adolescent faces stigmatization and rejection from the larger community, advances achieved through treatment may be quickly lost. For instance, adolescents under treatment for drug abuse are often unwelcome in public schools. This cuts them off from their natural nonabusing peer group and may deprive them of the opportunity to get an education.

Peer Factors in Recovery Through Treatment

Peer support can be an important element in treatment as well. Booth, Russell, Soucek, and Laughlin (1992), for instance, studied 61 consecutive admissions for alcoholism treatment at a midwestern medical center. They found that friends' reassurance of worth predicted greater time to readmission in survival analysis.

Therapy groups and self-help groups can be highly effective elements in drug-abuse treatment, at least in part, because they serve as a substitute peer group. Abusers, who have become socialized into the "addict culture" by drug-abusing peers, can be resocialized by this new artificial peer group. Supported by these new peers, they can learn the needed new skills for interpersonal coping (Duncan, 1975). On the other hand, peer pressure to resume drug taking can be a major cause of relapse. Marlatt (1985) found that direct and indirect social pressure to use drugs was a factor in one of five relapses. Such pressures, of course, are a problem only if the adolescent's reference group is composed of drug-abusing or at least drug-using peers.

SUMMARY

Adolescent drug use is heavily influenced by community, family, and peer factors. Three transitions are useful for understanding the development of drug use among young people. The first transition is from nonuse to use, which is made by almost all adolescents. The transition from use to abuse is made by 10% to 20% of young people. Contrary to popular belief, the transition from abuse back to use or nonuse is successfully made by most young drug abusers. This developmental model clearly illustrates the importance of social factors in the acquisition, shaping, and maintenance of drug-use patterns. For adolescents, drug use is a socially learned pattern of behavior.

Keys points made in this chapter include:

✓• Experimentation with drugs is normative for adolescents; abuse of drugs is not.
• For most healthy adolescents there are many social benefits and minimal negative health consequences of drug use.
✓• Typically a friend, older sibling, or parent introduces the adolescent to drugs.
• Rarely are adolescents exposed to coercive peer pressures to use drugs. Peer influence is most often a subtle, indirect process of modeling and social support.
• Maturity, independence, attractiveness, fun, and social acceptance are just a few of the social needs adolescents may associate with drug use.
• The transition from nonuse to use is facilitated by
  1. the local availability and affordability of drugs.
  2. the adolescent's learning the functional and social value of drug use.
  3. the neutralization of restraints against drug use.
  4. drug-using peers who tend to neutralize restraints against drug use.
  5. school environments with rigid, authoritarian policies. This approach tends to neutralize restraints against use.
  6. the use of scare tactics and "prophylactic lies." This approach tends to neutralize restraints against use.
• Although drug use is primarily a function of social influences, the transition from drug use to abuse also involves elements of genetic/ bological factors.

- The transition from drug use to abuse is gradual and rarely a cognizant choice.
- Drug abuse is characterized by
  1. drug use taking on a central role in the adolescent's life.
  2. the adoption of an addict role-identity.
  3. fears of withdrawal symptoms.
- The drug user typically takes drugs to achieve a pleasant state of mind; the abuser is more likely to take drugs to escape an unpleasant state of mind.
- The transition from drug use to abuse is facilitated by
  1. rejection by the non-drug-abusing community.
  2. increasing involvement with drug-abusing and delinquent peers.
  3. societal myths about the powerful addictiveness of drugs.
  4. severe punishment and parental rejection of drug use.
- Only one of four drug abusers ever receive treatment for their abuse.
- Most drug abusers recover within 4 years and do so without treatment.
- The transition from drug abuse to use or nonuse is facilitated by
  1. establishing a nonabusing peer group.
  2. avoiding social and physical environments associated with drug abuse.
  3. some degree of abstinence from drugs but not necessarily total abstinence; half of recovered abusers return to controlled use.

REFERENCES

Anthenelli, R. M., & Schuckit, M. A. (1992). Genetics. In J. H. Lowinson, P. Ruiz, R. B. Millman, & J. G. Landgrod (Eds.), *Substance abuse: A comprehensive textbook* (2nd ed.) (pp. 39-50). Baltimore, MD: Williams & Wilkins.

Anthony, J. C., & Helzer, J. E. (1991). Syndromes of drug abuse and dependence. In L. N. Robins & D. A. Regier (Eds.), *Psychiatric disorders in America* (pp. 116-154). New York: Free Press.

Bandura, A. (1986). *Social foundations of thought and action: A social cognitive theory.* Englewood Cliffs, NJ: Prentice Hall.

Baumrind, D. (1985). Familial antecedents of adolescent drug use: A developmental perspective. In C. Jones & R. Battjes (Eds.), *Etiology of drug abuse: Implications for prevention* (NIDA Research Monograph No. 56). Rockville, MD: National Institute on Drug Abuse.

Berger, E. E. (1974). Drug advertising and the "Pain, Pill, Pleasure" model. *Journal of Drug Issues, 4,* 208-212.

Biernacki, P. (1986). *Pathways from heroin addiction: Recovery without treatment*. Philadelphia: Temple University Press.

Blane, H., & Hewitt, L. (1977). *Alcohol and youth—An analysis of the literature, 1960-1975*. Report prepared for the National Institute on Alcohol Abuse and Alcoholism (NTIS #PB-268-698). Washington, DC: National Technical Information Service.

Booth, B. M., Russell, D. W., Soucek, S., & Laughlin, P. R. (1992). Social support and outcome of alcoholism treatment: An exploratory analysis. *American Journal of Drug and Alcohol Abuse, 18*, 87-101.

Bowker, L. H. (1974). Student drug use and perceived peer drug involvement. *International Journal of the Addictions, 9*, 851-861.

Brook, J. S., Cohen, P., Whiteman, M., & Gordon, A. S. (1991). Psychosocial risk factors in the transition from moderate to heavy use or abuse of drugs. In M. D. Glantz & R. W. Pickens (Eds.), *Vulnerability to drug abuse* (pp. 359-388). Washington, DC: American Psychological Association.

Brooke, D., Fudala, P. J., & Johnson, R. E. (1992). Weighing up the pros and cons: Help seeking by drug misusers in Baltimore, USA. *Drug and Alcohol Dependence, 31*, 37-43.

Cadoret, R. J. (1991). Genetic and environmental factors in initiation of drug use and the transition to abuse. In M. D. Glantz & R. W. Pickens (Eds.), *Vulnerability to drug abuse* (pp. 99-113). Washington, DC: American Psychological Association.

Choate, R., & Debevoise, N. (1976). Caution: Keep this commercial out of reach of children. *Journal of Drug Issues, 6*, 91-98.

Coate, D., & Grossman, M. (1985). *Effects of alcoholic beverage prices and legal drinking ages on youth alcohol use*. New York: National Bureau of Economic Research.

Cohen, S. (1982). Highlights of final discussion. In *Marijuana and youth: Clinical observations on motivation and learning* (DHHS Publication No. ADM 82-1186). Washington, DC: Government Printing Office.

Davies, D. L. (1962). Normal drinking in recovered alcohol addicts. *Quarterly Journal of Studies on Alcohol, 23*, 94-104.

Davies, D. L. (1969). Stabilized addiction and normal drinking in recovered alcohol addicts. In H. Sternberg (Ed.), *The scientific basis of drug dependence*. London: Churchill.

Davies, J. B. (1992). *The myth of addiction*. Philadelphia: Harwood Academic Press.

Downs, W. R., & Rose, S. R. (1991). The relationship of adolescent peer groups to the incidence of psychosocial problems. *Adolescence, 26*(102), 479-492.

Duncan, D. F. (1969). Stigma and delinquency. *Cornell Journal of Social Relations, 4*, 41-48.

Duncan, D. F. (1975). The acquisition, maintenance and treatment of polydrug dependence: A public health model. *Journal of Psychedelic Drugs, 7*, 209-213.

Duncan, D. F. (1988). Reasons for discontinuing hashish use in a group of Central European athletes. *Journal of Drug Education, 18*, 49-53.

Duncan, D. F., & Gold, R. S. (1985). *Drugs and the whole person*. New York & London: Macmillan.

Duryea, E., & Martin, G. (1981). The distortion effect in student perceptions of smoking prevalence. *Journal of School Health, 51*, 115-118.

Eckert, P. (1983). Beyond the statistics of adolescent smoking. *American Journal of Public Health, 73*(4), 439-441.

Elkind, D. (1978). Understanding the young adolescent. *Adolescence, 13*, 127-134.

Ellickson, P. L., & Hays, R. D. (1991). Antecedents of drinking among young adolescents with different alcohol use histories. *Journal of Studies on Alcohol, 52*, 398-408.

Esserman, J. (Ed.). (1981). *Television advertising and children: Issues, research and findings.* New York: Child Research Service.

Fejer, D., Smart, R. G., Whitehead, P. C., & Laforest, L. (1971). Sources of information about drugs among high school students. *Public Opinion Quarterly, 35*, 235-241.

Fors, S. W., & Rojek, D. G. (1983). The social and demographic correlates of adolescent drug use patterns. *Journal of Drug Education, 13*, 205-222.

Gerbner, G. (1977). Deviance and power: Symbolic functions of "drug abuse." In C. Winick (Ed.), *Deviance and mass media* (pp. 13-30). Beverly Hills, CA: Sage.

Gerbner, G. (1990). Stories that hurt: Tobacco, alcohol, and other drugs in the mass media. In H. Resnik, S. E. Gardner, R. P. Lorian, & C. E. Marcus (Eds.), *Youth and drugs: Society's mixed messages* (pp. 53-127). Rockville, MD: Office of Substance Abuse Prevention.

Gitlin, T. (1990). On drugs and mass media in America's consumer society. In H. Resnik, S. E. Gardner, R. P. Lorian, & C. E. Marcus (Eds.), *Youth and drugs: Society's mixed messages* (pp. 31-52). Rockville, MD: Office of Substance Abuse Prevention.

Glantz, M. D., & Pickens, R. W. (1991). Vulnerability to drug abuse: Introduction and overview. In M. D. Glantz & R. W. Pickens (Eds.), *Vulnerability to drug abuse* (pp. 1-14). Washington, DC: American Psychological Association.

Globetti, G., Alsikafi, M., & Morse, R. (1977). Alcohol use among black youth in a rural community. *Drug and Alcohol Dependence, 2*, 255-260.

Gold, M., & Williams, J. R. (1969). The effect of "getting caught": Apprehension of the juvenile offender as a cause of subsequent delinquencies. *Prospectus, 3*, 1-12.

Goodstadt, M., & Mitchell, E. (1990). *Prevention theory and research related to high risk youth. Breaking new ground for youth at risk: Program summaries* (DHHS Pub. No. ADM 90-1658). Rockville, MD: National Institute on Drug Abuse.

Grossman, M. (1989). *Health benefits of increases in alcohol and cigarette taxes—Working Paper No. 3082.* Cambridge, MA: National Bureau of Economic Research.

Hammersley, R., Morrison, V., Davies, J. B., & Forsyth, A. (1990). *Heroin use and crime: A comparison of heroin users and non-users in and out of prison.* Glasgow: Scottish Office Central Research Unit.

Helzer, J. E., Burnham, A., & McEvoy, L. T. (1991). Alcohol abuse and dependence. In L. N. Robins & D. A. Regier (Eds.), *Psychiatric disorders in America* (pp. 81-115). New York: Free Press.

Holland, J. G., & Skinner, B. F. (1961). *The analysis of behavior.* New York: McGraw-Hill.

Hughes, S. O., Power, T. G., & Francis, D. J. (1992). Defining patterns of drinking in adolescence: A cluster analytic approach. *Journal of Studies of Alcohol, 53*, 40-47.

Hulbert, J. (1974). Applying buyer behavior analysis to social problems: The case of drug use. *Proceedings of the American Marketing Association, 74*, 289-292.

Jacobson, R., & Zinberg, N. E. (1975). *The social basis of drug abuse prevention.* New York: McGraw-Hill.

Johnson, N. (1974). Junkie television. *Journal of Drug Issues, 4*, 227-231.

Johnston, L., O'Malley, P., & Bachman, J. (1991). *Drug use among high school senior, college students and young adults, 1975-1990.* Rockville, MD: National Institute on Drug Abuse.

Kandel, D. B., & Davies, M. (1991). Progression to regular marijuana involvement: Phenomenology and risk factors for near-daily use. In M. D. Glantz & R. W.

Pickens (Eds.), *Vulnerability to drug use* (pp. 211-253). Washington, DC: American Psychological Association.

Kaplan, H. B., & Johnson, R. J. (1991). Relationships between circumstances surrounding initial illicit drug use and escalation of drug use: Moderating effects of gender and early adolescent experiences. In M. D. Glantz & R. W. Pickens (Eds.), *Vulnerability to drug abuse* (pp. 299-358). Washington, DC: American Psychological Association.

Klingemann, H. K. (1991). The motivation for change from problem alcohol and heroin use. *British Journal of Addiction, 85,* 727-744.

Klingemann, H. K. (1992). Coping and maintenance strategies of spontaneous remitters from problem use of alcohol and heroin in Switzerland. *International Journal of the Addictions, 27,* 1359-1388.

Lewis, D. C. (1993, April). Coffee anyone? *The Brown University Digest of Addiction Theory and Application, 12*(4), 12.

Lukoff, I. F. (1974). Issues in the evaluation of heroin treatment. In E. Josephson & E. E. Carroll (Eds.), *Drug use: Epidemiological and sociological approaches.* New York: John Wiley.

Marlatt, G. A. (1985). Relapse prevention: Theoretical rationale and overview of the model. In G. A. Marlatt & J. R. Gordon (Eds.), *Relapse prevention* (pp. 3-70). New York: Guilford.

Martin, C. E., & Duncan, D. F. (1984). Televised OTC drug ads as surrogate dope pushers among young people: Fact or fiction? *Journal of Alcohol and Drug Education, 29*(4), 19-30.

Martin, C. E., Duncan, D. F., & Zunich, E. M. (1983). Students' motives for discontinuing illicit drug-taking. *Health Values, 7*(5), 8-11.

McCord, J. (1991). Another time, another drug. In M. D. Glantz & R. W. Pickens (Eds.), *Vulnerability to drug abuse* (pp. 473-489). Washington, DC: American Psychological Association.

McKechnie, R. (1976). Parents, children and learning to drink. In J. Madden, R. Walker, & W. Kenyon (Eds.), *Alcoholism and drug dependence* (pp. 451-456). New York: Plenum.

Milavsky, J. R., Pekowsky, B., & Stipp, H. (1976). TV drug advertising and proprietary and illicit drug use among teenage boys. *Public Opinion Quarterly, 39,* 457-481.

Newcomb, M., & Bentler, P. (1989). Substance use and abuse among children and teenagers. *American Psychologist, 44*(2), 242-248.

Newman, I. (1984). Capturing the energy of peer pressure: Insights from a longitudinal study of adolescent cigarette smoking. *Journal of School Health, 54,* 146-148.

O'Hare, T. M. (1990). Drinking in college: Consumption patterns, problems, sex differences and legal drinking age. *Journal of Studies of Alcohol, 51*(6), 536-541.

O'Malley, P. M., Johnston, L. D., & Bachman, J. A. (1985). Cocaine use among American adolescents and adults. In N. J. Kozel & E. H. Adams (Eds.), *Cocaine use in America: Epidemiologic and clinical perspectives* (pp. 50-75). Washington, DC: Government Printing Office.

Petosa, R. (1992). Developing a comprehensive health promotion program to prevent drug abuse. In G. Lawson & A. Lawson (Eds.), *Adolescent substance abuse: Etiology, treatment and prevention* (pp. 431-449). Gaithersburg, MD: Aspen Publications.

Regier, D. A., Narrow, W. E., Rae, D. S., Manderscheid, R. W., Locke, B. Z., & Goodwin, F. K. (1993). The de facto U.S. mental and addictive disorders service system: Epidemiologic catchment area prospective rates of disorders and services. *Archives of General Psychiatry, 50,* 85-94.

Robertson, T. S., Rossiter, J. R., & Gleason, T. C. (1979). Children's receptivity to proprietary medicine advertising. *Journal of Consumer Research, 6,* 247-255.

Robins, L. N., & Ratcliff, K. S. (1978). Risk factors in the continuation of childhood antisocial behavior into adulthood. *International Journal of Mental Health, 7,* 96-116.

Robins, L. N., & Regier, D. A. (1991). *Psychiatric disorders in America: The Epidemiologic Catchment Area Study.* New York: Free Press.

Robins, L. N., & Wish, E. (1977). Childhood deviance as a developmental process. In M. F. McMillan (Ed.), *Child therapy: Treatment and research.* New York: Brunner/Mazel.

Scheier, L. M., & Newcomb, M. D. (1991). Differentiation of early adolescent predictors of drug use versus abuse: A developmental risk-factor model. *Journal of Substance Abuse, 3,* 277-299.

Shaffer, H. J., & Jones, S. B. (1989). *Quitting cocaine: The struggle against impulse.* Lexington, MA: Lexington Books.

Sheppard, M. A. (1989). Adolescents' perceptions of cannabis use by their peers: Does it have anything to do with behavior? *Journal of Drug Education, 19,* 157-164.

Sher, K. J. (1991). *Children of alcoholics: A critical appraisal of theory and research.* Chicago: University of Chicago Press.

Skager, R., & Fisher, D. G. (1989). Substance use among high school students in relation to school characteristics. *Addictive Behaviors, 14,* 129-138.

Skinner, B. F. (1953). *Science and human behavior.* New York: Macmillan.

Smart, R., & Goodstadt, M. (1977). Effects of reducing the legal alcohol purchasing age on drinking and drinking problems: A review of empirical studies. *Journal of Studies on Alcohol, 38,* 1313-1323.

Stimson, G., & Oppenheimer, E. (1982). *Heroin addiction.* London: Tavistock.

Vaillant, G. E. (1983). *The natural history of alcoholism.* Cambridge, MA & London: Harvard University Press.

Waldorf, D., Reinarman, C., & Murphy, S. (1991). *Cocaine changes: The experience of using and quitting.* Philadelphia: Temple University Press.

Wallace, B. C. (1989). Psychological and environmental determinants of relapse in cocaine smokers. *Journal of Substance Abuse Treatment, 6,* 95-106.

Young, J. (1971). *The drugtakers: The social meaning of drug use.* London: MacGibbon & Kee.

Zinberg, N. E., Harding, W. M., & Winkeller, M. (1977). A study of social regulatory mechanisms in controlled illicit drug users. *Journal of Drug Issues, 7,* 117-133.

5. Substance Use and Abuse Among Urban Adolescents

Patricia Sivo Cole

Newington Children's Hospital School, Stafford Springs, Connecticut

Roger P. Weissberg

The University of Illinois at Chicago

INTRODUCTION

The problem of adolescent substance use in cities across the United States has become a topic of national concern. The escalating reports of drug-related gang violence, drug and alcohol addicted teenagers, and young people stricken with AIDS from intravenous drug use occupy a prominent space in the media coverage of urban areas. Research has established that substance abuse in adolescence is correlated with higher rates of suicide, homicide, violence, accidental death, unprotected sex, arrest, school failure, teen pregnancy and elevated infant mortality, poor physical and mental health, reduced potential earnings, and unstable relationships (e.g., Colton, Gore, & Aseltine, 1991; Donovan, Jessor, & Costa, 1988; Wallace & Bachman, 1991). Before any realistic solutions can be developed to combat adolescent substance use, a clear understanding of the scope of the problem is needed. This chapter will attempt to put the specter of drug and alcohol use among urban youth into perspective compared to the nation as a whole and begin to consider steps to address the problem in the future.

In order to begin the study of adolescent substance use and abuse in urban areas, several complex issues must be considered. First, it is important to clarify the definitions of seemingly simple terms. To begin, the word *adolescent* covers a relatively wide age range. Research has confirmed that substance use varies considerably among youth aged 12 to 18 years, with all studies finding higher proportions of older students using substances compared to those younger (e.g., National Institute on Drug Abuse [NIDA], 1992). Some studies focus solely on high school seniors (e.g., Johnston, O'Malley, & Bachman, 1992), whereas others combine students aged 12 to 17 years into one sample for reporting their findings (e.g., NIDA, 1992). Consequently, when comparing reports on "adolescent" substance use it is imperative to note the actual age ranges sampled to draw accurate conclusions.

Although adolescent substance use is typically talked about as a single entity, in reality it refers to many separate types of drugs, each with a differentiated pattern of behaviors and carrying different meanings to the user and to society as an observer. For example, an adolescent smoking a cigarette with friends creates a very different picture than a teenager doing a line of coke alone in his room or driving while intoxicated. This chapter will focus primarily on the most common substances used by adolescents—alcohol, cigarettes, and marijuana—with references to other illicit drugs when relevant.

A definition of adolescent substance use versus abuse has yet to find consensus among researchers. For several reasons most do agree that virtually any substance use among children up to age 11 years (with such exceptions as a sip of a parent's drink) constitutes a form of abuse. First, because even alcohol and cigarettes are not legal for children to use, any substance use exposes them to potential problems with the law, school, and their families (Newcomb & Bentler, 1989). Second, because they are still growing, children's nervous systems may be especially susceptible to the negative effects of drugs. Third, substance use may preclude their participation in the normal activities of childhood and thus interfere with healthy psychological and social development. Finally, childhood substance use has been linked to other serious behavior problems, such as truancy, school failure, delinquent activity, and precocious sexual activity (Hawkins, Lishner, Catalano, & Howard, 1986).

This agreement about what constitutes abuse breaks down when adolescents are considered. Although the increased probability of problems with the law and school remains for adolescents using any illegal substances, it is also true that some experimentation with drugs and alcohol is normative by the age of 18 years. For example, Johnston et al. (1992) report that 90% of all high school seniors have tried alcohol and 80% have used it in the past year despite laws in most states placing the legal drinking age at 21 years. In addition, most older adolescents who experiment with drugs and alcohol never develop any serious problems and gradually desist with no intervention as they get older (Newcomb & Bentler, 1989).

In general, it appears impossible to set a specific quantity or frequency of drug or alcohol use that will qualify definitively as abuse for every individual. People respond to substances differently, have different levels of tolerance, and have different psychological and social resources. In addition, the timing of the use (e.g., during the school day versus at a weekend party) can also signal abuse. The age of the adolescent significantly affects what might be considered abuse as well. A pattern of monthly alcohol use may be a dangerous warning sign at age 12 but normative at 18 years. Despite these caveats, even occasional *heavy* use of drugs or alcohol (e.g., five or more drinks on one occasion) can be considered temporary abuse that can lead to chronic abuse over time (Newcomb & Bentler, 1989). In addition, regular weekly use of substances can be viewed as potentially abusive for any adolescent. This rough guide can inform inspection of prevalence data, and although it does not include the data necessary for a clinical diagnosis of substance abuse, such as dependence, craving, withdrawal symptoms, interference with school/work, and impaired relationships (American Psychiatric Association, 1987), it captures the patterns that typically lead to abuse.

One exception to the rule of "heavy use" to identify abuse may be cigarettes. Research suggests that, unlike the use of other substances, cigarette smoking does not tend to diminish as adolescents become adults. Cigarette smoking contributes to the premature death of approximately 400,000 Americans each year through cancer, heart disease and stroke, lung disease, birth defects, and unintentional fires (U.S. Department of Health and Human Services [DHHS], 1989). Even without considering the long-term effects of smoking, Newcomb and Bentler (1987) found that cigarettes had more negative health effects and increased health service utilization than alcohol, marijuana, or hard drugs over a 4-year period. Consequently, *any* regular use of cigarettes could be viewed as abusive.

Another complexity to consider in studying urban adolescent substance use concerns the definition of *urban* itself. Although using a given population density is a common starting point and a reasonable beginning for attempting to compare substance use in different areas, it is clearly only a beginning. Such a measure does not reflect the heterogeneity of our cities. Vast differences exist between cities (e.g., downtown Manhattan vs. East St. Louis) and also within cities. In almost every city one can find the "good neighborhoods" and the "bad neighborhoods," and the experience of living in those two places may be worlds apart. The determining factors for these neighborhoods are typically not just socioeconomic status (SES) level but the degree of disorganization, support for a criminal subculture, physical deterioration, crime rate, and residential mobility (Hawkins, Catalano, & Miller, 1992). In looking only at population density, vastly different settings become combined and a clear understanding of any of them is obscured. A more precise vocabulary is needed that will address the differences within a given population density. To avert confusion, for the remainder of this chapter *urban* will refer to an area of high population density and *inner city* will refer only to those high-risk pockets located within those urban areas.

Beyond the question of definition, the greatest difficulty in studying urban adolescent substance use is that few representative studies have been conducted that compare inner-city and non-inner-city youth. The two major annual national surveys, the High School Senior Survey and the Household Survey, distinguish groups by population density, thus masking differences between and within cities (Hughes, 1992). Smaller studies that focus specifically on inner-city populations often are not representative and/or do not include a comparison group. Future studies and analyses of current data by the National Institute of Drug Abuse (NIDA) are planned but are not yet available to the public (NIDA, 1992).

An unavoidable complication of this research area is the heavy reliance on self-report. Questions have been raised about the reliability of such measures, especially in regard to minority youth (Mensch & Kandel, 1988). Such surveys may also become biased by sampling problems (e.g., nonparticipation of school absentees or dropouts, youth living in alternative settings, and homeless youth) or by false reporting due to deliberate deception or the inability to comprehend the questions adequately. Efforts have been made to compensate for these potential biases, but they remain a concern in interpreting results. This issue will be explored in greater depth later.

An additional factor that makes this topic difficult to study is that adolescent substance use is not a static problem. Levels of use and preferences for specific drugs change over time. This dynamic often creates confusing interactions with time and gender, ethnicity, population density, and region of the country (Johnston et al., 1992). For example, although use of one substance may be rising among white males in urban areas in the northeast, it may be dropping among minority females in rural areas in the south. Compressing all the data together into one large sample and looking at only one point in time may result in seriously misleading findings.

Acknowledging these unavoidable complications in studying this subject, this chapter will attempt to clarify the problem of adolescent substance use in urban areas by exploring a variety of topics. First, in order to provide a frame of reference, national survey data for adolescents in general will be reviewed followed by a summary of trends in substance use for the past 20 years. In order to grasp fully the severity of the problem today, it is important to examine the patterns that have emerged over time. Next, the limitations of national survey data will be explored to understand better the accuracy of the findings. The discussion will then turn to differences in adolescent substance use in urban versus nonurban areas, reviewing the national data supplemented by smaller studies of inner-city populations. The role of theory in identifying substance use in urban and nonurban areas will be considered, followed by a review of ethnic and gender differences in adolescent substance use. Finally, directions for future research and implications for preventive interventions will be offered.

PREVALENCE INFORMATION
PROVIDED BY NATIONAL SURVEYS

One major source for examining adolescent substance use in this country is the High School Senior Survey (Johnston et al., 1992). This national survey, which has been conducted annually since 1975, is a self-report questionnaire that students complete in school during their senior year. Johnston et al. utilize cluster sampling and select a sample of schools to represent different community sizes that cover the geographic regions of the 48 contiguous states. The survey established three levels of population density in order to compare the rates of substance use in urban versus nonurban areas. The first category is "large SMSA's," or the 16 largest Standard Metropolitan Statistical Areas in the 1980 Census (i.e., the country's largest cities); the second is "other SMSA's," or the remaining Standard Metropolitan Statistical Areas (i.e., smaller cities); and the third is "non-SMSA's," or sampling areas not designated as metropolitan (i.e., nonurban areas) (Johnston et al., 1992). Overall, less than 1.5% of seniors refuse to participate, although Johnston et al. (1992) reported that 18% of the seniors were absent on the day of the survey and were not included. School dropouts also are not represented in this sample, and according to the 1980 census this high-risk group represents 15% of the potential sample.

A second major source for national data is the National Household Survey on Drug Abuse (NIDA, 1992). For this survey, participants aged 12 to 17 years are interviewed in their homes with a response rate of 86%. A random sample of all U.S. households is selected, and consequently those living in institutions or with no permanent address are not included in the study.

According to these two major national surveys, the substance used most commonly by adolescents is alcohol. In the National Household Survey on Drug Abuse, 46% reported having tried alcohol in their lifetime with 40% having used it in the past year (NIDA, 1992). According to a recent national survey of high school seniors, 90% have at least tried alcohol by 12th grade and 80% of those have used it during their senior year (Johnston et al., 1992). These figures indicate that some familiarity with alcohol use during adolescence has become a normative experience despite laws against its use by minors.

Although researchers typically aggregate different types of alcohol to form a single variable, there are definite differences in the prevalence of beer, wine, and hard liquor use. For example, in a study of urban 9th-grade students, Cole (1992) reported that although 40% of the students had tried beer and 37% had tasted wine or wine coolers, only 16% reported drinking hard liquor. Understanding these differences can be important in linking theoretical frameworks and the prevalence of drug use. For example, Kandel (1982) suggested a stage theory of initiation to substance use with the first stage being the use of beer or wine, followed by cigarettes and/or hard liquor, then marijuana, and lastly, hard drugs. Although she does not suggest that there is a causal sequence of substance use in which involvement at one level causes progression to the next level or even indicates such progression will occur, her research indicated that very few students who use drugs at one stage have not also used those at the preceding level. These findings, coupled with the knowledge of the numerous health concerns associated with alcohol, highlight the importance of monitoring any level of experimentation or continued use by teens.

In addition to assessing the simple prevalence of alcohol use, studies have also focused on patterns of misuse. Several approaches have been developed to determine the extent of alcohol involvement. To supplement measures of frequency of use in the past year, surveys also explore monthly and daily use. Johnston et al. (1992) reported that more than half of seniors in high school used alcohol in the past 30 days, although less than 4% reported using it daily. The National Household Survey reported 20% of adolescents aged 12 to 17 years used alcohol in the past month, 14% drank 12 or more times in the past year, and 5% used it once a week or more (NIDA, 1992).

In order to understand the extent of alcohol misuse, quantity of use has been studied as well as simple frequency. Johnston et al. (1992) found that approximately one third of high school seniors reported they had five or more drinks on one occasion in the past 2 weeks and 21% reported that that happened more than once. Furthermore, initiation into the use of alcohol appears to begin at an increasingly early age (Horton, 1988). In the High School Senior Survey, 60% of the students reported drinking for the first time before high school and 40% reported being drunk for the first time before 10th grade. This trend of early involvement in alcohol and/or drug use has been linked to higher use in the future and greater involvement with more serious drugs (Kandel & Yamaguchi, 1985; Kandel, Yamaguchi, & Chen, 1992; Newcomb & Bentler, 1986a). In summary, the results of national surveys to date indicate that adolescent use of alcohol remains a common occurrence with a significant number of teens engaging in heavy use on a regular basis.

The second most commonly used substance by adolescents is cigarettes. Among high school seniors, 64% have tried smoking with 29% reporting that they smoked cigarettes in the past month (Johnston et al., 1992). In addition, the same survey found that cigarettes are used *daily* by more adolescents than any other drug. Among the seniors, 19% smoked at least once a day, and 11% reported smoking a half pack or more. One third of the smokers reported that they began in grades 7 to 9 with another 19% starting in elementary school. As expected, the figures for the Household Survey (NIDA, 1992) that included 12- to 17-year-old respondents are somewhat lower. In that survey, 38% reported having tried cigarettes, and of those 20% smoked in the past year and 11% in the past month.

Marijuana remains the most common illicit drug used by adolescents. More than 40% of high school seniors reported some use in their lifetime and 14% in the past month (Johnston et al., 1992). In contrast, among the 12- to 17-year-olds interviewed for the Household Survey, 13% reported having experimented but only 4% used in the past month (NIDA, 1992).

The level of use of other illicit drugs is significantly lower than for marijuana. For high school seniors, 18.5% have tried inhalants, 17.5% stimulants, 9.4% hallucinogens, 9% cocaine, 7.2% tranquilizers, 7.5% sedatives, 3.5% crack, and 1% heroin (Johnston et al., 1992). In contrast, although 7% of the 12- to 17-year-olds reported having tried inhalants, less than 4% have used any of the other illicits (NIDA, 1992).

PATTERNS OF CHANGE
WITHIN NATIONAL SURVEY SAMPLES

In order to understand better the meaning of the current prevalence statistics for adolescent substance use, it is necessary to explore how these figures have changed over time. The High School Senior Survey has been conducted since 1975 (Johnston et al., 1992). When looking at any involvement in illicit drug use among older adolescents, there was a steady increase until 1978, when approximately 54% of the seniors surveyed reported having tried at least one illicit substance in the previous year compared to 45% in 1975. For the next 6 years, the percentage of students reporting any involvement in illicit drugs dropped 1% to 2% annually. After a one-year hiatus, that trend continued to the present when 33% of seniors reported having used at least one illicit drug during the past year. This pattern of change was primarily driven by the decline in marijuana use. When marijuana was excluded from the calculations, a pattern of increasing involvement emerges from 1975 to 1982 followed by a steady drop-off since then.

In looking at the substances that are legal for adults, alcohol and cigarettes, different patterns unfold. In the late 1970s alcohol use increased slightly. Although lifetime prevalence rates have remained relatively stable since that time, monthly prevalence has been dropping gradually since the middle 1980s. Heavy drinking—five or more drinks on one occasion—has followed a similar pattern. In contrast, although rates of cigarette smoking appeared to decline in the late 1970s, there has been virtually no change in reported smoking since

1984 despite the dropping levels for other substances (Johnston et al., 1992; NIDA, 1992). Perhaps one reason for the lack of change in cigarette use lies in the recent concerns that some cigarette companies may be deliberately marketing certain brands of cigarettes to appeal to children.

The general pattern of declining rates of substance use, with the noted exception of cigarette smoking, has been viewed optimistically as a sign that youth are finally beginning to reject the use of illicit drugs. Several possible explanations for this pattern have been offered. Rhodes and Jason (1990) suggested that the increased interest in healthier lifestyles in the past decade also may have influenced adolescents. In addition, Johnston et al. (1992) found that adolescents' perceived disapproval by parents and peers of illicit drug use has increased steadily since the late 1970s. They also reported that the perceived risks associated with substance use have increased in the past decade as well. They suggested that their research, although purely correlational, indicates that changes in attitudes may be influencing the decline in use. Although their data did not support an overall move toward conservative values among teens, it is possible that they were influenced by the perception of society becoming more conservative linked to a change to a more conservative administration in the White House during the 1980s. Finally, it is possible that now widespread prevention programs may finally be creating the positive impact they were designed to produce (Oetting & Beauvais, 1990).

Despite this optimism, one viewing of the evening news demonstrates that drug use remains a serious problem, particularly in impoverished urban areas, where escalating violence has alarmed the nation. It is possible for an ambitious adolescent to make $3,000 in one day dealing drugs, and juvenile drug arrests have more than tripled in recent years (Rhodes & Jason, 1990). Consequently, the significance of declining numbers of youth reporting substance use has been questioned. Several more pessimistic explanations for the data have been offered.

The next section will outline some of the limitations of current research that may contribute to the discrepancy between the public's perceptions of the levels of adolescent substance use and the numbers generated by national surveys.

LIMITATIONS OF SELF-REPORT NATIONAL SURVEYS

Although the information they have provided over the years has been instructive, there are several inherent flaws in the data from the national surveys. First, school surveys, particularly the annual report of high school seniors, do not include dropouts or absentees —two important groups that account for a large percentage of the potential subjects. Using statistical methods, researchers have made modest corrections to approximate the prevalence of substance use if these two groups were included in their sample, but they have found no major changes in the patterns originally reported.

Certain basic assumptions about dropout rates and absenteeism may, however, be at least partially inaccurate. For example, although they report that the overall dropout rate for youth is approximately 15% and has remained relatively stable, marked differences do exist among the ethnic groups. According to the National Center for Education Statistics (Frahm, 1992), the dropout rate for black students aged 16 to 24 dropped from 21.3% in 1972 to 13.6% in 1991. The rate for white students similarly declined from 12.3% to 8.9% in the same time period. In contrast, the dropout rate among Hispanics rose slightly from 34.3% to 35.3% during the same time period. In addition, there is some evidence that dropout rates among urban black and Hispanic youth may be closer to 50% (Rhodes & Jason, 1988). The magnitude of these differences suggests that it is not appropriate to dismiss an overall steady national dropout rate as insignificant in understanding the pattern of changes in substance use when individual subgroups demonstrate such varying levels.

To further complicate the understanding of dropout rates, many students may leave school before 9th grade and are not officially included in measures that count how many freshmen complete their senior year. In addition, although one school may record that a child has left the system to attend school in another town following a family move, if that child never attends the new school the dropout rates are artificially suppressed when that child is not counted. This possibility is most relevant when considering lower SES families who are more likely to move frequently. Most studies that have assessed substance use among school dropouts have discovered significantly higher levels of substance use, and the above considerations suggest that the children most at risk may not even be counted in that group (Oetting & Beauvais, 1990).

A second limitation of the High School Senior Survey and to a lesser extent the Household Survey lies in the fact that those students who are placed outside of a regular school setting are not included. Thus students living at home but placed in special-education settings outside their home school, a subgroup of whom will have been out-placed because of identified substance-use problems, do not complete the school survey. Although the Household Survey may still reach those students in day programs and even makes an effort to reach those living in homeless shelters, it omits those who are hospitalized or living in residential facilities, group homes, or detention centers (NIDA, 1992). In sum, the complexities of accurately assessing substance use on a national level inevitably lead to an underestimate of use when those subjects who are most likely to engage in it are not included. This dilemma is endemic to any research attempting to study a phenomenon that by definition is not normally distributed in the general population.

A third limitation in the current research methodology emerges in examining studies that attempt to follow the same students over time. Chassin (1984) discovered that panel losses range from 15% to 50% of the sample, making it difficult to make generalizations to an entire population.

A fourth shortcoming of this type of research is its unavoidable reliance on self-report. For example, the current societal trend to view any substance use in a highly negative light may affect an entire cohort of respondents and lead to underreporting of use. In addition, concerns have been raised about the many individual pressures that may influence any one person's responses. For example, one student may overreport use in order to appear "cool" or at least to meet his or her own perceptions of normative use, but another may deliberately underreport to hide illegal behavior or out of pure defiance. Specific questions have been raised about the reliability of survey data among minority groups. Mensch and Kandel (1988) found a higher rate of discrepancy in the report of drug use among minorities, even after controlling for the frequency of use. This finding suggests that completing a survey may be interpreted as potentially threatening by different groups, especially when illegal behavior is being questioned. When the possibility of errors in the recall of substance-use frequency is factored in, it may seem as if gaining accurate estimates of use from the already limited available samples is practically impossible.

Fortunately, a great deal of research has been done to investigate the reliability of self-report measures of substance use; overall the findings suggest that they are adequately reliable. In a study by researchers at the Rand Corporation that correlated self-report of substance use in their sample of adults with urinalysis results, the comparison of the two results revealed a high correspondence (Marquis, Duan, Marquis, & Polich, 1981). In examining the same relationship with children and adolescents, several studies found similar high correlations between self-report and physiological measures in the study of cigarette smoking (Akers, Massey, Clarke, & Lauer, 1983; Botvin & Eng, 1980; Perry, Killen, Slinkard, & McAlister, 1980). In addition, Chassin et al. (1981) found no significant differences in self-report when comparing students who believed, via the bogus pipeline procedure, that their responses would be tested for accuracy and those who did not. Given the intrusiveness of physiological testing, the threat that it would carry to students' perceptions of anonymity combined with the tremendous cost of such procedures, the research to date suggests that self-report is preferable despite its limitations.

In order to increase the probability that students are answering honestly and carefully, several methods have regularly been included in the construction of surveys. First, including a fictitious drug within the list of substances being studied has served as a means to identify those students prone to exaggeration. Whitehead and Smart (1972) found that less than 1% of adolescents are likely to endorse a fake drug. More recent studies have reported similar results, which suggests that exaggeration of use is not a significant problem for interpreting survey results (e.g., Barnea, Rahav, & Teichman, 1987; Oetting & Beauvais, 1990).

Another way of determining the reliability of adolescents' responses to surveys has been to evaluate the internal consistency of the measures. For example, students who indicate that they used a substance during the past month should also report equal or higher levels of use of that substance in their lifetime. Research suggests that the more checks of accuracy included, the more subjects can be identified as inconsistent responders, but the level remains well below 10% (Oetting & Beauvais, 1990). Some of the discrepancies may be from innocent errors in remembering exactly how many times they engaged in an activity, careless marking, or poor reading skills and do not necessarily mean that they are deliberate attempts to mislead the researcher; however, their occurrence at all is something of which to be cognizant when interpreting the data.

In summary, all of these limitations in the current research—the absence from the survey of school dropouts and absentees and adolescents placed in alternative settings, the limited ability to follow the same students over time, and the problems of self-report data—do not completely discredit the reported trend of declining substance use, but they do suggest that it should be regarded with caution and explored further. Multiple methods are needed to increase our certainty of the finding. Understanding changes within subgroups of youth as compared to the nation as a whole may help clarify the discrepancy between the perceptions that drug use is producing escalating problems and national surveys that report an overall decline in use.

DIFFERENCES IN URBAN
VERSUS NONURBAN LEVELS OF USE

In this section the High School Senior Survey, which divides its data by population density as described earlier, and smaller studies of inner-city populations will be reviewed to provide some insight into the question of urban versus nonurban drug use. According to the High School Senior Survey's comparisons of large urban, other urban, and nonurban areas, there are small differences in overall illicit substance use among the different sized communities. Although 30% of seniors in nonurban areas reported using an illicit substance in the past year, the comparison numbers are slightly higher with 33% in the largest urban areas and 34% in the other urban areas. As mentioned earlier, it is important to consider the possibility of differential dropout rates for these communities when studying data from school samples. In the state of Connecticut, for example, dropout rates ranged from 6.5% in one small town to 21.6% in the capitol city in 1991 (Frahm, 1992). High school dropouts are more likely to use drugs, and consequently a survey in a city with a high dropout rate would probably underestimate adolescent substance use significantly. Until it is possible to integrate such information with substance-use rates, it is difficult to assess precise differences based on community size. This caveat applies to the remainder of the findings reported here.

When the findings were further broken down by the specific types of substances, minor differences did emerge among the three categories. For marijuana, the rate of annual prevalence for both large and other urban areas was 28%, whereas the annual prevalence in nonurban areas was only 24%. This pattern held for monthly prevalence rates, but there were no significant differences in daily use among the groups. Similarly, in the Household Survey of 12- to 17-year-olds monthly prevalence was highest for the different urban areas, whereas the nonurban areas had the lowest prevalence.

Although the annual prevalence for alcohol use among seniors was approximately 82% for large and other urban areas, it was only 76% for seniors living in nonurban areas (Johnston et al., 1992). Those differences were smaller for monthly prevalence; and the daily prevalence rates were 35% for large urban areas, 32% for other urban areas, and 31% for nonurban areas. The differences in the Household survey were less than one percentage point between the groups (NIDA, 1992). Finally, slight differences in cigarette smoking disappear completely when looking at daily prevalence, with 19% of seniors reporting smoking at least once a day regardless of community size.

The only substance that showed significantly greater involvement in nonurban areas was stimulants, with large urban, other urban, and nonurban communities exhibiting annual prevalence rates of 7%, 10%, and 11% respectively. For all of the other substances, any differences in prevalence were less than one percentage point. For example, the prevalence rate for cocaine was 5.6% in larger urban areas, 5.1% in other urban areas, and 4.8% in nonurban areas. For heroin, the rates were 0.4%, 0.5%, and 0.5%, respectively (Johnston et al., 1992).

In summary, the differences in adolescent substance use based on community size in this national survey ranged from none to slight, depending on the specific substance examined. Rural youth appeared to have access to the same drugs as youth in urban areas, including crack. Although it will be important to gain better data combining the dropout rates specific to the subgroup under study with prevalence data, this survey certainly does not support the idea that substance use is only an urban problem. The level of severity of substance use and the concomitant social problems may be somewhat different in different locales, but it is clear that drug use has also penetrated into the small towns of our country.

Although the findings of the national survey indicate that substance use is not just an urban problem, smaller studies focusing on inner-city youth in generally impoverished neighborhoods do point to a population within the broader category of "high population density" that deserves special attention. In inner-city neighborhoods where high crime, poverty, and violence are often normative, substance use has also been found to be more common (Dryfoos, 1990; Gottfredson, 1987; Nettles & Pleck, in press). For example, in two separate studies of inner-city 9th graders in different parts of the country, those students reported monthly use of marijuana and cigarettes at rates similar to those reported by seniors in the urban areas of the national survey (Cole, 1992; Farrell, Danish, & Howard, 1992). These data suggest that there may be enclaves of deprived areas within our cities with much greater problems of substance use that are obscured in the national survey data combining information on population density. Nettles and Pleck (in press) describe a possible bifurcation effect in adolescent substance use whereby middle-class and/or suburban teens are indeed using less alcohol and drugs but low-income minorities in the inner city are in fact using them at higher levels than in the past.

In order to understand current levels of substance use, it is helpful to examine trends in substance use across community size. According to the High School Senior Survey, the use of any illicit drug peaked in all communities in 1979 with annual prevalence rates of 61% in the large urban areas, 55% in other urban areas, and 48% in nonurban areas. With one minor exception, from 1979 to the present, substance use has decreased at a steady rate in all communities, with the greater decline occurring in the urban areas until the figures have basically converged as described above. The use of different substances appears to initiate in large cities and then to radiate outward over time.

The pattern of cocaine use demonstrates this phenomenon of convergence most clearly. In the late 1970s cocaine use increased dramatically in all communities, but the greatest rise was clearly in the large urban areas. When the rates began to drop off in 1987, the level of use in the large urban areas fell the fastest, leading once again to comparable current levels in all communities regardless of size. The initial surge to higher levels of use in the inner city and the accompanying media coverage on rising drug use as compared to the more gradual and less publicized diffusion to smaller communities have probably contributed to the perception that levels of use are significantly higher in urban areas.

THE ROLE OF THEORY IN IDENTIFYING SUBSTANCE USE IN URBAN AND NONURBAN AREAS

Despite the lack of large consistent differences between urban and nonurban prevalence of substance use overall, it is likely that there is variation in the relative importance of different risk factors in the initiation and maintenance of adolescent substance use, especially in subgroups such as the inner city. One of the shortcomings of the current state of research on rural versus urban adolescent substance use is that the two populations are typically studied in separate research projects (e.g., Fagan, Weis, & Cheng, 1990; Kovach & Glickman, 1986) or else combined as one sample and not compared with each other (e.g., Hundleby, 1987; Johnson & Marcos, 1988; Johnson & Pandina, 1991; Newcomb & Harlow, 1986). The risk factors for adolescent substance use related to intrapersonal characteristics such as nonconformity and rebelliousness, extroversion, depression, low self-esteem, poor coping skills, and individual personality traits would probably remain similar across community size (e.g., Chassin, 1984; Hawkins et al., 1986; Hawkins & Weis, 1985; Jessor & Jessor, 1977; Oetting & Beauvais, 1987). In contrast, theories that include an emphasis on a social component as a potential risk factor may provide an avenue for studying whether certain variables are more predictive of substance use among adolescents living in urban versus rural areas.

The number of theoretical frameworks developed in the past 20 years to explain and predict adolescent involvement in substance use are too numerous to list and would take several volumes to describe adequately. The following is an outline of important risk and protective factors in the social environment that can be used to further explore potential differences within urban settings as well as between urban and nonurban populations.

The first category centers on social stress in the school environment and the broader community. Researchers have proposed that substance use may be initiated as a coping mechanism to deal with a variety of stressors (Rhodes & Jason, 1990; Wills & Shiffman, 1985). The number and intensity of daily stressors experienced by adolescents may vary significantly depending on the environment in which they live. For example, the perceived threat of violence and crime, the physical manifestations of poverty such as inadequate housing, and general lack of fundamental resources differ from neighborhood to neighborhood and from urban to rural areas. The overall quality of an adolescent's neighborhood, such as high population density, a criminal subculture, high residential mobility, physical deterioration, and a low level of attachment to the neighborhood, has been linked to adolescent substance use (Dryfoos, 1990; Hawkins et al., 1992). Developing a qualitative as well as quantitative method for evaluating the stress of the teens' daily living environment will be an important task in understanding adolescent substance use as a whole.

A second category of importance is the role of peer groups and peer group dynamics. Particularly with the popularity of gangs in the inner city, which are known to be frequently linked to drugs and crime, it is vital to understand the dynamics of the peer group in different environments. Given the strong relationship between individual substance use and friends' use (e.g., Barnes & Welte, 1986; Brook, Brook, Gordon, Whiteman, & Cohen, 1990; Newcomb & Bentler, 1986b), the role of peers in initiating *and* preventing substance use will be important to examine in different settings. The support of immediate and extended family in the day-to-day lives of teenagers is another area worthy of further exploration in looking at urban adolescent substance use. Disorganized or chaotic households, low parental support, lack of parental monitoring, and general lack of closeness in the family have all been found to be related to adolescent substance use (e.g., Brook et al., 1990; Hawkins et al., 1992; Kandel, Kessler, & Margulies, 1978). Nettles and Pleck (in press) noted that although adolescents in rural towns, particularly black youth, are often faced with poverty and all the accompanying difficulties, they are frequently assisted by strong family ties and positive peer support to a greater extent than those in the inner city. In fact, Dryfoos (1990) reported that rural, southern blacks are the least likely of any group to experiment with drugs. Understanding the powerful role of family support and the extended family network in different settings is critical to developing relevant programs to prevent adolescent substance use.

In sum, these are just a few of the areas that can be included in a comprehensive framework for identifying the precursors and protective factors for adolescent substance use in both urban and nonurban settings. Learning the relative contributions of specific variables in rural, suburban, and urban settings and also within subgroups of those environments will be useful for the development of preventive interventions. In order to address a community's weaknesses, such as adolescent substance use, it will be important to have a full understanding of its strengths.

ETHNIC DIFFERENCES
IN SUBSTANCE USE

Any study that includes ethnicity as a variable inevitably has several confounding factors. First, as described earlier, differential dropout rates, especially in urban areas, may significantly affect data collected in schools. Interestingly, Wallace and Bachman (1991) found that differential dropout rates disappeared when factors such as parental education and occupation, income, and family size were held constant. Second, in this country ethnicity is often confounded with SES levels and population density. Consequently, any statements about differences in substance use by ethnic group need to be seen not as a statement about a "race" of people but rather as a reference to a unique combination of culture, economic opportunity, and environment (Betancourt & Lopez, 1993). Finally, as mentioned earlier, research has suggested that minority groups are more likely to underreport drug and alcohol use (Mensch & Kandel, 1988). With those caveats in mind, the following is a review of the major findings on ethnic group differences in adolescent substance use.

Almost every study on substance use that compares different ethnic groups has found that Native Americans tend to report the highest level of illicit drug use with a lifetime incidence twice as high compared to any other subgroup (Welte & Barnes, 1987). They are followed closely by whites, then blacks, and lastly Asians, with the different groups of Hispanics falling somewhere in the middle (Barnes & Welte, 1986; Johnston et al., 1992; NIDA, 1992; Welte & Barnes, 1987).

Alcohol is the substance of choice across the different ethnic groups. In the High School Senior Survey, which included several different ethnic categories, whites reported the highest proportion of drinkers followed by Native Americans, Puerto Ricans/Latinos, Mexican Americans, blacks, and Asians (Johnston et al., 1992). In the Household Survey of 12- to 17-year-olds, although blacks reported a lower annual prevalence rate compared to whites and Hispanics (35%, 42%, and 40%, respectively), there was very little difference in the proportion who reported using 12 or more times a year or at least once a week (NIDA, 1992).

In a study of students in 7th to 12th grade, Barnes and Welte (1986) found the same pattern of results among the different ethnic groups for lifetime prevalence. When looking at the proportion of students reporting heavy drinking, the disparities become even more marked. Native Americans had the highest rate of heavy drinking at 18% with the proportion of whites close behind at 16%. In contrast, the prevalence rates for Hispanics, blacks, and Asians were 8%, 5%, and 6%, respectively. In other words, twice as many whites reported heavy drinking compared to Hispanics and three times as many compared to blacks. Windle's (1990) longitudinal research further supports these findings. He reports that being "non-black" in his study was predictive of later adolescent alcohol use, alcohol-related aggression, and dependency symptoms.

Finally, pronounced differences exist among different ethnic groups' cigarette use with the highest proportion of white youth reporting use, followed by Hispanics and blacks (Johnston et al., 1992; NIDA, 1992). Although the rate of cigarette use has remained level in recent years for whites, the prevalence rate for black youth has continued to fall, contributing to a growing disparity between the groups. In general, across substances, black adolescents report lower levels of use compared to whites and Hispanics.

Despite the fact that minority groups appear to use less drugs and alcohol than white adolescents, they report experiencing more substance-use-related problems when the quantity used is held constant (e.g., Welte & Barnes, 1987). One explanation may be that the confound of SES contributes to that finding. For example, an adolescent under the influence is more likely to be picked up by the police if he or she lives in a heavily policed area. This possibility may also contribute to the public perception that minority youth abuse alcohol more. Nonetheless, the consistent findings of lower substance use among black youth are somewhat surprising in light of the fact that black adults are overrepresented among people who visit an emergency room for drug- and alcohol-related problems (Kopstein & Roth, 1993). Several explanations have been offered to clarify this seeming paradox. For example, some have suggested that the discrepancy can be explained by the underreporting of minority youth on surveys (e.g., Mensch & Kandel, 1988). Bachman et al. (1991) point out, however, that there was no significant underreporting of alcohol and cigarettes, which revealed the greatest differences between blacks and whites.

A second explanation may be the bias of those studies relying on self-report, which typically exclude children living in alternative settings, the homeless, and school dropouts, statuses that overrepresent minorities. In addition, Kandel and Davies (1991) suggest that more whites may use private physicians when faced with drug and alcohol problems and consequently are less likely to be found in the emergency room or public treatment centers where the data on adults are usually collected. Another possible factor contributing to this puzzling discrepancy is that national rates of substance use by black youth are weighted by rural southern blacks who are the least likely to experiment with drugs (Dryfoos, 1990). Finally, there is growing evidence that although blacks in general may be less likely to initiate substance use in adolescence, those who do appear to be more likely to continue using and move toward heavy use (Botvin et al., 1989; Kandel & Davies, 1991). Similarly, Barnes and Welte (1986) found that although few Hispanic adults used alcohol, those who did were more likely to drink heavily.

Although the data on substance use among minority youth may be accurate for each ethnic group as a whole, there is evidence that the highest rates of drug use occur in places where ethnic minorities live in separate areas such as Indian reservations, ghettos, and barrios (Oetting & Beauvais, 1990). For example, Brunswick (1988) describes a sample of inner-city black youth who reported much higher rates of substance use than the national samples. In addition, when Hispanics are broken down into subgroups such as Mexican, Puerto Rican, and Cuban, very different patterns of use emerge that are obscured by using one category of "Spanish speaking" (Gans, Blyth, Elster, & Gaveras, 1990). Thus, without tying ethnicity to the setting, any statements are only broad generalizations.

In summary, keeping in mind the possible confounds of differential dropout rates, SES, setting, and other potential limitations on the current research, the research projects to date concur that, overall, white adolescents are more likely to engage in substance use compared to their Hispanic and black peers. Research focused on places where minority populations are segregated from the general population has found much higher incidence of drug and alcohol use. Thus the inner-city ghettos and Native American reservations deserve special attention, especially because substance abuse among the adults in those communities is also elevated compared to the national average.

GENDER DIFFERENCES IN SUBSTANCE USE

In general, the data from the major national surveys suggest that adolescent boys are somewhat more likely to use most illicit drugs than girls, with larger differences emerging at the higher frequency levels (Johnston et al., 1992; Kolbe, 1990; NIDA, 1992). In contrast, girls' use of stimulants, sedatives, and tranquilizers are the same as or slightly higher than boys. Among 12- to 17-year-olds, although boys reported slightly higher rates of lifetime and annual prevalence for illicit drugs compared to girls, those differences disappeared for monthly prevalence (NIDA, 1992). Overall, any differences are relatively small and have been diminishing for the past several years. Boys' substance use peaked in the late 1970s, and girls' peaked later in 1981. Since that time the levels of substance use have been declining for both groups (Johnston et al., 1992). In smaller studies of inner-city youth, neither Cole (1992) nor Farrell et al. (1992) found gender differences in substance use reported for the past month.

Using a sample of high school sophomores, juniors, and seniors, Colton et al. (1991) reported no overall gender differences in the frequency or quantity of substance use. When the data were broken down by age, however, they found that in the 10th grade a higher proportion of girls used drugs compared to boys. This difference disappeared for the later grades. They explained this finding by suggesting that because sophomore girls tend to associate with boys in higher grade levels, they may engage in more use earlier.

In a study designed to look at the motivations for substance use, Newcomb, Chou, Bentler, and Huba (1988) found that more boys used drugs to enhance positive affect or increase social cohesion compared to girls. In addition, Stein, Newcomb, and Bentler (1987) reported that when a group of adolescents were followed into young adulthood, males used marijuana more often and they reported more problems stemming from drug and alcohol use. As the differences in amount of substance use between boys and girls shrink, there may still be important variation in the motivations for them to initiate use and the long-term outcomes for engaging in drug use. Consequently, studies exploring gender differences in substance use continue to offer valuable insight into the predictors and patterns of substance use.

The majority of published studies report that although the difference in the frequency of alcohol use between boys and girls is slight and has been diminishing steadily, a greater proportion of boys continue to report occasions of heavy drinking (Barnes & Welte, 1986; Colton et al., 1991; Johnston et al., 1992; NIDA, 1992; Windle, 1990). Johnston et al. (1992) reported no differences in annual prevalence of alcohol use, although boys had a higher monthly prevalence (61% vs. 52%). The largest difference emerged when the students were asked about occasions of heavy drinking. Among the boys, 39% reported having five or more drinks on one occasion within the prior 2 weeks compared to 24% of the girls. Drinking beer appears to account for most of the disparity. In a sample of 7th- to 12th-grade students in New York State, no gender differences were found for light to moderate drinking, but 18% of the boys compared to 8% of the girls reported drinking heavily at least once per week (Barnes & Welte, 1986).

Similarly, boys reported more problems associated with drinking, such as car accidents or driving while intoxicated, trouble at home or school, and fighting (Colton et al., 1991). In addition, in a national survey of 14- to 15-year-olds, Windle (1990) found that male gender predicted alcohol use, alcohol-related aggression, and alcohol dependency symptoms in a longitudinal study. In a study that followed high school students into young adulthood, Stein et al. (1987) also found that boys reported a greater number of problems with alcohol use after graduation.

Researchers have found that among high school seniors, girls have a slightly higher probability of being daily smokers compared to boys (19.3% vs. 18.6%), but fewer girls than boys smoke at the half-pack per day level (Johnston et al., 1992). Similarly among younger students, 12 to 17 years old, although lifetime prevalence remains higher for boys (40% vs. 35%) there is only a 2% difference in monthly prevalence (NIDA, 1992). Historically, more boys smoked than girls, although the proportion of girls smoking increased to match boys in 1977. Since that time, smoking declined in both groups until the late 1980s, but the rates fell faster for boys. The levels have remained relatively stable for both groups since then (Johnston et al., 1992; Thorne & DeBlassie, 1985).

In summary, with the single exception of diet pills (the proportion of girls who use them outnumbers the boys by 28% to 7%), the differences between the prevalence of boys' and girls' substance use is minimal (Johnston et al., 1992; NIDA, 1992). Of greater concern is that boys appear to be at an increased risk for heavier use and associated problems. To date, this pattern of gender differences appears similar for inner-city groups. Some have suggested that it is important to look at these gender differences in a larger context considering delinquency, teen pregnancy, and mental health problems. For example, although girls may report less substance abuse, they also report greater levels of depression and higher use of mental health services than boys (Elliott, Huizinga, & Menard, 1989). More research is needed to determine if the cause of these differences is more biological, social, or psychological in nature.

DIRECTIONS
FOR FUTURE RESEARCH

The scope of the national surveys that continue to be conducted annually is impressive and the associated studies have been informative in studying adolescent substance use. The next necessary step will be to plan studies designed to focus specifically on those youth who are not already included. First, this would require an extensive study to survey absentees and dropouts that cannot be reached in school surveys. Using community members as research assistants, it is possible to track down adolescents who can fall through the cracks in the national surveys. Such a venture would require a large, multicultural staff, but advances in sampling technology can enable researchers to target representative communities and limit the necessity of studying every city and town. A second area that deserves more attention is the numbers of youth who are in detention, special-education schools, and other special settings that typically are missed by national surveys. A percentage of these students are placed there expressly because they are having difficulties with drugs and/or alcohol and it will be important to include them in an overall picture of adolescent substance users.

More in-depth longitudinal studies will be helpful to learn more about the long-term outcomes of engaging in adolescent drug or alcohol use. It may be as important to understand why some youth use heavily in adolescence only to go on to become successful adults as why others are not so fortunate. Conversely, it is important to identify protective factors that delay or prevent certain adolescents from engaging in drug use and to examine long-term outcomes for these groups. Again, panel loss in the studies to date has made generalizations difficult to make, and a great deal of effort needs to be expended to maintain contact with the subjects over time.

Developing a more explicit method for differentiating between substance use and abuse that takes into consideration the adolescent's age, frequency and quantity of use, type of drug involvement, and the combinations used will be important to identify those youth who are especially at risk for chronic abuse and its attendant problems. In addition, given recent NIDA reports that youth between ages 11 and 14 are vulnerable to pressures to begin drug use (Kopstein & Roth, 1993), it is important to extend the national surveys to the younger grades for more accurate assessments of factors that contribute to the initiation of such behaviors.

Finally, more in-depth epidemiological studies are needed to document factors associated with the causes and consequences of drug use and abuse for different racial/ethnic groups in urban and rural areas. Special attention must be given to the heterogeneity of our cities. Studies that focus at the neighborhood level will be necessary to capture true differences in the experiences of adolescents. Similarly, even more important than studying ethnic differences, the differential impact of culture, SES, and environment should be examined (Betancourt & Lopez, 1993). In addition, the differences reported between boys' and girls' substance use as well as the reasons for their steady decline require further exploration. Studying substance use within the broader scope of problem behavior, such as delinquency and psychiatric disorders, may lead to insights into these gender differences. This information is needed most urgently to inform community prevention programs so they can be most effective.

IMPLICATIONS FOR
PREVENTIVE INTERVENTIONS

The first and most obvious implication of the research on adolescent substance use is that experimentation with drugs and alcohol begins at a young age, and consequently, prevention efforts must be started even earlier. Although it may not be necessary to provide explicit information about specific substances to elementary-school students, it is vital that personal and social competencies—such as peer resistance, stress management, self-esteem, and social problem solving, to name only a few—be introduced as early as preschool (Caplan et al., 1992; Consortium on the School-based Promotion of Social Competence, 1992; Dusenbury, Botvin, & James-Ortiz, 1989).

Substance use is not evenly distributed in the population, and much research points to the fact that certain students are at increased risk of developing problems. For example, early antisocial behavior, academic failure, disruptive or chaotic family environment, and parental substance use or criminality are among many variables linked to adolescent substance use. Targeted prevention programs that could address the specific concerns of those students at highest risk may be necessary to achieve significant effects (Emshoff, 1989).

In addition, fueled by the introduction of problem behavior theory by Jessor and Jessor (1977), researchers have been studying the relationships between adolescent drug and alcohol use, sexual activity, school failure, and delinquent behavior for almost two decades. Many studies have confirmed that these behaviors co-occur, and they have begun to identify the common precursors and predictors of such problem behavior (e.g., Barnes, 1984; Barone et al., in press; Donovan et al., 1988; Fagan et al., 1990; Farrell et al., 1992; Hundleby, 1987). Instead of developing separate prevention programs to combat teen pregnancy, delinquency, and substance abuse, which has been the pattern to date, some researchers are advocating a more systematic approach. High-quality, comprehensive, competence-promotion programs that are designed to influence both the children and their immediate environments are the new wave for addressing these complex problems (Weissberg, Caplan, & Harwood, 1991).

Taking advantage of school and community resources, recent studies indicate that long-term positive effects on children's behavior can be achieved by having them participate in age-appropriate social-competence training that is conducted over several years (Botvin, Baker, Dusenbury, Tortu, & Botvin, 1990; Elias et al., in press). Comprehensive social-competence and health education (C-SCAHE) emphasizes both teaching children to use new social skills that may help avert problem behaviors, and attempting to change the child's school, peer, family, and community environments to nurture and support the development of prosocial behaviors and interactions (Weissberg et al., 1991). Although schools are one excellent way of reaching large numbers of children efficiently, including other community resources will enhance the positive effects of such programs (Dryfoos, 1990; Elias et al., in press). For example, churches, community centers, recreation programs, and so forth could be included in developing prevention programs. Involving community members in outreach to the most vulnerable may provide the most effective way to communicate to dropouts and others who will not benefit from school-based programs. C-SCAHE efforts may represent the most powerful way to address realistically the complex and interrelated problems facing adolescents today.

SUMMARY AND CONCLUSIONS

In reviewing the current research in the area of adolescent substance use and abuse in urban areas, several conclusions can be drawn.

- With the exception of cigarettes, the use of drugs and alcohol among adolescents in general has been dropping since the mid-1980s.
- In general, differences in adolescent substance use based on population density alone are relatively slight. Research suggests, however, that inner-city neighborhoods and other areas where ethnic minorities live separately from the greater society may be witness to higher levels of use.
- Among different ethnic groups, Native American youth report the highest level of drug and alcohol use, followed closely by whites, then blacks, and Asians, with the different groups of Hispanics falling somewhere in between.

- Minority youth are often more susceptible to the negative consequences of substance use.
- Adolescent boys are more likely to abuse illicit substances than are girls, with larger differences emerging with respect to heavy usage of certain substances such as alcohol.
- Conclusions about substance use and abuse rates, especially for subgroups such as those based on ethnicity or population density, must be considered within the context of the limitations of the studies, which may be unintentionally biased by differential dropout rates and absenteeism, the lack of data from alternative settings for youth, panel loss, and the problems of self-report in general.

In closing, although a great deal of work has been done in the area of adolescent substance use, the answers found have produced many more questions. It is no longer possible to look at substance use in a vacuum. The problem is part of a complex web of individual, family, and societal influences. Although a first look at national surveys obscures differences in substance use based on setting, in order to address adolescent substance use in our inner cities it will be imperative to examine the precursors unique to that environment. Interventions will need to consider the entire ecological context in order to be successful.

REFERENCES

Akers, R. L., Massey, J., Clarke, W., & Lauer, R. M. (1983). Are self-reports of adolescent deviance valid? Biochemical measures, randomized response, and the bogus pipeline in smoking behavior. *Social Forces, 62*, 234-251.

American Psychiatric Association. (1987). *Diagnostic and statistical manual of mental disorders* (3rd ed., rev.). Washington, DC: Author.

Bachman, J. G., Wallace, J. M., O'Malley, P. M., Johnston, L. D., Kurth, C. L., & Neighbors, H. W. (1991). Racial/ethnic differences in smoking, drinking, and illicit drug use among American high school seniors, 1976-89. *American Journal of Public Health, 81*, 372-376.

Barnea, Z., Rahav, G., & Teichman, M. (1987). The reliability and consistency of self-reports on substance use in a longitudinal study. *British Journal of Addiction, 82*, 891-898.

Barnes, G. M. (1984). Adolescent alcohol abuse and other problem behaviors: Their relationships and common parental influences. *Journal of Youth and Adolescence, 13*, 329-348.

Barnes, G. M., & Welte, J. W. (1986). Patterns and predictors of alcohol use among 7-12th grade students in New York State. *Journal of Studies on Alcohol, 47*, 53-62.

Barone, C., Weissberg, R. P., Kasprow, W. J., Voyce, C., Arthur, M., & Shriver, T. P. (in press). Involvement in multiple problem behaviors of young urban adolescents. *Journal of Primary Prevention, 15*.

Betancourt, H., & Lopez, S. R. (1993). The study of culture, ethnicity, and race in American psychology. *American Psychologist, 48*, 629-637.

Botvin, G. J., Baker, E., Dusenbury, L., Tortu, S., & Botvin, E. M. (1990). Preventing adolescent drug abuse through a multimodal cognitive-behavioral approach: Results of a 3-year study. *Journal of Consulting and Clinical Psychology, 58*, 437-446.

Botvin, G. J., Batson, H. W., Witts-Vitale, S., Bess, V., Baker, E., & Dusenbury, L. (1989). A psychosocial approach to smoking prevention for urban black youth. *Public Health Reports, 104*, 573-582.

Botvin, G. J., & Eng, A. (1980). A comprehensive school-based prevention program. *Journal of School Health, 50*, 209-213.

Brook, J. S., Brook, D. W., Gordon, A. S., Whiteman, M., & Cohen, P. (1990). The psychosocial etiology of adolescent drug use: A family interactional approach [Special issue]. *Genetic, Social, and General Psychology Monographs, 116*(2), 111-267.

Brunswick, A. F. (1988). Young black males and substance use. In J. T. Gibbs, A. F. Brunswick, M. E. Connor, R. Dembo, T. E. Larson, R. J. Reed, & B. Solomon (Eds.), *Young, black, and male in America: An endangered species*. Dover, MA: Auburn House.

Caplan, M., Weissberg, R. P., Grober, J. H., Sivo, P. J., Grady, K., & Jacoby, C. (1992). Social competence promotion with inner-city and suburban young adolescents: Effects on social adjustment and alcohol use. *Journal of Consulting and Clinical Psychology, 60*, 56-63.

Chassin, L. (1984). Adolescent substance use and abuse. *Advances in Child Behavioral Analysis and Therapy, 3*, 99-152.

Chassin, L., Presson, C. C., Bensenberg, M., Corty, E., Olshavsky, R. W., & Sherman, S. J. (1981). Predicting adolescents' intentions to smoke cigarettes. *Journal of Health and Social Behavior, 22*, 445-455.

Cole, P. S. (1992). *A longitudinal study of stress, coping, substance use, and minor delinquency among young adolescents in an urban school*. Unpublished doctoral dissertation, Yale University, New Haven, CT.

Colton, M. E., Gore, S., & Aseltine, R. H. (1991). The patterning of distress and disorder in a community sample of high school aged youth. In M. E. Colton & S. Gore (Eds.), *Adolescent stress: Causes and consequences* (pp. 157-180). Hawthorne, NY: Aldine de Gruyter.

Consortium on the School-based Promotion of Social Competence. (1992). Drug and alcohol prevention curricula. In J. D. Hawkins, R. F. Catalano, & Associates (Eds.), *Communities that care: Action for drug abuse prevention* (pp. 129-148). San Francisco: Jossey-Bass.

Donovan, J. E., Jessor, R., & Costa, F. M. (1988). Syndrome of problem behavior in adolescence: A replication. *Journal of Consulting and Clinical Psychology, 56*, 762-765.

Dryfoos, J. G. (1990). *Adolescents at risk*. New York: Oxford University Press.

Dusenbury, L., Botvin, G. J., & James-Ortiz, S. (1989). The primary prevention of adolescent substance abuse through the promotion of personal and social competence. *Prevention in Human Services, 7*, 201-224.

Elias, M. J., Weissberg, R. P., Hawkins, J. D., Perry, C. L., Zins, J. E., Dodge, K. A., Kendall, P. C., Gottfredson, D., Rotheram-Borus, M. J., Jason, L. A., & Wilson-Brewer, R. (in press). The school-based promotion of social competence: Theory, research, practice, and policy. In R. J. Haggerty, N. Garmezy, M. Rutter, & L. R. Sherrod (Eds.), *Stress, risk, and resilience in children and adolescents: Processes, mechanisms, and interventions.* New York: Cambridge University Press.

Elliott, D. S., Huizinga, D., & Menard, S. (1989). *Multiple problem youth: Delinquency, substance use, and mental health problems.* New York: Springer-Verlag.

Emshoff, J. G. (1989). A preventive intervention with children of alcoholics. *Prevention in Human Services, 7,* 225-253.

Fagan, J., Weis, J. G., & Cheng, Y. (1990). Delinquency and substance use among inner-city students. *Journal of Drug Issues, 20,* 351-402.

Farrell, A. D., Danish, S. J., & Howard, C. W. (1992). Relationship between drug use and other problem behaviors in urban adolescents. *Journal of Consulting and Clinical Psychology, 60,* 705-712.

Frahm, R. A. (1992, September 17). Dropout rates high for Hispanics, but decline among blacks, whites. *Hartford Courant,* p. A8.

Gans, J. E., Blyth, D. A., Elster, A. B., & Gaveras, L. L. (1990). *America's adolescents: How healthy are they?* Chicago: American Medical Association.

Gottfredson, G. D. (1987). American education: American delinquency. *Today's Delinquent, 6,* 5-71.

Hawkins, J. D., Catalano, R. F., & Miller, J. Y. (1992). Risk and protective factors for alcohol and other drug problems in adolescence and early adulthood: Implications for substance abuse prevention. *Psychological Bulletin, 112,* 64-105.

Hawkins, J. D., Lishner, D., Catalano, R. F., & Howard, M. O. (1986). Childhood predictors of adolescent substance abuse: Toward an empirically grounded theory. *Journal of Children in Contemporary Society, 8,* 11-48.

Hawkins, J. D., & Weis, J. G. (1985). The social development model: An integrated approach to delinquency prevention. *Journal of Primary Prevention, 6,* 73-97.

Horton, L. (1988). The education of most worth: Preventing drug and alcohol abuse. *Educational Leadership, 45,* 4-8.

Hughes, A. L. (1992). The prevalence of illicit drug use in six metropolitan areas in the United States: Results from the 1991 National Household Survey on Drug Abuse. *British Journal of Addiction, 87,* 1481-1485.

Hundleby, J. D. (1987). Adolescent drug use in a behavioral matrix: A confirmation and comparison of the sexes. *Addictive Behaviors, 12,* 103-112.

Jessor, R., & Jessor, S. L. (1977). *Problem behavior and psychosocial development: A longitudinal study of youth.* New York: Academic Press.

Johnson, R. E., & Marcos, A. C. (1988). Correlates of adolescent drug use by gender and geographic location. *American Journal of Drug and Alcohol Abuse, 14,* 51-63.

Johnson, V., & Pandina, R. J. (1991). Effects of the family environment on adolescent substance use, delinquency, and coping styles. *American Journal of Drug and Alcohol Abuse, 17,* 71-88.

Johnston, L. D., O'Malley, P., & Bachman, J. G. (1992). *Drug use among American high school seniors, college students and young adults, 1975-1990: Vol. I.* Rockville, MD: National Institute on Drug Abuse.

Kandel, D. B. (1982). Epidemiological and psychosocial perspectives on adolescent drug use. *Journal of the American Academy of Child Psychiatry, 21,* 328-347.

Kandel, D. B., & Davies, M. (1991). Cocaine use in a national sample of U.S. youth (NLSY): Ethnic patterns, progression, and predictors. In S. Schober & C. Schade

(Eds.), *The epidemiology of cocaine use and abuse* (pp. 151-188). Rockville, MD: National Institute on Drug Abuse.

Kandel, D. B., Kessler, R. C., & Margulies, R. S. (1978). Antecedents of adolescent initiation into stages of drug use: A developmental analysis. *Journal of Youth and Adolescence, 7,* 13-40.

Kandel, D. B., & Yamaguchi, K. (1985). Developmental patterns of the use of legal, illegal, and medically prescribed psychotropic drugs from adolescence to young adulthood. In C. L. Jones & R. J. Battjes (Eds.), *Etiology of drug abuse: Implications for prevention* (pp. 193-235). (DHHS Publication No. ADM 85-1335). Washington, DC: Government Printing Office.

Kandel, D. B., Yamaguchi, K., & Chen, K. (1992). Stages of progression into drug involvement from adolescence to adulthood: Further evidence for the gateway theory. *Journal of Studies on Alcohol, 53,* 447-457.

Kolbe, L. J. (1990). An epidemiological surveillance system to monitor the prevalence of youth behaviors that most affect health. *Health Education, 21,* 44-47.

Kopstein, A. N., & Roth, P. T. (1993). *Drug abuse among racial/ethnic groups, January 1993.* Rockville, MD: National Institute on Drug Abuse.

Kovach, J. A., & Glickman, N. W. (1986). Levels and psychosocial correlates of adolescent drug use. *Journal of Youth and Adolescence, 15,* 61-77.

Marquis, K. H., Duan, N., Marquis, M. S., & Polich, J. M. (1981). *Response errors in sensitive topic surveys* (Report Nos. R1710/1-HHS Executive Summary; R-1710/2-HHS Estimates, Effects, and Correction Options). Santa Monica, CA: Rand Corporation.

Mensch, B. S., & Kandel, D. B. (1988). Underreporting of substance use in a national longitudinal youth cohort. *Public Opinion Quarterly, 52,* 100-124.

National Institute on Drug Abuse. (1992). *National household survey on drug abuse: Population estimates 1991.* Rockville, MD: Author.

Nettles, S. M., & Pleck, J. H. (in press). Risk, resilience, and development: The multiple ecologies of black adolescents. In R. J. Haggerty, N. Garmezy, M. Rutter, & L. R. Sherrod (Eds.), *Stress, risk, and resilience in children and adolescents: Processes, mechanisms, and interventions.* New York: Cambridge University Press.

Newcomb, M. D., & Bentler, P. M. (1986a). Frequency and sequence of drug use: A longitudinal study from early adolescence to young adulthood. *Journal of Drug Education, 16,* 101-120.

Newcomb, M. D., & Bentler, P. M. (1986b). Substance use and ethnicity: Differential impact of peer and adult models. *Journal of Psychology, 120,* 83-95.

Newcomb, M. D., & Bentler, P. M. (1987). The impact of late adolescent substance use on young adult health status and utilization of health services: A structural equation model over four years. *Social Disease and Medicine, 24,* 71-82.

Newcomb, M. D., & Bentler, P. M. (1989). Substance use and abuse among children and teenagers. *American Psychologist, 44,* 242-248.

Newcomb, M. D., Chou, C., Bentler, P. M., & Huba, G. J. (1988). Cognitive motivations for drug use among adolescents: Longitudinal tests of gender differences and predictors of change in drug use. *Journal of Counseling Psychology, 35,* 426-438.

Newcomb, M. D., & Harlow, L. L. (1986). Life events and substance use among adolescents: Mediating effects of perceived loss of control and meaninglessness in life. *Journal of Personality and Social Psychology, 51,* 564-577.

Oetting, E. R., & Beauvais, F. (1987). Peer cluster theory, socialization characteristics, and adolescent drug use: A path analysis. *Journal of Counseling Psychology, 34,* 205-213.

Oetting, E. R., & Beauvais, F. (1990). Adolescent drug use: Findings of national and local surveys. *Journal of Consulting and Clinical Psychology, 58,* 385-394.

Perry, C. L., Killen, J., Slinkard, L. A., & McAlister, A. L. (1980). Peer teaching and smoking prevention among junior high school students. *Adolescence, 15,* 277-281.

Rhodes, J. E., & Jason, L. A. (1988). *Preventing substance abuse among children and adolescents.* Elmsford, NY: Pergamon.

Rhodes, J. E., & Jason, L. A. (1990). A social stress model of substance abuse. *Journal of Consulting and Clinical Psychology, 58,* 395-401.

Stein, J. A., Newcomb, M. D., & Bentler, P. M. (1987). An 8-year study of multiple influences on drug use and drug use consequences. *Journal of Personality and Social Psychology, 53,* 1094-1105.

Thorne, C. R., & DeBlassie, R. R. (1985). Adolescent substance use. *Adolescence, 20,* 335-347.

U.S. Department of Health and Human Services. (1989). *Reducing the health consequences of smoking: 25 years of progress. A report of the Surgeon General.* Washington, DC: U.S. Department of Health and Human Services.

Wallace, J. M., & Bachman, J. G. (1991). Explaining racial/ethnic differences in adolescent drug use: The impact of background and lifestyle. *Social Problems, 38,* 333-357.

Weissberg, R. P., Caplan, M., & Harwood, R. L. (1991). Promoting competent young people in competence-enhancing environments: A systems-based perspective on primary prevention. *Journal of Consulting and Clinical Psychology, 59,* 830-841.

Welte, J. W., & Barnes, G. M. (1987). Alcohol use among adolescent minority groups. *Journal of Studies on Alcohol, 48,* 329-336.

Whitehead, P. C., & Smart, R. G. (1972). Validity and reliability of self-reported drug use. *Canadian Journal of Criminology and Corrections, 14,* 1-7.

Wills, T. A., & Shiffman, S. (1985). Coping and substance use: A conceptual framework. In S. Shiffman & T. A. Wills (Eds.), *Coping and substance use* (pp. 3-24). New York: Academic Press.

Windle, M. (1990). A longitudinal study of antisocial behaviors in early adolescence as predictors of late adolescent substance use: Gender and ethnic group differences. *Journal of Abnormal Psychology, 99,* 86-91.

6. Substance Misuse Among Rural Adolescents

Fay E. Reilly
University of Alaska, Anchorage

Carl G. Leukefeld
University of Kentucky in Lexington

Jingwei Gao
Sheila Allen
Regional Action Partnership

INTRODUCTION

This chapter examines alcohol and drug use among rural adolescents by focusing on the current state of knowledge. We begin the chapter by reviewing research related to rural adolescent alcohol and drug use and conclude with a presentation of rural Appalachia as a context to understand better how cultural environment affects adolescents.

The general public is concerned about the use of drugs among adolescents. Frequently, alcohol and other drug use begins during adolescence (Johnston, O'Malley, & Bachman, 1984; Oetting & Beauvais, 1990). Substance abuse as a teenager has been found to be related to continuing adult use and abuse, school dropout rate, and teenage traffic fatalities (Sarvela, Newcomb, & Duncan, 1988). Rural adolescent alcohol and drug abuse is a concern because rural use rates by adolescents are approaching, and in some cases exceeding, urban rates (Hahn, 1982; Kirk, 1979; Sarvela & McClendon, 1987; Napier, Carter, & Pratt, 1981), which has a high cost to society.

Researchers have focused on understanding the etiology and antecedents of adolescent drug use in both rural and urban youth. Several factors that contribute to the initiation and maintenance of adolescent drug use have been examined more extensively. These factors include peer influence, family as well as adult influences, early age of use onset, psychosocial factors, and multiple drug use (Leukefeld, 1990). These factors have not, however, consistently explained the onset or maintenance of substance-use behaviors. Rural patterns of alcohol and drug use have also been reported to be different from urban patterns (Blazer, Crowell, & George, 1987; Globetti, Alsikafi, & Morse, 1978).

ADOLESCENCE

In this chapter, *adolescence* is defined as the period of time between the ages of 13 and 18. Other definitions consider biological, social, psychological, cultural, and developmental factors. Biologically, adolescents undergo physical development by producing secondary sex characteristics and growing to their adult height. Socially, adolescents are experiencing changes related to differences in expectations between children and adults. Peer relationships take on added significance during adolescence. Psychologically, adolescents are adjusting to multiple changes in their bodies and in their social expectations. In addition, adult cognitive processes begin to develop during adolescence. The length of adolescence is affected by the need for society to have children function as adults. In contemporary U.S. society, the length of adolescence seems to be getting longer as U.S. society becomes more complex (Adams, Gullotta, & Markstrom, 1994; Lewis & Volkmar, 1990).

DRUG AND ALCOHOL ABUSE

Donovan and Jessor (1978) define *alcohol misuse* among adolescents as drunkenness at least six times in the previous year or experiencing negative consequences due to drinking. In this chapter, a more stringent definition is used. *Use, misuse,* and *abuse* are synonymous and are defined as any use of substances by an adolescent and including medications that are not prescribed. This definition includes smoking before the age of 16, drinking before the age of 21, any use of illegal drugs, and any use of a substance in a manner not intended or prescribed (e.g., solvents, prescription drugs, or over-the-counter drugs).

RURAL

An historical motivation to distinguish between *rural* and *urban* arose from the need to understand how the United States was growing and industrializing. Later, classifications of rural became important when resources were distributed. With each emphasis, different definitions of *rural* were used. As a result, the term *rural* has many meanings. The two definitions used by the U.S. Government were developed by the Office of Management and Budget and the U.S. Bureau of the Census. The Office of Management and Budget uses the Metropolitan Statistical Area (MSA). The designation of rural is given to existing counties within a state that include an integrated area with 50,000 or fewer residents. On the other hand, the Bureau of the Census defines a rural population to include all those people living outside (a) urban areas that are named, or (b) incorporated places of 2,500 or more people. The Bureau of the Census further divides rural populations into farm and nonfarm residents (U.S. Bureau of the Census, 1940-1990).

Besides these two definitions, there have been other ways of categorizing rural. In these schemes, a variety of characteristics of the rural area are examined. For example, classification schemes have examined economic activity, county demographics, commuting patterns, and population density (Zube & Zube, 1977).

RURAL ADOLESCENCE

The above rural definitions suggest that variations in social networks including family interaction patterns, concentrations of populations, economic influences, access to services, history, and access to urban areas currently exist. Indeed, many of these factors have been found to be associated with adolescent alcohol and drug-abuse patterns and are examined here.

EARLY ADOLESCENT
USE PATTERNS IN RURAL AREAS

Several studies have reported that lifetime prevalence of drug use among rural adolescents steadily increases with each successive school year (Kirk, 1979; Napier et al., 1981), particularly for alcohol, tobacco, and marijuana (Harris & Ford, 1988; McIntosh, Nyberg, Fitch, Wilson, & Staggs, 1979). School grade and substance-abuse behavior were highly associated in rural areas, with students in higher grade levels consistently reporting more substance use (Sarvela, Pape, Odulana, & Bajracharya, 1990; Winfree & Griffiths, 1983a).

Compared with urban adolescents, rural youth were found to have experiences with most drugs such as solvents, LSD, heroin, and uppers at a younger age than urban youth (Napier, Goe, & Bachtel, 1984; Sarvela & McClendon, 1987; Sarvela, Newcomb, & Duncan, 1988; Sarvela et al., 1990). Urban adolescents had higher use rates overall. Others have reported, however, that rural drug use and drug initiation begins as early as the fourth to sixth grades (Oetting & Beauvais, 1990). Rural youth are obviously not protected from drug use by their apparent isolation. In fact, it has been suggested that the rural adolescent's initiation and prevalence of risky behaviors are related to higher-than-national prevalence rates of alcohol misuse among rural adolescents (Napier et al., 1984; Sarvela & McClendon, 1987; Sarvela, Newcomb, & Duncan, 1988; Sarvela et al., 1990).

Rural children develop and form their opinions and attitudes about substance use at a very early age, and these opinions have been found to be related to their prospective substance-abuse behavior. A willingness to use drugs in rural areas greatly increases as adolescence approaches (Blau, Gillespie, Felner, & Evans, 1988; Oetting & Beauvais, 1990). Sarvela and McClendon (1987) believe that opinions and related substance-abuse behaviors may begin at an earlier age in rural areas than in the United States as a whole. Carman's (1979) study on motivations for drug use and problematic outcomes among rural Wyoming junior high school students lends support to this theory that the formation of opinions toward drugs—"personal effects motivations"—has implications for patterns of drug-use problems, frequency of intoxication, and social complications among rural students.

MULTIPLE DRUG USE AMONG RURAL ADOLESCENTS

Several rural studies have reported that the use of one drug can predict other drug use (Ellinwood, 1974; McGlothlin, 1974; Patch,

1973). These findings generally are supported in both urban and rural settings. For example, in a study conducted in an agriculturally based county in southwestern Ohio, Napier et al. (1981) indicated that the frequency of alcohol use correlated moderately with the frequency of marijuana use. Cockerham (1977) examined the relationship between patterns of alcohol and multiple drug use among rural white and American Indian adolescents and reported that those who used any drug had a favorable attitude toward drugs, other than alcohol, and would be more likely to use another drug when compared to nonusers. Napier, Bachtel, and Carter (1983) found that rural frequent users of an illegal substance were also multiple drug users.

Skager and Fisher (1989) identified school characteristics that demonstrate different patterns of alcohol and other drug use. After surveying 44 high schools in California, they found different patterns of drug use in three types of schools. Substance use was highest in rural, predominantly white schools; second highest in large schools where parents came from high socioeconomic status groups; and lowest in predominantly minority, low socioeconomic status, rural, or small town schools.

PEER PRESSURE

Several rural studies have noted that peer influence is one of the strongest predictors of adolescent drug use (Carman, 1977; Globetti et al., 1978; Sarvela & McClendon, 1987; Tolone & Dermott, 1975). Pruitt, Kingery, Mirzaee, Heuberger, and Hurley (1991) concluded that perceived drug use among friends, in addition to receiving information about drugs from friends, was found to be associated with rural adolescent drug use. A rural adolescent's perception of his or her friends' involvement in illegal drug use was more powerful in predicting their own use than their perceptions of the information about drugs they received from friends. Students at highest risk for illegal drug use have more friends who use drugs and receive more information about drugs from their friends. Conversely, rural students who report lower drug use among their friends and receive less drug information from friends seem to be at lower risk of personal involvement with illegal drug use. Thus the association between peer influence and illegal drug use in rural areas as reported by Pruitt et al. (1991) is high.

Older rural adolescents receive information about drugs from their peers (Sarvela, Newcomb, & Littlefield, 1988). Dating is related to increases in drug use as is identifying with the drug culture (Napier et al., 1983). Sarvela and McClendon (1987) posited the assumption that the high rate of rural adolescent alcohol misuse is related to peer alcohol use and that drug use is a behavior that can be learned through peer socialization. Exposure to role models early in life also encourages the use of illegal drugs. Rural students who associated with or identified with drug users exhibited a much higher probability of involvement in illegal drug use (Napier et al., 1984; Tolone & Dermott, 1975). In fact, the peer influence and psychosocial identification variables in Napier et al.'s (1984) analysis explained nearly 70% of the variance of all drug use in a group of rural high school students.

Socialization level was also found to be significantly related to all types of drug use among rural high school students (Jurkovic, 1979). One early study (Carman, 1977) reported that junior high students had a similar pattern of drug choice when compared with senior high students, which suggests that socialization into drug use is strongly related to adolescent drug behavior. In another study, Globetti et al. (1978) reported that a majority of rural students indicated that friends served as drinking companions, as sources of alcohol, and provided a place for their first drink—in a friend's home. Social pressure is also cited as a reason why rural students become engaged in deviant activity (Terre, Drabman, & Meydrech, 1990). Drinking with friends dramatically increased as grade level increased. Thus Pruitt et al. (1991) suggest that drug prevention efforts could be more effective and appropriate if peer pressure is targeted.

FAMILY INFLUENCE ON USE

Open communication between parent and child has been found to have a positive impact on a decreased level of substance use by rural adolescents. Conversely, parents' problematic attitudes and behaviors toward substance use are associated with their children's use behavior. In fact, a father's substance-use behavior was found to be significantly correlated with adolescent substance use (Kafka

& London, 1991). Query (1985) reported, in his study of drug-abusing youth aged 10 to 13 in an adolescent chemical treatment program, that more than half of those from rural areas had parents with alcohol and/or drug problems and that almost two thirds had blood relatives with such problems, thus highlighting the family as a primary source of socialization into drug abuse.

Sarvela and McClendon (1987) suggested that adolescent patterns of alcohol use may reflect patterns of use in their own families. Braucht (1983) identified four family characteristics related to problem adolescent drinking. They include less parental disapproval, less involved parents, parents who were heavy drinkers, and parents with less positive attitudes or who were less affectionate toward the adolescent. Napier et al. (1983) also identified a relationship between rural adolescent drug use and parental drinking. The presence of at least one "open" parental figure was associated with lower levels of substance use; however, this relationship did not exist when the open figure was a peer (Kafka & London, 1991). The authors suggest that the difference between parent and friend may be the moral authority that parents represent.

The interpersonal relationships of parents to each other and to their children are related to a child's alcohol and drug use. Napier et al. (1983) found parental marital status not to be a precursor of illegal drug use among teens. Predictors of alcohol and other drug use related to family life included stressful home life in addition to parent relationships. Napier et al. (1981) found that adolescents with intact married parents and good interpersonal relationships tended to be low users of alcohol and marijuana.

FACTORS ASSOCIATED
WITH RURAL ADOLESCENT USE

Predictors and correlates of rural adolescent alcohol and drug abuse include psychosocial factors. Low self-esteem, depression, and anxiety were associated with increasing willingness to use drugs (Blau et al., 1988). Blazer et al. (1985; Blazer et al., 1987) reported that alcohol abuse and depression were more prevalent in rural areas, whereas other drug use or dependence and depression were more prevalent in urban areas. Carman (1977) examined locus of control and drug use among a sample of rural adolescents and found that external locus of control negatively correlated with marijuana, hallucinogen, and barbiturate use. In another study, Carman (1979) found personal effects motivations were significantly related to rural adolescent drug use. Problem use was thus associated with the desire or perceived need for personal change.

Several studies have suggested different drug-using characteristics between rural and urban adolescents. Hahn (1982) concluded, in a study of 11,277 rural Indiana students in the 7th, 9th, 10th, and 12th grades, that there was a different drug-use pattern between rural and urban students in those grades. Urban students reported more marijuana use but rural students used significantly more alcohol—both in quantity and frequency. He also added that the gulf between urban and rural student drug use may no longer exist. Findings from another study indicate that driving after drinking and using other drugs was prevalent among rural youth (Sarvela et al., 1990), so that driving under the influence (DUI) rates reached epidemic proportions in certain rural areas.

Differences between male and female rural adolescents in their substance-use patterns have diminished, and sometimes females show higher use rates than males in rural areas (Johnston et al., 1984; Newcomb, Maddahian, & Bentler, 1986; Sarvela, Newcomb, & Duncan, 1988; Sarvela et al., 1990). In other studies, Carman (1974) predicted that adolescents with low expectations for success and high values for achieving goals would be heavy drug users, and the findings supported this hypothesis. Napier et al. (1983) reported that more religious adolescents used drugs less frequently. Income was not found to be associated with rural adolescent drug use, except for barbiturates (Napier et al., 1983). Alexander and Klassen (1988) found that rural student smokers were more likely to be absent from school.

RURAL DRUG
INFORMATION AND EDUCATION

Although several studies have reported a gradual reduction in heroin and cocaine use by adolescents after drug education efforts (Oetting & Beauvais, 1990), there are a limited number of rural studies that have examined sources of drug information and adolescent education programs (Mirzaee, Kingery, & Pruitt, 1991; Sarvela,

1987; Sarvela, Newcomb, & Littlefield, 1988). Mirzaee et al. (1991) studied 1,023 students in the 8th and 10th grades in small- to medium-sized central Texas rural school districts. They reported that a majority of students indicated that TV was their main source of drug information on depressants, stimulants, hallucinogens, and alcohol —indicating the importance of media as a source of drug information.

The media and teachers have been found to be important sources of drug information for rural adolescents (Mirzaee et al., 1991; Sarvela, Newcomb, & Littlefield, 1988). School-based drug education programs have been reported more likely to be effective if all teachers are involved. Physicians, according to Mirzaee et al. (1991), were reported to be the most reliable and believable sources of drug information for rural respondents. Mirzaee et al. also found it was important to use peers in school drug education programs to provide positive peer influence on adolescents' health behavior. The police also were reported to contribute to the success of drug education with such programs as Drug Abuse Resistance Education (D.A.R.E).

After limited success with general drug prevention models in the 1960s and 1970s, which used information and a general life skills model, a social influence model based on social learning theory has been used nationally (Evans et al., 1981; Evans et al., 1978). This drug prevention approach combines social skills training, decision making, and psychological inoculation to teach students to live without drugs. The results from a rural study carried out by Ellickson and Bell (1990), targeted at preventing junior high school drug use, indicates that education programs based on the social influence model can be effective in lowering rates of initiation and lowering rates of cigarette and marijuana use.

Studies have noted conflict associated with knowledge about substance use and attitudes toward use. In a study of 7th-grade students in two North Carolina rural school systems, Dignan, Block, Steckler, and Cosby (1985) found that student attitudes toward smoking behavior were unchanged after a risk reduction program, although students agreed that prevention and intervention programs were positive. In rural North Carolina smoking was such a predominant social norm, and a symbol of willingness to support the local economy, that students were in favor of smoking, thus, a "boomerang" effect. In another study Sarvela and McClendon (1987) did not find lower substance use, particularly lower alcohol use, among 6th and 7th grade students in rural northern Michigan and northeastern Wisconsin after they received drug education programs. The authors noted that economic, cultural, and family background may sustain student substance-use behavior. Different characteristics of substance use may also be associated with prevention and treatment efforts (Hahn, 1982; Leukefeld, Clayton, & Myers, 1992). Several early studies (Mirzaee, Kingery, & Pruitt, 1991) found that the family could be a valuable source of information about drugs. For example, parent involvement in drug education activities and programs has the potential for more effective drug education.

RACE/ETHNICITY AND CULTURE

Data from national surveys can be used to draw an overall picture of alcohol and drug use. The very nature of national survey sampling, however, can mask, hide, or wash out the influence of rural or minority segments of the population. Studies have reported that the initiation, use maintenance, use rates, use frequency, and prevalence among adolescents are related to society's attitudes, cultural background, race, ethnicity, and other social variables (Ellickson & Bell, 1990; Martin & Pritchard, 1991). The following presents a discussion of alcohol and drug-use research that has focused on rural adolescents and their race/ethnicity. These studies target rural adolescent alcohol and other drug research for three groups: African American, Spanish-speaking (e.g., Hispanic, Latino, Cuban, Puerto Rican, Mexican American), and Native American/Native Alaskan adolescents.

African American

In a review of research on African American youth, Harper reported that African American rural youth reported slightly less drinking and fewer heavy drinkers than rural white youth (Dawkins, 1980, in Harper, 1988; Napier et al., 1983). Also, African American rural adolescents were more likely to receive their first drink from their parents, more likely to drink at social occasions, and had less knowledge about alcohol or other drugs than did white rural youth (Dawkins, 1980, in Harper, 1988).

Okwumabua, Okwumabua, Winston, and Walker (1989), in their study of 7th to 12th graders in a rural Alabama county, found alcohol to be the entry drug, rather than tobacco; they reported an onset of use at 5 years of age for tobacco and 7 to 8 years of age for solvents and marijuana. Both similarities and differences between rural and urban African American youth in their drug-use patterns were reported in this study. Although onset patterns for rural youth were similar to urban rates, the rate of decline in rural use occurred by age 16 compared with age 18 in the urban areas. In a large adolescent study, McIntosh et al. (1979) reported that urban and rural African American females had the lowest overall drug-use rates of all subgroups. However, their use rates of hallucinogens, heroin, cocaine, and solvents equaled or exceeded all other subgroups.

Spanish Speaking

Chavez, Beauvais, and Oetting (1986), reporting on a Hispanic and Anglo sample in a southwestern community, found higher use rates of alcohol, uppers, tranquilizers, and heroin than in a national sample. Among Hispanics there was higher reported "ever tried" for cigarettes, marijuana, stay-awake pills, tranquilizers, and PCP. Hispanic females reported higher rates for alcohol, cigarettes, uppers, and diet pills than for all other groups.

Cockerham and Alster (1983) examined marijuana use among Mexican American and Anglo rural youth from 12 to 18 years of age. The Mexican American youth had a more positive attitude about marijuana and higher rates of reported use. The authors go on to suggest that difference in marijuana use may be a result of Mexican American cultural identity. Guinn and Hurley (1976) reported higher rates of alcohol and other drug use in a predominantly white urban sample than in a Mexican American rural sample. The drugs that both groups reported using were alcohol, tobacco, stimulants, and marijuana. The rural sample also reported higher use of cough syrup and solvents than the urban sample.

Mata and Andrew (1988) examined inhalant use among a rural Anglo and Mexican American sample from 6th to 12th grades. The Mexican American students were more likely to have used inhalants than the Anglos in their sample. A low rate of use by females was also noted and higher use rates were related to friends' approval more than to availability. Findings from another study of Mexican

American and Anglo rural youth indicated that Mexican American youth had more favorable attitudes toward both drug use in general and marijuana use in particular (Cockerham & Alster, 1983). They also found that the Mexican American culture may play an important role in promoting drug attitudes and drug use. McIntosh et al. (1979) also reported high rates of hallucinogen, uppers, and solvents use among rural Mexican American females. They found this despite the recognized general conservatism of Mexican American females related to alcohol and tobacco use.

Native Americans and Native Alaskans

Cockerham, Forslund, and Raboin (1976), when examining attitudes related to drug use among American Indians and white youth, reported that American Indians were more favorable toward drug use than white youth. Higher percentages of American Indian youth had tried marijuana and other drugs as well as initiated use at an earlier age. Once marijuana was tried, however, there were no differences between white and American Indian youth in their frequency of use, reasons for use, or with the type of other drugs tried. Although American Indians who used marijuana were more likely to experiment with other drugs, they were no more likely than whites to continue using these drugs.

Cockerham (1977) studied the attitudes and practices of a sample of white and Native American adolescents between the ages of 12 and 18 with regard to their use of alcohol and other drugs. They reported that both whites and American Indians approved of drinking but American Indians got drunk more frequently. American Indians were more likely to approve of using drugs other than alcohol, were more likely to have tried marijuana, and were more likely to use hard drugs than were whites. Cockerham also suggests in the study that rural American Indian youth are encouraged culturally to appreciate the importance of social needs of affiliation, social acceptance, pleasant sensation, and relief from stress in social activities.

Both American Indians and non-Indians stated that they use drugs to experience an alteration in their senses (Binion, Miller, Beauvais, & Oetting, 1988). American Indian and non-Indian youth also reported alcohol and other drug use during social occasions and with friends to facilitate socializing. The importance of the combination of pleasant effect and ease of socializing seems to be stronger for

American Indians. Compared to non-Indians, reservation American Indian youth attribute more importance to their alcohol use to experience independence; for sensation seeking; and to deal with boredom, friends, feelings, and social needs according to this study.

Cockerham (1975) reported that Native American adolescents, surveyed at a reservation junior high school, were aware that alcohol and drug use was a prime activity that could get them in trouble with the police. Despite this, the majority approved of drinking. In addition, 80% of the sample identified themselves as drinkers and 92% of those who approved of drinking identified themselves as drinkers. There were no reported differences between girls and boys, however, in their drinking rates, drinking frequency, or amount consumed in each drinking episode. Although boys started drinking earlier, both boys and girls had begun a pattern of regular drinking before they were 13 years old.

Okwumabua and Duryea (1987), in a study of American Indian high school students, reported that 81% of students had tried cigarettes, alcohol, marijuana, solvents, or cocaine. The age at which these students stated they first used these substances was as early as 5 to 7 years old. By age 14, the majority had tried the substances. Onset of drug use was earlier for boys than for girls. Of those who reported using substances, 91% were multiple drug users. Winfree and Griffiths (1985) examined the results of three surveys on attitudes toward marijuana and marijuana use over an 8-year period by rural youth aged 13 and 16. They found heavier marijuana use by Native Americans in the cohort. At the end of the 8 years, the authors noted a difference in attitudes between the younger and older cohorts. The younger cohort became more conservative; however, use by Native Americans continued to be greater than among whites. This more conservative attitude was not reflected in the older cohort, and their attitudes toward marijuana use remained liberal.

Weibel-Orlando, Weisner, and Long (1984), in a study of urban and rural American Indian drinking patterns, reported that drinking patterns were not acquired in the urban environment. Rather, they report that these patterns were formed in rural areas and on reservations prior to migrating to urban areas. Drinking in the family of origin strongly predicted both past and current drinking frequency, and rural Native Indians in the study tended to have higher alcohol consumption in a drinking session.

Oetting and Goldstein (1979) indicated that young Native Americans were more heavily involved in drug use than a national sample of adolescents. They reported particularly high use of alcohol, marijuana, and inhalants. Social factors related to drug use were rejection, alienation, poverty, broken families, and religion. Nationally, when compared to a white student population from Minnesota, before 12th grade, fewer Native American/Native Alaskan youth drink on a daily or weekly basis. By the 12th grade, however, Native American/Native Alaskan youth surpass the white reference group rates. Blum, Harmon, Harris, Bergeisen, and Resnick (1992) found in a survey of eight Native American Health Service areas that female American Indian/Alaska Native populations used cigarettes at higher rates than other ethnic or racial groups. Other commonly used substances included marijuana, peyote, and inhalants. Alaska Natives were twice as likely as other native groups to report daily cigarette use. They also reported a higher rate of suicide attempts and having experienced physical abuse.

Query (1985) conducted an adolescent study in a youth chemical dependency unit located in the north central plains and reported that American Indians were overrepresented in the patient population on the basis of their representation in the general population. In a 6-month follow-up after treatment, 27% of the white clients remained drug free; however, none of the American Indians were drug free. This raises questions about the effectiveness of standard chemical dependency treatment for the American Indian youth population. Chavez et al. (1986) suggest that rural communities demonstrate greater variability than urban communities in their drug-use/drug-abuse patterns. Swaim, Beauvais, Edwards, and Oetting (1986) agree and go on to suggest that the potential of rural communities is to develop idiosyncratic patterns of drug use among its youth.

In a study of marijuana use among Native American and Caucasian youth, Winfree and Griffiths (1983b) found that Native American and Caucasian marijuana use was associated with different social factors. Drug law attitude, peer use, and parents' views of drugs had stronger prediction on Caucasian youth marijuana involvement than on Native American youth. According to this study, Native Americans begin using marijuana at an earlier age than Caucasians and as grade level advances, their involvement increases. The authors believed that ethnicity of those students played a key role in their drug-related values, attitudes, and behavior.

Cockerham and his colleagues (1976) indicated that American Indian youth presented more favorable attitudes, both from friends and from themselves, toward marijuana and other drug use than did white youth. American Indians reported that they tried marijuana and other drugs at a younger age and were more socially oriented to use drugs than white youth. It is interesting to note that American Indian youth, compared with white youth, were no more likely to continue using other drugs, although they were more likely to try drugs.

APPALACHIAN KENTUCKY:
A RURAL EXAMPLE

This section presents an example of a geographical setting in which adolescents live and mature. It is presented here to help those readers who might be unfamiliar with rural areas so that they may better understand the environmental influences that may impinge upon adolescents and set the stage for alcohol and drug use among rural adolescents.

Appalachians represent a distinct group on the basis of their history, economy, culture, and service availability (Raitz & Ulack, 1984). Most of the Appalachian Kentucky region fits the Bureau of the Census definition of *rural*. Similarities between Appalachian Kentucky and other rural areas include low population density, lower levels of education, poorer health status relative to urban areas, greater distance from formal health care services than in urban areas, and fewer services than in urban areas (Bagby, 1989; DeLeon, Wakefield, Schultz, Williams, & VandenBos, 1989; Raitz & Ulack, 1984).

Other features found in Eastern Appalachian Kentucky that are common to some but not all rural areas are high poverty rates, breakdown of the traditional kinship structures, out-migration from the geographic region, and distrust of outsiders. All of these factors place Appalachians at high risk for untreated health and mental health as well as other problems (Hoover et al., 1988; Keefe, 1986, 1988a, 1988b; Weller, 1965).

The overall geographical area of Appalachia makes it one of the largest geographic regions in the United States. The total Appalachian region consists of an area 600 miles long, 250 miles wide, and comprising 80,000 square miles in 12 states: Kentucky, Virginia, West Virginia, Tennessee, North Carolina, Alabama, Georgia, New York,

Pennsylvania, Ohio, South Carolina, and Mississippi (Appalachian Regional Commission, 1985).

Appalachian geography, and particularly Appalachian Kentucky, has contributed to its isolation from mainstream culture. Difficult access, scarcity of roads, and steep mountainous terrain have all contributed to this isolation (Raitz & Ulack, 1984; Weller, 1965). Geography has also reinforced family structure and proximity. Appalachia has little bottomland, few valleys, and narrow hollows. Families first settled in the area, picking the prime land. As families grew, they found the solution to the paucity of flat land was for the younger generation to settle very near their kinfolk. The result is to have large extended family clans settled close to each other, forming the traditional "hollows." The result of this geographic closeness is emotional closeness, with the extended family being extremely important to Appalachians (Raitz & Ulack, 1984).

Keefe (1988a, 1986) and Raitz and Ulack (1984) argue that Appalachian Kentuckians have many features that set them apart as a distinct group. Features that distinguish Appalachian Kentuckians from other groups include a geographic location, a common history, a sense of belonging to the mountains, and a sense of the place being inseparable from the person (Keefe, 1986). Appalachian reliance on the extended family for support mediates the effects of stress, even in the face of economic impoverishment and disregard by the mainstream culture. This mediating effect may be disappearing, however, for those Appalachian Kentuckians who have experienced breakdown of the extended family. Adolescents without extended family support are at high risk for developing more emotional problems (Halperin & Slomowitz, 1988).

Appalachian Kentuckians have their own cultural style of accepting care, especially health care. Appalachian health care includes herbal medicine and informal care received from family and friends, as well as emergency hospital care (Keefe, 1988b). This pattern was necessary because of the relative isolation, lack of rapid transportation, and lack of professional health services. Thus individuals in these situations were more likely to develop a tradition of helping themselves.

The Appalachian region of Kentucky is noted for high poverty rates, lack of industrial diversity and community development, and high unemployment (Raitz & Ulack, 1984). This region is among the poorest in the nation with poverty rates of more than two to three times the national average.

Alcohol and Other Drugs

The Appalachian region of Kentucky has a salient history and continuing experience with alcohol and other drug production and use. Appalachian Kentuckians have a tradition as independent producers of alcohol. Conflict between Appalachian alcohol producers and federal "revenuers" is legendary. The literature related to alcohol and other drug abuse as well as prevention activities focused on Appalachian adolescents and youth is, however, extremely limited (Bagby, 1989; Keefe, 1988a).

There is a peculiar relationship with alcohol on a societal level. Virtually all the counties in the Appalachian region of Kentucky are dry, with a few of the major population centers being wet, resulting in moist counties. The forces that contribute to the continuing dryness of the area are said to be both bootleggers who want to maintain their source of income and churches who oppose alcohol use.

A relationship similar to alcohol production and use exists for marijuana production. The region is considered to be a major marijuana producer. Even though the economic indicators show high unemployment and low per capita income, this may not reflect the true state of the economy. The impact of marijuana on the economy causes ambivalence in some about tackling issues related to marijuana and other drugs, including alcohol. Tobacco has also been a cash crop in this region of Appalachia for many years, and the rate of tobacco use is among the highest in the state of Kentucky at more than 40%.

The use of prescription drugs also has an interesting history in the Appalachian region of Kentucky. The use of prescription drugs is said to have begun with coal companies and coal camps in the late 19th and early 20th centuries. Thus a tradition of prescribing "nerve pills" developed and the demand for these prescriptions became associated with what is now called "nerves." This tradition was particularly relevant to wives of coal miners and currently continues for many women. In the region, prescription drug use is as acceptable as tobacco or alcohol with little risk associated with use (University of Kentucky, unpublished data, 1993).

CONCLUSION

In this chapter we presented the following major points:

- The level of drug use among rural adolescents is at a high level.
- Rural adolescents use a variety of drugs and, like their urban counterparts, use multiple drugs.
- Students at highest risk for illegal drug use are those who have more friends/peers who use drugs.
- The acceptance and use of substances by parents is related to their adolescent children's drug use.
- Media, teachers, and peers have been found to be important sources of drug information for rural adolescents.
- Drug use and initiation patterns can be different for different racial/ethnic and cultural groups of adolescents.
- Appalachian adolescents are a distinct group of rural adolescents.

The number of studies focused on adolescents in rural areas are fewer and more out of date than those for urban areas. In fact, it is apparent from the literature reviewed in this chapter that there is a paucity of substance-abuse information about rural adolescents. In addition, these studies do not present uniform findings. On the one hand, they report differential drug-abuse patterns between rural and urban youth (Brown, Voskuhl, & Lehman, 1977; Swaim et al., 1986), but on the other hand, they indicate that the differential drug and alcohol use rates between rural and urban youth are diminishing, and in some cases, rural adolescent drug-use rates are higher than those of urban adolescents (Alexander & Klassen, 1988; Globetti et al., 1978; Hahn, 1982; Kirk, 1979; Lowman, 1981; Napier et al., 1981; National Insitute on Drug Abuse, 1980; Swaim et al., 1986; Winfree & Griffiths, 1983a).

A shortcoming of the adolescent research reviewed is that it is largely school based. Studies are needed that examine the impact of rural adolescent school dropouts and their drug-use rates. For example, Alexander and Klassen (1988) reported that students who are absent for more than 3 days a month were more likely to be involved in drug use and less likely to have been surveyed in the initial mass survey. It has also been suggested that school dropouts are more likely to be users of alcohol and other drugs (Bachman et al., 1991;

Oetting & Beauvais, 1990). Thus lower rates of alcohol and other drug use frequently noted in specific race/ethnic populations may be a result of absenteeism and/or higher dropout rates, particularly in rural areas.

There is also a paucity of research on substance abuse among specific racial/ethnic rural adolescents. Research on race/ethnicity and rural adolescence reveals a variety of substance-abuse patterns, but these patterns need to be further examined. For example, substance-abuse patterns are associated with economic status (Skager & Fisher, 1989), cultural attitudes/ethnic identity (e.g., Cockerham & Alster, 1983; Cockerham et al., 1976), and race/ethnic group membership (e.g., Dawkins, 1980).

Rural adolescent studies suggest that alcohol and other drug abuse by racial/ethnic group youth both has similarities with and is distinct from urban drug abuse. The most obvious similarity is that a large number of adolescents reported use/abuse of alcohol and other drugs. The idea that rural residents are protected from the influences of alcohol and other drugs because of their rural residence should be dispelled by the findings presented here. The exact interplay between alcohol and other drug abuse and other factors needs to be more fully examined. Although research has examined onset patterns, use, and attitudes toward alcohol and other drugs, additional research is needed to focus on examining risk factors associated with and predictors of alcohol and other drug use among rural adolescents.

The community environment within which adolescents grow up is important when developing alcohol and other drug prevention programming, as noted in the description of Appalachian Kentucky. An important point to remember here, which needs further scrutiny, is that rural communities demonstrate greater variability than urban communities in drug-use/drug-abuse patterns (Chavez et al., 1986), and that rural communities have potential for developing idiosyncratic patterns of drug use among their youth (Swaim et al., 1986).

Finally, rural alcohol and other drug databases are limited, especially for examining longitudinal changes in adolescent drug and alcohol use over time. It seems that these types of databases should be developed to assist communities, counties, and states plan alcohol or other drug activities and projects. The idiosyncratic drug-use patterns that may develop in rural communities suggest that information collection and intervention strategies need to be connected in order to tailor better rural community and county prevention activities for adolescents.

REFERENCES

Adams, G. R., Gullotta, T. P., & Markstrom, C. (1994). *Adolescent life experiences* (3rd ed.). Pacific Grove, CA: Brooks/Cole.

Alexander, C. S., & Klassen, A. C. (1988). Drug use and illnesses among eighth grade students in rural schools. *Public Health Reports, 103*(4), 394-399.

Appalachian Regional Commission. (1985). *Appalachia: Twenty years of progress.* Washington, DC: Author.

Bachman, J. G., Wallace, J. M., O'Malley, P. M., Johnston, L. D., Kurth, C. L., & Neighbors, H. W. (1991). Racial/ethnic differences in smoking, drinking, and illicit drug use among American high school seniors, 1976-89. *American Journal of Public Health, 81*, 372-377.

Bagby, J. (1989). Introduction. In *Health in Appalachia: Proceedings from the 1988 Conference on Appalachia* (pp. 1-2). Lexington: The University of Kentucky, The Appalachian Center.

Binion, A., Miller, C. D., Beauvais, F., & Oetting, E. R. (1988). Rationales for the use of alcohol, marijuana, and other drugs by eighth-grade Native American and Anglo youth. *International Journal of the Addictions, 23*(1), 47-64.

Blau, G. M., Gillespie, J. F., Felner, R. D., & Evans, E. G. (1988). Predisposition to drug use in rural adolescents: Preliminary relationships and methodological considerations. *Journal of Drug Education, 18*(1), 13-22.

Blazer, D., Crowell, B. A., Jr., & George, L. K. (1987). Alcohol abuse and dependence in the rural south. *Archives of General Psychiatry, 44*(8), 736-740.

Blazer, D., George, L. K., Landerman, R., Pennybacker, M., Melville, M. L., Woodbury, M., Manton, K. G., Jordon, K., & Locke, B. (1985). Psychiatric disorders: A rural/urban comparison. *Archives of General Psychiatry, 42*(7), 651-656.

Blum, R. W., Harmon, B., Harris, L., Bergeisen, L., & Resnick, M. (1992). American Indian-Alaska Native youth health. *Journal of the American Medical Association, 267*, 1637-1644.

Braucht, C. (1983). Problem drinking among adolescents: A review and analysis of the psychosocial research. In *Alcohol and Health Monograph 4: Special population issues* (DHHS Pub. #ADM 82-1193). Washington, DC: Government Printing Office.

Brown, B. S., Voskuhl, T. C., & Lehman, P. E. (1977). Comparison of drug abuse clients in urban and rural settings. *American Journal of Drug and Alcohol Abuse, 4*(4), 445-454.

Carman, R. S. (1974). Internal-external locus of control, alcohol use and adjustment among high school students in rural communities. *Journal of Community Psychology, 2*, 129-133.

Carman, R. S. (1977). Internal-external control and drug use among junior high school students in a rural community. *International Journal of the Addictions, 12*(1), 53-64.

Carman, R. S. (1979). Motivations for drug use and problematic outcomes among rural junior high school students. *Addictive Behaviors, 4*, 91-93.

Chavez, E., Beauvais, F., & Oetting, E. R. (1986). Drug use by small town Mexican American youth: A pilot study. *Hispanic Journal of Behavioral Sciences, 8*, 243-258.

Cockerham, W. C. (1975). Drinking attitudes and practices among Wind River Reservation Indian youth. *Journal of Studies on Alcohol, 36*(3), 321-326.

Cockerham, W. C. (1977). Patterns of alcohol and multiple drug use among rural white and American Indian adolescents. *International Journal of the Addictions, 12*(2-3), 271-285.

Cockerham, W. C., & Alster, J. M. (1983). A comparison of marijuana use among Mexican-American and Anglo rural youth utilizing a matched-set analysis. *International Journal of the Addictions, 18*(6), 759-767.

Cockerham, W. C., Forslund, M. A., & Raboin, R. M. (1976). Drug use among white and American Indian high school youth. *International Journal of the Addictions, 11*(2), 209-220.

Dawkins, M. P. (1980). *Alcohol and the black community: Exploratory studies of selected issues.* Saratoga and Palo Alto, CA: Century Twenty-One Publishers.

DeLeon, P. H., Wakefield, M., Schultz, A. J., Williams, J., & VandenBos, G. R. (1989). Rural America: Unique opportunities for health care delivery and health services research. *American Psychologist, 44*, 1298-1306.

Dignan, M. B., Block, G. D., Steckler, A., & Cosby, M. (1985). Evaluation of the North Carolina risk reduction program for smoking and alcohol. *Journal of School Health, 55*(3), 103-106.

Donovan, J. E., & Jessor, R. (1978). Adolescent problem drinking: Psychosocial correlates in a national sample study. *Journal of Studies on Alcohol, 39*, 1506-1524.

Ellickson, P. L., & Bell, R. M. (1990). Drug prevention in junior high: A multi-site longitudinal test. *Science, 247*, 1299-1305.

Ellinwood, E. (1974). The epidemiology of stimulant abuse. In E. Josephson & E. Carroll (Eds.), *Drug use: Epidemiological and sociological approaches* (pp. 303-329). Washington, DC: Hemisphere Publishing.

Evans, R. I., Rozelle, R. M., Maxwell, S. E., Raines, B. E., Dill, C. A., Guthrie, T. J., Henderson, A. H., & Hill, P. C. (1981). Social modeling films to deter smoking in adolescents: Results of a three-year field investigation. *Journal of Applied Psychology, 66*(4), 399-414.

Evans, R. I., Rozelle, R. M., Mittelmark, M. B., Hansen, W. B., Bane, A. L., & Havis, J. (1978). Deterring the onset of smoking in children: Knowledge of immediate physiological effects and coping with peer pressure, media pressure, and parent modeling. *Journal of Applied Social Psychology, 8*(2), 126-135.

Globetti, G., Alsikafi, M., & Morse, R. (1978). High school students and the use of alcohol in a rural community: A research note. *Journal of Drug Issues, 8*(4), 435-441.

Guinn, R., & Hurley, R. (1976). A comparison of drug use among Houston and Lower Rio Grande Valley secondary students. *Adolescence, 11*, 455-459.

Hahn, D. B. (1982). A statewide comparison of student alcohol and marijuana use patterns at urban and rural public schools. *Journal of School Health, 52*(4), 250-255.

Halperin, R. H., & Slomowitz, M. (1988). Hospitalized Appalachian adolescents. In S. E. Keefe (Ed.), *Appalachian mental health* (pp. 188-205). Lexington: University of Kentucky Press.

Harper, F. D. (1988). Alcohol and black youth: An overview. *Journal of Drug Issues, 18,* 7-14.

Harris, M. B., & Ford, V. L. (1988). Tobacco use in a fifth-grade southwestern sample. *Journal of Early Adolescence, 8,* 83-96.

Hoover, G. A., Carter, M. V., Heinrich, M. A., O'Connell, L., Scott, D. R., Daulton, M., & Tilson, J. E. (1988). Toward an understanding of the health care needs of the rural homeless in Appalachia: The case of the sheltered homeless in east Tennessee. In *Health in Appalachia: Proceedings from the 1988 Conference on Appalachia* (pp. 76-85). Lexington: The University of Kentucky, The Appalachian Center.

Johnston, L. D., O'Malley, P. M., & Bachman, J. G. (1984). *Highlights from "Drugs and American high school students 1975-1983"* (National Institute on Drug Abuse). Washington, DC: Government Printing Office.

Jurkovic, G. J. (1979). Dimensions of moral character and drug use among rural high school students. *Journal of Clinic Psychology, 35*(4), 894-896.

Kafka, R. R., & London, P. (1991). Communication in relationships and adolescent substance use: The influence of parents and friends. *Adolescence, 26*(103), 587-598.

Keefe, S. E. (1986). Southern Appalachia: Analytical models, social services, and native support systems. *American Journal of Community Psychology, 14,* 479-498.

Keefe, S. E. (Ed.). (1988a). *Appalachian mental health.* Lexington: University of Kentucky Press.

Keefe, S. E. (1988b). Mental health in Appalachia: An anthropologist's perspective. In *Health in Appalachia: Proceedings from the 1988 Conference on Appalachia* (pp. 23-32). Lexington: The University of Kentucky, The Appalachian Center.

Kirk, R. S. (1979). Use of alcohol and other drugs by rural teenagers. *Currents in Alcoholism, 6,* 233-237.

Leukefeld, C. (1990). Drug prevention research needs. In K. Rey, C. L. Faegre, & P. Lowery (Eds.), *Prevention research findings: 1988* (pp. 46-52). Washington, DC: Government Printing Office.

Leukefeld, C., Clayton, R. R., & Myers, J. A. (1992). Rural drug and alcohol treatment. *Drugs and Society, 7*(12), 95-116.

Lewis, M., & Volkmar, F. (1990). *Clinical aspects of child and adolescent development* (3rd ed.). Philadelphia: Lea & Febiger.

Lowman, C. (1981). Facts of planning: Prevalence of alcohol use among U.S. senior high school students. *Alcohol Health and Research World, 6*(1), 29-40.

Martin, M. J., & Pritchard, M. E. (1991). Factors associated with alcohol use in later adolescence. *Journal of Studies on Alcohol, 52*(1), 5-9.

Mata, A. G., & Andrew, S. R. (1988). Inhalant abuse in a small rural south Texas community: A social epidemiological overview. *NIDA Research Monograph, 85,* 49-76.

McGlothlin, W. (1974). The epidemiology of hallucinogenic drug use. In E. Josephson & E. Carroll (Eds.), *Drug use: Epidemiological and sociological approaches* (pp. 279-301). Washington, DC: Hemisphere Publishing.

McIntosh, A. M., Nyberg, K. L., Fitch, S. D., Wilson, J. B., & Staggs, F. M. (1979). Age and drug use by rural and urban adolescents. *Journal of Drug Education, 9*(2), 129-142.

Mirzaee, E. M., Kingery, P. M., & Pruitt, B. E. (1991). Sources of drug information among adolescent students. *Journal of Drug Education, 21*(2), 95-106.

Napier, T. L., Bachtel, D. C., & Carter, M. V. (1983). Factors associated with illegal drug use in rural Georgia. *Journal of Drug Education, 13,* 119-140.

Napier, T. L., Carter, T. J., & Pratt, M. C. (1981). Correlates of alcohol and marijuana use among rural high school students. *Rural Sociology, 46*(2), 319-332.

Napier, T. L., Goe, R., & Bachtel, D. C. (1984). An assessment of the influence of peer association and identification on drug use among rural high school students. *Journal of Drug Education, 14*(3), 227-248.

National Institute on Drug Abuse. (1980). *Treatment research report: Drug abuse in rural America* (Publication #ADM 81-1040). Rockville, MD: National Institute on Drug Abuse.

Newcomb, M. D., Maddahian, E., & Bentler, P. M. (1986). Risk factors for drug use among adolescents: Concurrent and longitudinal analysis. *American Journal of Public Health, 76*(5), 525-531.

Oetting, E. R., & Beauvais, F. (1990). Adolescent drug use: Findings of national and local surveys. *Journal of Consulting and Clinical Psychology, 58*(4), 385-394.

Oetting, E. R., & Goldstein, G. S. (1979). Drug use among Native American adolescents. In G. M. Beschner & A. S. Friedman (Eds.), *Youth drug abuse: Problems, issues, and treatment* (pp. 409-441). Lexington, MA: Lexington Books/D. C. Heath.

Okwumabua, J. O., & Duryea, E. J. (1987). Age of onset, periods of risk, and patterns of progression in drug use among American Indian high school students. *International Journal of the Addictions, 22*(12), 1269-1276.

Okwumabua, J. O., Okwumabua, T. M., Winston, B. L., & Walker, H. (1989). Onset of drug use among rural black youth. *Journal of Adolescent Research, 4,* 238-246.

Patch, V. D. (1973). Public health aspects of adolescent drug use. In Drug use in America: Problem in perspective [Special issue]. *National Commission on Marijuana and Drug Abuse, 1,* 975-1077.

Pruitt, B. E., Kingery, P. M., Mirzaee, E., Heuberger, G., & Hurley, R. (1991). Peer influence and drug use among adolescents in rural areas. *Journal of Drug Education, 21*(1), 1-11.

Query, J. M. N. (1985). Comparative admission and follow-up study of American Indians and whites in youth chemical dependency unit on the north central plains. *International Journal of the Addictions, 20*(3), 489-502.

Raitz, K. B., & Ulack, R. (1984). *Appalachia, a regional geography: Land, people and development.* Boulder, CO: Westview.

Sarvela, P. D. (1987). Early adolescent alcohol abuse in rural northern Michigan. *Community Mental Health Journal, 23*(3), 183-191.

Sarvela, P. D., & McClendon, E. J. (1987). Indicators of rural drug use. *Journal of Youth and Adolescence, 17*(4), 335-347.

Sarvela, P. D., Newcomb, P. R., & Duncan, D. F. (1988). Drinking and driving among rural youth. *Health Education Research, 3*(2), 197-201.

Sarvela, P. D., Newcomb, P. R., & Littlefield, E. A. (1988). Sources of drug and alcohol information among rural youth. *Health Education, 19*(3), 27-31.

Sarvela, P. D., Pape, D. J., Odulana, J., & Bajracharya, S. M. (1990). Drinking, drug use, and driving among rural midwestern youth. *Journal of School Health, 60*(5), 215-219.

Skager, R., & Fisher, D. G. (1989). Substance use among high school students in relation to school characteristics. *Addictive Behaviors, 14,* 129-138.

Swaim, R., Beauvais, F., Edwards, R. W., & Oetting, E. R. (1986). Adolescent drug use in three small rural communities in the Rocky Mountain region. *Journal of Drug Education, 16*(1), 57-72.

Terre, L., Drabman, R. S., & Meydrech, E. F. (1990). Relationships among children's health-related behavior: A multivariate, developmental perspective. *Preventive Medicine, 19,* 134-146.

Tolone, W. L., & Dermott, D. (1975). Some correlates of drug use among high school youth in a midwestern rural community. *International Journal of the Addictions, 10*(5), 761-777.

U.S. Bureau of the Census. (1940-1990). *United States census.* Washington, DC: U.S. Department of Commerce.

University of Kentucky Center on Drug and Alcohol Abuse, Lexington. [Unpublished data, 1993.]

Weibel-Orlando, J. W., Weisner, T., & Long, J. (1984). Urban and rural Indian drinking patterns: Implications for intervention policy development. *Substance and Alcohol Actions/Misuse, 5,* 45-57.

Weller, J. E. (1965). *Yesterday's people.* Lexington: University of Kentucky Press.

Winfree, L. T., & Griffiths, C. T. (1983a). Youth at risk: Marijuana use among Native American and Caucasian youths. *International Journal of the Addictions, 18*(1), 53-70.

Winfree, L. T., & Griffiths, C. T. (1983b). Social learning and adolescent marijuana use: A trend study of deviant behavior in a rural middle school. *Rural Sociology, 48*(2), 219-239.

Winfree, L. T., & Griffiths, C. T. (1985). Trends in drug orientations and behavior: Changes in a rural community, 1975-1982. *International Journal of the Addictions, 20,* 1495-1508.

Zube, E. H., & Zube, M. J. (1977). *Changing rural landscapes.* Amherst: University of Massachusetts Press.

7. The Pharmacologic Aspects of Psychoactive Substances: Implications for Medical Management

Paul V. Trad

Cornell University Medical Center

INTRODUCTION

Effective diagnosis and treatment of an individual using alcohol or illicit drugs requires that the clinician be familiar with the pharmacologic mechanisms of action of these agents. This discussion focuses on the following psychoactive substances: nicotine, alcohol, marijuana, cocaine, phencyclidine (PCP), and heroin. Each exerts a distinctive effect on the individual's central nervous system as well as on other systems of physiologic function. In some instances, the substance acts to accelerate the individual's neurological system, but in other cases the substance functions to depress the neurological system. Moreover, these effects may be compounded if the individual mixes various psychoactive agents. When mixtures of these drugs have been ingested, the clinician may have difficulty distinguishing among the effect of the various agents. In addition, although the use of most of these substances is illegal, both alcohol and nicotine use are legal and, as a result, diagnosing abuse of these substances can be a complicated process because individuals may resist or deny admitting that they have a problem with the substance.

Among the important tasks for the clinician is the identification of the symptoms manifested by the individual and the evaluation of the individual's mental status in order to formulate a comprehensive treatment plan. In this regard, the clinician should also be aware that comprehensive treatment mandates addressing all the side effects a psychoactive agent may precipitate. Comprehensive diagnostic screening also requires the clinician to investigate any factors in the patient's environment that may influence use of these agents, including significant relationships, home environment, and stressful confrontations. In addition, clinicians should be acquainted with the management of severe intoxications caused by each agent in the event of an emergency.

The discussion below begins by outlining the mechanism of action of each psychoactive substance. Subsequently, procedures for diagnostic screening are outlined. This form of screening involves an assessment of the individual's psychosocial environment. The neurobiological response to addiction is then reviewed, and an overview of treatment guidelines is then provided. The discussion concludes with comments relating to interventions in cases of acute intoxication.

THE NEUROBIOLOGICAL
EFFECTS OF NICOTINE

Sixty-four percent of adolescents from the senior high school class of 1990 have used cigarettes. Nearly 6% smoked half a pack daily (Johnston, O'Malley, & Bachman, 1991). Nicotine exerts a strong stimulating effect on the user that is unique from the effect of other drugs. The agent acts on stereospecific receptors for nicotine as well as on dopaminergic pathways. When taken in the form of cigarettes, nicotine is inhaled into the lungs. From there, the substance is absorbed into the bloodstream and reaches the brain within 8 seconds following inhalation. Peak concentrations of nicotine in the plasma after a cigarette is smoked are generally 25 to 50 ng/ml (Benowitz, Porchet, Sheiner, & Jacob, 1988). The agent is also eliminated rapidly from the body. After one cigarette has been smoked, concentrations decline rapidly over a period of 5 to 10 minutes, a pattern primarily reflecting distribution of the agent through the body. For a habitual smoker, the half-life of nicotine is approximately 2 hours. The agent is oxidized to form its primary metabolite, cotinine, which has relatively fewer cardiovascular effects. In turn, cotinine is cleared slowly from the body (half-life of about 19 hours), and this lingering metabolic effect makes it a more accurate barometer of overall nicotine intake than the nicotine itself (Benowitz et al., 1988).

The external effects of nicotine are well known. The substance is absorbed systematically during smoking, triggering such signs as hand tremor, an alerting pattern of low voltage and fast activity on the electroencephalogram (EEG), decreased tone in skeletal muscles (reflected by a diminished amplitude in the electromyogram), and a decrease in deep tendon reflexes (Jaffe, 1990). Nicotine also causes an elevation in the concentration of several hormones and neurotransmitters in the plasma. Excessive use of nicotine may provoke nausea and vomiting by stimulating the medulla oblongata as well as by activating the vagal reflexes. Most of these effects have been attributed to the increase in mesolimbic dopaminergic neurons caused by the intake of nicotine (Jaffe, 1990).

Other physiological responses associated with nicotine abuse are also familiar. For example, nicotine has been shown to decrease weight gain, reduce aggression, and enhance memory. Smokers tend to weigh approximately 5 to 10 pounds less than nonsmokers. Nicotine is posited to have this effect because it suppresses the appetite for sweets, while increasing energy expenditure both at rest and during exercise (Perkins, Epstein, Marks, Stiller, & Jacob, 1989).

Theorists have hypothesized that the effects of nicotine are reinforcing. Specifically, in one study, smokers given 1.5 mg of nicotine intravenously reported sensations of well-being and displayed increased scores on scales measuring the euphorigenic effects of morphine and amphetamine (Henningfield, Miyasato, & Jasinski, 1983). These pleasurable feelings may enhance memory and attention capacities, decrease irritability, and alter the appetite of the nicotine user.

Long-term use of tobacco products containing nicotine has been causally linked to a broad spectrum of illnesses, ranging from cardiovascular disease to lung cancer. In fact, tobacco smoking remains the most widespread preventable cause of death in the United States. Statistics indicate that for male smokers the overall mortality ratio is approximately 1.7 compared with nonsmokers, and the ratio is 2.0 for males who smoke two packs per day and even higher for those who inhale the smoke. Among women, smoking more than one pack a day has been associated with a fivefold increase in fatal coronary heart disease (Willett et al., 1987).

The probability of illness may be decreased if cigarette smoking is stopped. By 5 to 10 years after cessation, risk of disease reduces to a level only slightly above that of the nonsmoker. Although the destruction of lung tissue that occurs during smoking is not reversible, once smoking ends the rate of decline in pulmonary function begins to resemble that of the nonsmoker. Conversely, the neurobiological effects of nicotine persist for as long as the individual continues to smoke. Specifically, smokers metabolize a variety of drugs more rapidly than do nonsmokers, most probably as a result of the induction of enzymes in the intestinal mucosa and the liver. Among the drugs whose potency is compounded by the presence of tobacco are theophylline, phenacetin, propranolol, imipramine, caffeine, oxazepam, and nordazepam (Benowitz et al., 1988). In addition, smokers may need higher doses of painkillers than nonsmokers in order to experience relief from discomfort, may be less sedated by benzodiazepines than nonsmokers, and may obtain a lower level of antianginal effect from certain cardiovascular drugs.

Even chronic smokers are not immune to the short-term neurobiological effects of nicotine. To illustrate: After one or more cigarettes the smoker will exhibit increases in blood pressure and pulse rate, hand tremors, decreases in skin temperature, and increases in the plasma concentrations of certain hormones. By the same token, however, the habitual smoker develops tolerance for some other effects of nicotine. In particular, smokers do not experience the dizziness, nausea, and vomiting experienced by nontolerant individuals exposed to nicotine. Moreover, regular smokers find injections of nicotine pleasant, but nonsmokers report an unpleasant reaction (Henningfield et al., 1983). The most plausible explanation for these differences is that tolerance is due primarily to pharmacodynamic changes rather than to alterations in drug disposition.

Investigations of the duration of tolerance vary. In some animal studies, tolerance disappears within 24 to 48 hours of abstinence, but in other studies tolerance endures for months. Among humans, nicotine tolerance has been found to decline rapidly. For example, the first cigarette of the day inaugurates a far more pronounced cardiovascular and neurological response than do those that follow.

Termination of tobacco use is apt to initiate a withdrawal syndrome that varies in intensity depending on the individual. The most frequently reported symptoms other than tobacco craving, which subsides within a few weeks, include irritability, anxiety, restlessness, impatience, and difficulties in concentration. Cognitive impairment, in the form of decreased short-term memory, has also been demonstrated, and some smokers complain that increases in appetite and concentration deficits persist for weeks or months. Clinical investigations have shown that the cessation of smoking also results in changes in the EEG, as well as a decrease in high-frequency activities typical of arousal and an elevation of low-frequency activities associated with drowsiness (Jaffe, 1990).

NEUROBIOLOGICAL
EFFECTS OF ALCOHOL

Alcohol continues to be the most used of all drugs by adolescents. Nearly 90% of the senior high school class of 1990 used alcohol, with 9% acknowledging having consumed five or more drinks in a row on several occasions in a recent 2-week period (Johnston et al., 1991). The use of alcohol has become a seminal feature of the culture of the United States, with almost two thirds of adults using the agent at least occasionally and an estimated 12% of adults falling into the category of "heavy drinkers." Over the course of a lifetime, an estimated 13% of the population will become alcohol dependent, a risk substantially higher for men than for women (Cloninger, Dinwiddie, & Reich, 1989).

Chronic use of alcohol leads to an increased ability to metabolize the substance and to establish pharmacologic tolerance. This means that a higher blood concentration of alcohol is needed in order to produce an intoxicating effect in a chronic user, as opposed to an infrequent user or a nonuser. The amount of alcohol consumption necessary for a lethal dose remains unpredictable, however, and clinicians should be cautioned that severe acute intoxication with respiratory depression may occur at virtually any time (Mendelson & Mello, 1979). Two particularly invidious outcomes of chronic alcohol use are that the user may become cross-tolerant to a wide range of other drugs or that the alcohol may combine with other chemical substances to exert an additive effect. Cross-tolerance between alcohol and other agents may be triggered by changes in the central nervous system (CNS) or a more rapid metabolism, because alcohol stimulates hepatic microsomal enzyme activity. Chronic alcohol users are generally more tolerant of anesthetics and sedatives than nondrinkers. Of significance is that cross-tolerance is typically a phenomenon in the sober alcoholic. That is, when the user's level of blood alcohol is high, the effect of other pharmacologic agents is actually compounded (Sellers & Busto, 1982; Smith, 1977).

Chronic alcohol abuse results in physical dependence. Human beings can metabolize the alcoholic content of approximately 30 ml (1 oz) of whisky in an hour. Provided intake is spread out over the course of a day, each administration of alcohol may be metabolized without substantial increases in blood concentration levels. In contrast, ingestion of only moderately larger amounts of alcohol at closer intervals of time may exceed the body's metabolic capacity and can produce higher blood concentrations that result in physical dependence within a few days. Symptoms of withdrawal characteristically appear within 12 to 72 hours after the total cessation of drinking. Nevertheless, even a mild decline in blood concentration levels may precipitate withdrawal symptoms. Declines of this type may be brought about by decreases in the total daily intake of alcohol (Mendelson & Mello, 1979).

The classic symptoms of withdrawal include nausea, weakness, anxiety, tremors, and alterations in sleep patterns. If alcohol dependency is extreme, the individual may undergo severe tremulousness, seizure disorders, and delirium tremens. Tremors, surfacing within a few hours following the last drink, may range from mild to so disruptive that the individual is unable to lift a glass. Concurrently, the individual may undergo nausea, sweating, cramps, vomiting, hyperreflexia, and elevated blood pressure. Nightmares are a common feature of this clinical picture. The REM phase of sleep, suppressed by chronic alcohol use, reemerges with alcohol cessation. The individual may experience visual and auditory hallucinations that, depending on the degree of alcoholism, may be transient or persistent. Seizure activity often appears within the first 24 hours after withdrawal. If the withdrawal progresses untreated, the individual may become physically weaker, cognitively disoriented, and, with the onset of persecutory hallucinations, increasingly more agitated. Hyperthermia, along with exhaustion and cardiovascular collapse, may also occur. This pronounced state of alcohol withdrawal is frequently labeled delirium tremens or alcohol withdrawal delirium. Assuming the individual survives this phase of withdrawal, recovery customarily occurs within 5 to 7 days. Even if abstinence continues, however, altered brain function may continue for many months (Grant, 1987).

A variety of unique problems are encountered in chronic abusers of alcohol that are not as evident with abusers of other types of drugs. For example, infants born to mothers who have consumed large amounts of alcohol during pregnancy may not only experience withdrawal symptoms after delivery but also be mentally retarded and harbor a host of developmental disabilities. Chronic alcoholics also experience nutritional deficiencies because of alcohol's capacity to supply calories and depress appetite without offering nutritional value. Among the disorders encountered in chronic alcoholics are peripheral neuropathies, glossitis, pellagra, amblyopia, anemia, encephalopathy, and psychotic episodes characterized by an impairment of recent memory. Other disorders, including acute gastritis, pancreatitis, fatty liver, cirrhosis of the liver, cardiopathy, and skeletal muscle insults, are more likely caused by the toxic effects of alcohol. Alcohol use has also been implicated in adult-onset seizures that are unrelated to withdrawal. Additional complications include malabsorption, disturbances in the regulation of glucose metabolism, and altered gonadal functioning, which may be caused by impaired pancreatic and/or hepatic functioning. The regular ingestion of moderate to high levels of alcohol has also been associated with certain types of cancer, such as breast cancer in women (Korsten & Lieber, 1985; Lieber, 1988; Ng, Hauser, Brust, & Susser, 1988). In one study of 7,188 women aged 25 to 74, Schatzkin et al. (1987) found that consumption of any amount of alcohol increased the risk of breast cancer by 40% to 50% among women who drank fewer than three drinks per day. The link between drinking and breast cancer was more pronounced among younger, thinner, and premenopausal women. Moreover, alcoholics who have recently been detoxified commonly exhibit symptoms of clinical depression as well as subtle cognitive deficits that may be caused by the direct toxic effects of alcohol on the brain and generally improve if abstinence persists.

Alcoholism in women poses some special problems. Investigations suggest that women may be more prone to the serious medical consequences of heavy drinking than men (Gomberg & Lisansky, 1984). Some studies have suggested that alcoholism in women may begin as a response to stress. Specifically, difficulty in conceiving, difficulty in carrying to term, miscarriage, spontaneous abortion, childbirth, and hysterectomy have been associated with female alcoholism (Gomberg & Lisansky, 1984). Among the events women mentioned most frequently as contributing to and even causing a drinking problem were biological incidents, including childbirth, breast removal, and hysterectomy (Rathbone-McCuan & Roberds, 1980). Blood alcohol level is known to vary with the phases of the menstrual cycle, a finding that suggests a connection between hormonal status and the effects of alcohol (Jones & Jones, 1976). Premenstrual and menstrual difficulties may be antecedents to excessive drinking—a theory that remains to be verified (Gomberg & Lisansky, 1984). In this regard, clinicians should be alert to correlations between drinking level and the phase of the woman's menstrual cycle (Braiker, 1984, p. 349).

Significantly, women become intoxicated more rapidly than men even if body weight is the same, because women generally have less muscle tissue, which ordinarily contains water to break down the alcohol. An individual's body weight, metabolic rate, emotional state, and previous experience with alcohol also affect alcohol consumption (Humphrey & Friedman, 1986). For example, women may develop cirrhosis of the liver at low levels of alcohol consumption and after a shorter period of pronounced drinking than do men (Saunders, Davis, & Williams, 1981). In one study, Krasner, Davis, Portmann, and Williams (1977) determined that 11.5% of alcoholic women had hepatitis and central sclerosing hyaline necrosis in comparison to 3.3% of alcoholic men. Moreover, Saunders et al. (1981) found that women with alcoholic cirrhosis had been excessive drinkers for a mean period of 13.5 years in comparison to 20 years for men with cirrhosis. Recent evidence indicates that besides the direct hepatotoxic effects of alcohol, immunologic reactions directed against the liver contribute to alcoholic liver problems.

Female alcoholics also manifest more gynecologic problems than do light or moderate women drinkers. Among the roster of complaints are infertility, miscarriage, stillbirth, fetal alcohol syndrome, and defects among offspring (Wilsnack, Klassen, & Wilsnack, 1984). Thresholds were six or more drinks per day at least three times a week for miscarriages, stillbirths, and prematurity, and six or more drinks per day at least five times per week for infertility and birth defects. Fetal alcohol syndrome, fetal alcohol defects, dysmenorrhea, abruptio placentae, spontaneous abortion, and preterm delivery have also been correlated with abnormal drinking patterns.

Jacobson (1986) investigated clinical associations between computerized tomographic (CT) scan changes and drinking among 26 female alcoholics and 41 controls. The study revealed that female alcoholics had larger ventricles and a greater degree of widening of the interhemispheric fissures than did controls. Moreover, the CT scans of all the alcoholic women were significantly different from the scans of the healthy female controls. In particular, almost all of the female alcoholics manifested neurological signs of alcohol dependence syndrome.

Although the death rate for women is generally lower than for men, alcoholism reduces this advantage, making mortality the same or even greater for women (Schmidt & Popham, 1980). In addition, alcoholic women are significantly younger at time of death than women in the general population (Smith, Cloninger, & Bradford, 1983). Specifically, Smith et al. found that the approximate mean age of study subjects was 66.5 for nonalcoholic women and 51 for alcoholic subjects, indicating that the life span of alcoholic women may be shortened by as much as 15 years. In the Smith et al. study, the leading causes of death were digestive system disorders, cirrhosis of the liver and other liver diseases, and pancreatitis. The researchers concluded that the earlier the onset, the higher the correlation with various symptoms, and that women who are older when they seek treatment, who have become heavy drinkers before the age of 30, and who have a history of frequent binges are at the highest risk for death.

NEUROBIOLOGICAL EFFECTS OF MARIJUANA

Marijuana remains the most commonly used illicit drug in the United States, with an estimated 41% of the senior high school 1990 class reporting some lifetime experience with the drug (Johnston et al., 1991). Marijuana is derived from the hemp plant, which synthesizes at least 400 chemicals of which more than 60 are cannabinoids. The psychoactive isomer that causes the majority of psychological effects associated with marijuana is tetrahydrocannabinol (THC) (Dewey, 1986; Razdan, 1986).

Cannabinoids have multiple routes of action and not all of these agents appear to produce the same effects in humans. The mechanism of action of the substance is not well understood and it is hypothesized that a single receptor site or mechanism accounts for the diverse effects of marijuana. Among the proposed mechanisms of action are interactions with lipids in cell membranes that increase the agent's fluidity. Another suggested mechanism of action is that cannabinoids alter the synthesis of prostaglandins. The increase or decrease in synthesis seems to depend on the tissue studied, however, and some THC metabolites appear to have actions opposite of those of the parent compound (Martin, 1986; Reichman, Nen, & Hokin, 1988).

THC can exert a significant effect on both the CNS and the cardiovascular system. The behavioral responses the individual manifests as a result of ingestion may vary as a function of dosage, route of administration, expectations, and individual vulnerability to psychotoxic effects. Most frequently, marijuana is smoked and, as with tobacco, the amount of active derivatives that reach the bloodstream is dependent on the specific smoking method.

Marijuana exerts its most prominent effect on the CNS. For example, smoking a cigarette containing 2% THC or taking an oral dose of 20 mg of THC will be likely to modify mood, memory, motor coordination, cognitive and sensory abilities, and perceptions of time and of the self. The individual will often experience an initial euphoria that is followed by relaxation (Hollister, 1986; Maykut, 1985). Short-term memory will be impaired, as will the ability to implement tasks requiring multiple steps, an outcome labeled "temporal disintegration," which is associated with the tendency to confuse past, present, and future, along with feelings of depersonalization— the perception that the self is not real (Jaffe, 1990).

Motor coordination may also be affected to a significant degree. In this regard, balance and stability of stance may deteriorate after only low doses of the agent, and these effects become exaggerated when the eyes are closed. Muscle strength diminishes, reflected in a decrease in hand steadiness. Tasks involving fairly intricate cognitive processes, such as perception, attention, and information processing, become impaired at doses equivalent to one or two cigarettes. This type of impairment may persist for 4 to 8 hours and can impede performance of activities such as driving (Hollister, 1988).

Increased hunger, dry mouth, enhanced hearing, and intense visual images have also been reported by marijuana users. Visual and auditory stimuli, ordinarily ignored, may acquire a unique quality, although sensations of touch, taste, and smell often become accentuated. The psychological effects of the agent are even more pronounced. THC in high doses is known to cause hallucinations, delusions, and feelings of paranoia. As sensations of depersonalization may engulf the individual, cognition becomes confused and disorganized. A psychotic response may also occur at extremely high doses (Andreasson, Allebeck, Engstrom, & Rydberg, 1987). For chronic marijuana users, symptoms may persist even when the individual is not smoking the agent. For example, the individual may manifest apathy, dullness, impairments of judgment and concentration, and memory lapses. These responses are compounded by a loss of interest in pursuing conventional goals. Combined, this constellation of symptoms has been referred to as "amotivational syndrome." Although no specific evidence has established that these personality changes are due to irreversible organic brain damage, it is possible that chronic, long-term use of marijuana may result in structural and functional neurologic change (Jaffe, 1990).

Marijuana has been shown to exert specific effects on the cardiovascular system. In particular, users experience an increase in heart rate, and systolic blood pressure while supine, decreased blood pressure when standing, and a notable reddening of the conjunctivae of the eye. Heart rate acceleration correlates with the amount of THC in the blood. Myocardial oxygen demand is also increased and for patients with angina, exercise time to angina is reduced by nearly 50% after one marijuana cigarette (Hollister, 1988).

The immune and endocrine systems are affected by marijuana use as well. Specifically, cellular and humoral immune responses are suppressed to a degree. Marijuana may also interfere with the synthesis of nucleic acids and proteins. The data regarding the effect of chronic marijuana use on human sexual function remain unclear. Among men, lowered concentrations of testosterone and reversible inhibition of spermatogenesis have been reported. Women may be more susceptible to endocrinologic dysfunction following marijuana use. Specifically, smoking one marijuana cigarette may suppress plasma LH during the lutheal phase of the menstrual cycle (Mendelson et al., 1986). As a result, the woman may fail to ovulate. When an expectant mother uses marijuana, the effect is manifested in the offspring. Infants born to such mothers have lower birth weight, shorter gestation periods, and a greater percentage of congenital malformations than offspring of nonusers. Meconium staining is also more frequent, as is longer labor. Moreover, such children may have learning difficulties and impairments in stimulus response (Hollister, 1986).

Long-term marijuana smoking has been associated with bronchitis and asthma, indicating that the agent has an adverse effect on pulmonary function and the bronchial epithelium, even among young people. Because the smoke is inhaled more deeply and held longer in the lungs than cigarette smoke, marijuana smoking results in four times more tar accumulation in the lungs than cigarette smoking (Wu, Tashkin, Djahed, & Rose, 1988), suggesting that chronic marijuana use significantly heightens the risk of lung cancer. Plasma concentrations of THC achieve their peak within 7 to 10 minutes, and the physiologic effects become maximal within a half hour. A withdrawal syndrome has been reported for chronic users who stop using the substance. Among the documented symptoms of withdrawal are irritability, restlessness, nervousness, decreased appetite, weight loss, insomnia, tremors, chills, and increased body temperature (Jones, Benowitz, & Bachman, 1976).

NEUROBIOLOGICAL EFFECTS OF COCAINE

Slightly more than 9% of the senior high school class of 1990 acknowledged using cocaine at least once in their lifetime (Johnston et al., 1991). An estimated 20 million people in the United States have used cocaine at some time. As a psychostimulant, cocaine has a variety of subjective effects that are dependent on the user, the environment, drug dosage, and route of administration. The most pronounced symptom reported is a sensation of euphoria that appears to be indistinguishable from the euphoria induced by amphetamines. Laboratory experiments reveal that subjects cannot distinguish between these two substances (Fischman & Schuster, 1982). Cocaine endures for a relatively brief period, however, with a half-life of only 50 minutes. The agent reduces fatigue and seems to erase performance impairments that are caused by sleep deprivation. Cocaine is usually administered either intranasally or intravenously.

Along with other amphetamine-like psychostimulants, cocaine produces mood elevation as well as an enhanced perception of self-esteem, and mental and physical aptitude. Hunger and the need to sleep are diminished. Initially, the user may experience increased energy and sociability, which motivate greater use of the drug. Over time, however, these social benefits may be replaced by a kind of drug-induced euphoria (Gawin & Ellinwood, 1988). Frequent use of cocaine may heighten interest in sexual activities. The disinhibition, grandiosity, and impaired judgment the substance triggers may cause the individual to behave in a sexually promiscuous manner. While under the influence of the agent, the cocaine user is likely to become excited and hyperactive. If heavy use persists, toxic CNS symptoms may ensue, including anxiety, hypervigilance, suspiciousness, and fears of persecution.

Shortly after inhalation or intravenous use of the drug, the user experiences an intense sensation—a "rush" that persists for several minutes and has been described as being highly pleasurable. Cocaine crosses the blood-brain barrier rapidly. In fact, shortly after administration of the agent, concentrations of cocaine in the brain far surpass concentrations in the plasma. Redistribution to other organs occurs next. Researchers have posited that the sharp contrast between these high but brief concentrations in the brain and the subsequent rapid decline of the pleasurable sensation underlies the strong drive for additional doses of the drug. Although some individuals may be able to use psychostimulants for months or years without developing toxic paranoia, many individuals develop symptoms of this condition after brief usage (Cregler, 1989). An individual may, for example, continue to inject the drug every 2 to 3 hours around the clock for several days, abandoning both food and sleep. Episodes of this type typically end when the user is out of the drug or becomes too cognitively disorganized to continue. After usage ceases, the individual generally falls into a deep sleep that lasts for 12 to 18 hours, depending on the duration of the initial episode. Cocaine is also highly psychotoxic. Within a few hours after drug administration, users report increased anxiety as euphoric sensations fade. Suspiciousness and paranoia soon follow (Sherer, Kumor, Cone, & Jaffe, 1988) and full-fledged paranoid ideation with visual hallucinations may surface within the course of a 24-hour period of use. Among heavy users, pseudohallucinations are common.

Cocaine is posited to have a psychologically reinforcing quality because it increases synaptic concentrations of dopamine by inhibition of its uptake into neurons originating in the ventral tegmental area of the brain and projecting to structures such as the nucleus accumbens, ventral pallidima, and frontal cortex (Koob & Bloom, 1988; Ritz, Lamb, Goldberg, & Kuhar, 1987; Wise, 1988). The agent is powerful and may produce severe toxicity, even under conditions of monitored clinical use. Among the most serious toxic effects induced by cocaine are cardiac arrhythmias, myocardial ischemia or infarction, myocarditis, high-output congestive heart failure, dilated cardiomyopathy, cerebrovascular spasm with transient neural ischemia or infarct of the brain or spinal cord, intracerebral hemorrhage, aortic dissection, rhabdomyolysis with acute renal and hepatic failure, disseminated intravascular coagulation, convulsions, hyperpyrexia, and respiratory depression. Medical complications tend to be more common after large doses of cocaine are taken intravenously or by inhalation but may also be encountered after relatively modest doses or intranasal use (Cregler, 1989; Gawin & Ellinwood, 1988; Isner et al., 1986; Mody, Miller, McIntyre, Cobb, & Goldberg, 1988; Roth, Alarcon, Fernandez, Preston, & Bourgoignie, 1988).

The cocaine user who relies on subjective perceptions to regulate dosage may easily reach levels of the agent that have toxic effects. For example, dopamine, which plays a primary role in reinforcing the effects of cocaine, most likely blocks the reuptake of norepinephrine while promoting the release of adrenal catecholamines. Coronary vasoconstriction and myocardial sensitization are probably the main factors responsible for ischemia, arrhythmias, and infarcts, although ischemia of the skeletal muscle or direct toxic action may account for rhabdomyolysis with cocaine use. Endothelial injury induced by the vasoconstriction may lead to formation of thrombi or other adverse cardiovascular effects. Finally, long-term use of cocaine may induce myocarditis or dilated cardiomyopathy even when there is no acute event (Karch & Billingham, 1988). Cocaine lowers the seizure threshold, making seizures the most common neurological complication of cocaine use. This form of toxicity most likely results from the local anesthetic actions of cocaine that manifest themselves with high dosages of the agent. Moreover, seizures and loss of consciousness may be secondary effects of a coronary event induced by cocaine.

When cocaine is used during pregnancy, the woman is more likely to experience a spontaneous abortion during the first trimester and placental abruption, infarction, and fetal death when used late in the pregnancy. When cocaine is ingested, it may cause uterine contractions, fetal tachycardia, and excessive fetal activity (Cregler, 1989). The risk of precipitous labor and maternal hemorrhage is also enhanced. Most of this toxicity is caused by the vasoconstrictive effects of the drug. It is not certain whether cocaine is teratogenic, but there appears to be an increased incidence of sudden infant death among babies born to cocaine-dependent mothers (Chasnoff, Hunt, & Kaplan, 1989; Ryan, Ehrlich, & Finnegan, 1987).

NEUROBIOLOGICAL
EFFECTS OF PHENCYCLIDINE (PCP)

Since 1979, when 12.8% of the senior high school class admitted using PCP at least once, lifetime usage of the drug has declined. Only 2.8% of the 1990 senior high school class have ever used the drug (Johnston et al., 1991). PCP was a chemical compound, one of a group of agents known as arylcyclohexylamines, developed in the 1950s as an animal anesthetic and was used briefly as an anesthetic in humans. The agent was abandoned as a human anesthetic, however, because patients manifested delirium upon awakening from the anesthesia. PCP became popular in the 1970s as an illicit agent that was usually smoked or snorted. Relatively easy to synthesize in a laboratory, phencyclidine is commonly known by several street names, including PCP and "angel dust."

PCP exerts a variety of pharmacological actions in the human body. For example, it has CNS-stimulatory as well as depressant effects and has hallucinogenic and analgesic actions. The phrase "dissociative anesthetic" has also been used to characterize this agent because its effect appears to be unique (Aniline & Pitts, 1982). During the heyday of its popularity, users reported that once-a-week use was typical. Some users engaged in 2- to 3-day binges that were followed by intervals of prolonged sleep, from which the user would generally waken depressed and disoriented (Jaffe, 1990).

PCP binds with high affinity to several distinct sites in the CNS. The compound is believed to block the cation channel that is regulated by a type of receptor for excitatory amino acids (Monaghan, Bridges, & Cotman, 1989; Wroblewski & Danysz, 1989). Moreover, PCP and related agents may lower the incidence of neuronal death caused by prolonged ischemia or the local application of excitatory neurotoxins. The agent can also inhibit the uptake of dopamine and norepinephrine and, when administered to animals, it can trigger increased levels of dopamine in the nucleus accumbens (Dunwiddie & Alford, 1987; Hernandez, Auerbach, & Hoebel, 1988).

PCP is well absorbed following all routes of administration. Only a small amount of the drug is excreted unchanged. After ingestion, considerable gastroenteric recirculation occurs, and continuous gastric suction may be of value for treating an overdose. The half-life of the drug is about 3 days (Aniline & Pitts, 1982). Clinical observations suggest that humans can develop tolerance to PCP. Chronic users report such effects as persistent difficulties with short-term memory, speech, and cognition, problems that endure from 6 months to one year following cessation of use. Changes in overt personality have also been reported and include social withdrawal and isolation, states of anxiety, nervousness, and severe depression. Although the onset of adverse effects is unpredictable, deaths, violent behavior, and accidents have occurred as a result of direct toxicity. PCP can also cause acute behavioral toxicity—such as intoxication, aggression, and brief confusional states—comas, convulsions, and psychotic states (Aniline & Pitts, 1982; Giannini, Loiselle, DiMarzio, & Giannini, 1987).

NEUROBIOLOGICAL
EFFECTS OF HEROIN

Although the use of heroin has risen dramatically for adults since the late 1960s, it has remained statistically flat for adolescents. Only 1.3% of the 1990 senior high school class have ever used the drug (Johnston et al., 1991). A user's first experience with opioids is frequently unpleasant, marked by an excessive amount of nausea and vomiting. Other individuals, however, report initial satisfaction with the first dose. Rapid intravenous injection of an opioid produces a warm flushing of the skin and sensations in the lower abdomen described by addicts as resembling a sexual orgasm. This pleasurable perception endures for approximately 45 seconds and is referred to as a "rush." Heroin crosses the blood-brain barrier rapidly. In the brain, the substance is deacetyelated into pharmacologically active 6-monoacetyl morphine and then converted to morphine (Jaffe, 1990).

The behavior, social adjustment, and medical problems encountered among opioid abusers are surprisingly varied. Although good health and productivity are not necessarily incompatible with regular heroin use and addiction, the behavior of an addicted individual prior to receiving a heroin hit may have serious social and physiological consequences. Heroin reduces pain, aggression, and the sexual drive; as a result, use of the agent per se does not cause crime. Most users lack the funds to purchase sufficient heroin on a regular basis, however, and users may therefore commit crimes prior to the use of heroin in order to obtain the agent (Anglin, McGlothlin, & Speckart, 1981; Nurco, Kinlock, Hanlon, & Ball, 1988).

Within a short period of regular usage of heroin, significant tolerance develops to the drug's respiratory-depressant, analgesic, sedative, emetic, and euphorigenic effects. The rate at which tolerance builds up, however, in either an addict or a medical patient, depends on the pattern of use. When heroin is used intermittently it is possible to obtain the desired analgesic and sedative effects from moderate doses for an infinite period—but when the drug action is used on a continuous basis significant tolerance develops. As a result, if the drug is used frequently, the addict will need to increase the dosage. In this manner, some addicts may build up to phenomenally high doses. Nevertheless, the higher the dosage, the greater the risk of potential death from respiratory depression.

The nature and severity of the withdrawal symptoms that appear when heroin use is discontinued depend on various factors, including previous daily dosage, duration of use, and the health of the addict. Symptoms such as lacrimation, rhinorrhea, yawning, and sweating typically appear about 8 to 12 hours after the last dose. Approximately 12 to 14 hours after the last dose, the addict may lapse into a restless and turbulent sleep. As the withdrawal syndrome progresses, additional signs and symptoms appear, including dilated pupils, anorexia, gooseflesh, irritability, and tremors. Weakness, depression, nausea, and vomiting are common, as heart rate and blood pressure become elevated. Marked chilliness, alternating with flushing and excessive sweating, is also characteristic (Jaffe, 1990).

At this juncture, pilomotor activity causes prominent gooseflesh and the skin begins to resemble a plucked turkey. This characteristic has led to the common sobriquet "cold turkey" that is associated with withdrawal from heroin. The individual at this phase may also suffer abdominal cramps and pains in the joints and extremities.

As the withdrawal syndrome progresses, anorexia occurs, combined with vomiting, sweating, and diarrhea. Although occasionally cardiovascular collapse occurs, the withdrawal syndrome generally does not place the individual in a life-threatening situation. Without treatment virtually all of the gross symptomatology recedes in 7 to 10 days. Reestablishing psychological equilibrium depends on each individual, however.

DIAGNOSTIC SCREENING

Diagnosing an individual dependent on alcohol or one of the illicit drugs described above is not necessarily an easy task. Extensive research suggests that it is hard to identify the profile of a chemically dependent person and that no particular personality type, family history, socioeconomic situation, or stressful experience unequivocally predicts chemical dependency (Lawson, Ellis, & Rivers, 1984). Nonetheless, assessments of chemically dependent individuals have suggested that several factors may contribute to the likelihood that the individual will use and eventually abuse these substances. In this regard, the individual's physiological, sociological, and psychological functioning may provide clues concerning likely addiction and should be evaluated.

A comprehensive physiological assessment requires determining if physical addiction is present. In this regard, the clinician should obtain a detailed history of the patient's drug or alcohol use at the beginning of the treatment. A medical practitioner should perform this assessment and should be trained to overcome patient resistance to probing questions. In addition, the patient should be evaluated for the presence of certain physical conditions, including chronic depression, schizophrenia, or other mental conditions likely to respond to psychotropic medications.

Sociologic factors in the individual's life should also be examined. Specifically, it is important to assess family background to determine if a family history of substance abuse exists. Tarter and Schneider (1976) identified a group of variables that appears to influence the individual's decision to start, continue, or stop drinking. Among these variables are childhood exposure to alcohol, familial messages concerning appropriate quantities of alcohol, drinking customs, symbolic meaning attached to alcohol, and the use of alcohol in a social or private context. A similar form of family analysis may be applied with other types of drugs.

A comprehensive assessment also involves evaluating the psychological factors motivating the individual to engage in addictive behavior and the abuse of alcohol and illicit drugs. In this regard, the clinician should investigate how the individual interacts with his or her environment, the nature of the person's defense mechanisms, and the rules governing the individual's behavior. Moreover, has the individual's current life situation sparked dissatisfaction or dysphoria? Key psychological qualities to be alert to are mental obsessions and compulsions, a poor self-image, negative and defeatist attitudes, rigid defense systems, and delusions. Problem areas may include minimal identification with appropriate role models, poor identification with the family, and impaired interpersonal skills for communication, cooperation, negotiation, empathy, listening, and sharing (Lawson et al., 1984). Significantly, weaknesses in these areas may be manifested through the use of alcohol and illicit drugs as well as patterns of self-destructive behavior such as suicide attempts (Glenn, 1981).

THE NEUROBIOLOGICAL RESPONSE OF ADDICTION

One of the most intriguing aspects of addiction to alcohol and illicit drugs remains the phenomenon of addiction itself. Medical researchers generally view disease processes as having a pathophysiologic effect with molecular, cellular, and behavioral repercussions (Blois, 1988). According to Bloom (1988), drug and alcohol addiction may be analyzed in a similar manner, because these agents have been shown to have molecular, cellular, and behavioral effects on the central nervous system.

Yet the addiction that results from alcohol and drug abuse also generates some extraneous effects not encountered with other forms of disease pathogenesis. Among these effects are tolerance, sensitization, and drug craving. The development of tolerance to the drug being abused is a significant component of the addictive state (Bloom, 1993). To explain the onset of tolerance, traditional pharmacological explanations have pointed to alterations in the metabolism of the primary neurotransmitters or to alterations of their receptor mechanisms (Bloom, 1993). Another theory posits that tolerance signifies the body's attempt to reassert the homeostasis that is associated with a drug-free condition. As Koob and Bloom (1988, 1989) explain, tolerance generally develops and decays with a similar time course, suggesting that as the user reacts to the drug, the brain initiates adaptive processes to counter these effects and clear the drug from the body.

Sensitization is another unusual physiologic response associated with the use of some of these illicit agents. This process generally occurs with stimulants, such as amphetamines, but may also occur with other addictive agents and has been described as progressive enhancement of the response to the agent (Bloom, 1993).

Perhaps the most significant and least understood phenomenon associated with alcohol and drug addiction remains, however, the craving that accompanies abuse of these substances. Of relevance is the fact that not only does the craving sensation occur between episodes of drug intake, but this sensation may linger to haunt the addict even after there has been an apparent functional recovery (Koob, Wall, et al., 1989). Consequently, any effective long-term solution to the problem should consider the underlying basis for this residual craving (Bloom, 1993).

TREATMENT GUIDELINES FOR ALCOHOL AND DRUG ABUSE

Given the seemingly intractable nature of drug addiction, one may ask whether any forms of treatment are effective. An answer to this question requires an understanding of addictive conditions. Unlike acute diseases, addictive conditions are more like chronic illnesses in the sense that although there may be an initial crisis intervention, treatment ultimately becomes a long-term process (O'Brien, McLellan, & Alterman, 1993). Moreover, by the time treatment begins the patient may be facing a host of ancillary problems, such as unemployment, mental illness, the breakdown of social support, and homelessness.

Before an intervention is made clinicians should recognize that a wide variety of treatment programs are available. These programs may be inpatient or outpatient, may be based on the type of abused substance involved, and often take into account unique features relating to the life of the abuser. Once it has been determined that treatment will be pursued, the first step is for the clinician to assess the severity of the addiction. As O'Brien et al. (1993) note, simply determining that the addiction is present is not particularly helpful. Nor does determining the amount of the substance the patient uses provide information that will lead to an effective treatment program. Rather, it is recommended that the clinician rely on the Addiction Severity Index, a structured 45-minute clinical research interview that is administered by a trained technician. The Index was designed to assess problem severity in seven areas typically affected by substance abuse, including alcohol and drug use, medical, legal, employment, family/social, and psychiatric problems (McLellan, Luborsky, O'Brien, & Woody, 1980).

A second step involves determining an appropriate treatment program. In this regard, the Treatment Service Review may be administered. This Review is a 5-minute interview administered by a technician that offers a quantitative profile of treatment programs in terms of the number and types of services actually provided to patients (McLellan, Alterman, Cacciola, Metzger, & O'Brien, 1992). When administering the Review, the following questions may be answered:

- Do patients in the same programs receive similar types and amounts of services, and do these services differ for different types of substance-abuse problems?
- Do patients who receive more services display greater improvement and better post-treatment outcomes?

According to O'Brien et al. (1993), this form of thorough evaluation is required in order to ensure that the most appropriate treatment program is selected for each patient.

EMERGENCY MANAGEMENT OF ACUTE INTOXICATION

Acute intoxication with any of the agents discussed will generally mandate supervised withdrawal that is best accomplished in an inpatient setting in which access to the drug is minimized and the withdrawal syndrome can be handled appropriately from a medical standpoint. A series of general principles apply in these cases, irrespective of the particular drug the patient has been abusing. For example, the evaluation should begin with a thorough medical history and physical examination to determine if any of the customary withdrawal techniques are contraindicated. As an illustration, Jaffe (1990) explains that for a patient with angina pectoris, ulcerative colitis, pulmonary insufficiency, or another debilitating illness, a more gradual withdrawal program may be recommended. Next, the degree of the patient's physical dependence should be estimated. Patients experiencing severe pain are not appropriate candidates for withdrawal until a strategy for managing the pain is devised. Clonidine, which has analgesic qualities, is occasionally helpful in this situation.

Estimating the patient's degree of physical dependence on any of these substances from history alone may be difficult, because patients may themselves be unaware of the full scope of their habit. Or they may exaggerate or dissimulate considerably concerning usage. Conversely, other patients may deny use of these agents, even when they have been taking enough of the drug to produce physical dependence. In still other cases, the individual may be oblivious to the amount of the agent consumed, a phenomenon often present among alcoholics. Ultimately, obtaining an accurate history necessitates reliance on patient observation and the results of a physical examination.

The clinician should also be familiar with particular types of withdrawal patterns. With heroin, for example, most patients perceive some withdrawal symptoms, even when dosage is reduced gradually. In these cases, methadone may be helpful for suppressing withdrawal syndrome, causing the patient to experience influenza-like symptoms. Alcohol withdrawal requires a unique approach, because chronic ingestion of large amounts of alcohol is frequently linked to various forms of malnutrition and vitamin deficiencies. Many alcoholics will be dehydrated because of vomiting caused by alcoholic gastritis or withdrawal. Vitamins and attention to fluid balance therefore become essential components of the treatment. Although the abrupt withdrawal of cocaine, PCP, marijuana, and nicotine have not been associated with acute physiologic syndromes that mandate medical intervention, the patient may undergo aversive physiologic and psychological disturbances. Administration of dopaminergic agonists or tricyclic antidepressants has been suggested for the treatment of the fatigue, irritability, depression, and hypersomnolence that may develop after withdrawal of agents such as cocaine. Nicotine, administered in the form of chewing gum, transdermal patches, or nasal sprays, may ameliorate tobacco withdrawal syndrome and may be used for a protracted period as an adjunct to a more comprehensive effort to alter drug-taking behavior.

CONCLUSION

As suggested by the above discussion, the pharmacokinetic aspects of alcohol and illicit drugs are important to understand in order that effective diagnostic and treatment protocols may be devised. Each of the agents discussed—including nicotine, alcohol, marijuana, cocaine, heroin, and PCP—exerts a unique effect on the neurological and cardiovascular functioning of the individual. As a result, each of these agents may trigger a distinctive form of behavior in the individual and has the potential to endanger the individual's life.

Among the key pharmacologic aspects of these substances are:

- Nicotine use, associated with both immediate reinforcing effects and long-term deleterious effects, is considered the most widespread preventable cause of death in the United States.
- Alcohol, the most widely used drug among adolescents, causes dependency in an estimated 13% of the general population.
- Marijuana, the most commonly used illicit drug in the United States, has been used by an estimated 41% of high school seniors.
- Cocaine, which produces euphoric sensations as well as cardiovascular damage and neuromuscular impairment in neonates, has been used by an estimated 20 million people in the United States.
- PCP, originally developed as an animal anesthetic, produces depressant, hallucinogenic, and analgesic effects as well as unpredictable deaths and violence.
- Heroin, a highly addictive agent that can have debilitating effects on physiologic functioning, has risen dramatically in use among adults since the 1960s.

Consequently, clinicians should be sensitive to the unique qualities of each of these substances. In addition, clinicians should also strive to promote preventive behavior by discussing these issues with patients. Prevention requires a candid assessment of the likelihood that the individual will be exposed to the substance and will or will not have sufficient psychological resources to resist usage of the agent. In this regard, the clinician should investigate the patient's typical environment as well as the patient's knowledge of the effect of the agents. Peer use of these agents is an additional issue that should be investigated. The clinician should clarify whether the patient's peers place value on using these substances and are currently using them. Moreover, legal substances, such as nicotine and alcohol that are known to have addictive and detrimental effects should not be ignored, because these agents may be just as powerful physiologically as illicit substances.

In addition, clinicians should be familiar with the typical withdrawal symptoms associated with these agents as well as with recommended forms of managing withdrawal. This familiarity will enable the clinician to make the most beneficial decision regarding the patient's treatment. In short, the capacity to diagnose and treat such patients successfully requires extensive knowledge of the pharmacologic mechanisms of action of these agents.

REFERENCES

Andreasson, S., Allebeck, P., Engstrom, A., & Rydberg, U. (1987). Cannabis and schizophrenia: A longitudinal study of Swedish conscripts. *Lancet, 2,* 1483-1486.

Anglin, M. D., McGlothlin, W. H., & Speckart, G. (1981). The effect of parole on methadone patient behavior. *American Journal of Drug and Alcohol Abuse, 8,* 153-170.

Aniline, O., & Pitts, F. N., Jr. (1982). Phencyclidine (PCP): A review and perspectives. *Critical Reviews in Toxicology, 10,* 145-177.

Benowitz, N. L., Porchet, H., Sheiner, L., & Jacob, P., III. (1988). Nicotine absorption and cardiovascular effects with smokeless tobacco use: Comparison with cigarettes and nicotine gum. *Clinical Pharmacology and Therapeutics, 43,* 23-28.

Blois, M. S. (1988). Medicine and the nature of vertical reasoning. *New England Journal of Medicine, 318*(13), 847-851.

Bloom, F. E. (1988). Neurotransmitters: Past, present and future directions. *FASEB Journal, 2*(1), 32-41.

Bloom, F. E. (1993). The neurobiology of addiction: An integrative view. In S. G. Korenman & J. D. Barchas (Eds.), *Biological basis of substance abuse* (pp. 3-16). New York: Oxford University Press.

Braiker, H. (1984). Therapeutic issues in the treatment of alcoholic women. In S. C. Wilsnack & L. J. Beckman (Eds.), *Alcohol problems in women* (pp. 330-359). New York: Guilford.

Chasnoff, I. J., Hunt, C. E., & Kaplan, D. (1989). Prenatal cocaine exposure is associated with respiratory pattern abnormalities. *American Journal of Diseases of Children, 143,* 583-587.

Cloninger, C. R., Dinwiddie, S. H., & Reich, T. (1989). Epidemiology and genetics of alcoholism. *Annual Review of Psychiatry, 8,* 331-346.

Cregler, L. L. (1989). Adverse consequences of cocaine abuse. *Journal of the National Medical Association, 81,* 27-38.

Dewey, W. L. (1986). Cannabinoid pharmacology. *Pharmacological Reviews, 38,* 151-178.

Dunwiddie, T. V., & Alford, C. (1987). Electrophysiological actions of phencyclidine in hippocampal slices from the rat. *Neuropharmacology, 26,* 1267-1273.

Fischman, M. W., & Schuster, C. R. (1982). Cocaine self-administration in humans. *Federal Procedure, 41,* 241-246.

Gawin, F. H., & Ellinwood, E. H., Jr. (1988). Cocaine and other stimulants: Actions, abuse, and treatment. *New England Journal of Medicine, 318,* 1173-1182.

Giannini, A. J., Loiselle, R. H., DiMarzio, L. E., & Giannini, M. C. (1987). Augmentation of haloperidol by ascorbic acid in phencyclidine intoxication. *American Journal of Psychiatry, 144,* 1207-1209.

Glenn, S. (1981, January). *Directions for the eighties.* Paper presented at the Nebraska Prevention Center, Omaha.

Gomberg, E. S. L., & Lisansky, J. (1984). Antecedents of alcohol problems in women. In S. C. Wilsnack & L. J. Beckman (Eds.), *Alcohol problems in women* (pp. 238-249). New York: Guilford.

Grant, I. (1987). Alcohol and the brain: Neuropsychological correlates. *Journal of Consulting and Clinical Psychology, 55,* 310-324.

Henningfield, J. E., Miyasato, K., & Jasinski, D. R. (1983). Cigarette smokers self-administer intravenous nicotine. *Pharmacology, Biochemistry and Behavior, 19,* 887-890.

Hernandez, L., Auerbach, S., & Hoebel, B. G. (1988). Phencyclidine (PCP) injected in the nucleus accumbens increases extracellular dopamine and serotonin as measured by microdialysis. *Life Sciences, 42,* 1705-1712.

Hollister, L. E. (1986). Health aspects of cannabis. *Pharmacological Reviews, 38,* 1-20.

Hollister, L. E. (1988). Cannabis 1988. *Acta Psychiatrica Scandinavica, Suppl. 345, 78,* 108-118.

Humphrey, J., & Friedman, J. (1986). The onset of drinking and intoxication among university students. *Journals of Studies on Alcohol, 47,* 455-458.

Isner, J. M., Estes, N. A. M., III, Thompson, P. D., Costanzo-Nordin, M. R., Subramanian, R., Miller, G., Katsas, G., Sweeney, K., & Sturner, W. Q. (1986). Acute cardiac events temporally related to cocaine abuse. *New England Journal of Medicine, 315,* 1438-1443.

Jacobson, R. (1986). Female alcoholics: A controlled CT brain scan and clinical study. *British Journal of Addiction, 81,* 661-669.

Jaffe, J. H. (1990). Tobacco smoking and nicotine dependence. In S. Wonnacott, M. A. H. Russell, & I. P. Stolerman (Eds.), *Nicotine psychopharmacology: Molecular, cellular and behavioural aspects* (pp. 1-37). Oxford: Oxford University Press.

Johnston, L. D., O'Malley, P. M., & Bachman, J. G. (1991). *Drug use among American high school seniors, college students, and young adults, 1975-1990: Vol. I. High school seniors.* Washington, DC: Department of Health and Human Services.

Jones, B. M., & Jones, M. K. (1976). States of consciousness and alcohol: Relationship to the blood alcohol curve, time of day, and the menstrual cycle. *Alcohol Health and Research World, 1*(1), 10-15.

Jones, R. T., Benowitz, N., & Bachman, J. (1976). Clinical studies of cannabis tolerance and dependence. *Annals of the New York Academy of Sciences, 282,* 221-239.

Karch, S. B., & Billingham, M. E. (1988). The pathology and etiology of cocaine-induced heart disease. *Archives of Pathology and Laboratory Medicine, 112,* 225-230.

Koob, G. F., & Bloom, F. E. (1988). Cellular and molecular mechanisms of drug dependence. *Science, 242,* 715-723.

Koob, G. F., & Bloom, F. E. (1989). Opponent process theory of motivation: Neurobiological evidence from studies of opiate dependence. *Neuroscience and Biobehavioral Reviews, 13*(2-3), 135-140.

Koob, G. F., Wall, T. L., et al. (1989). Nucleus accumbens as a substrate for the aversive stimulus effects of opiate withdrawal. *Psychopharmacology* (Berlin), *98*(4), 530-534.

Korsten, M. A., & Lieber, C. S. (1985). Medical complications of alcoholism. In J. H. Mendelson & N. K. Mello (Eds.), *The diagnosis and treatment of alcoholism* (pp. 21-64). New York: McGraw-Hill.

Krasner, N., Davis, M., Portmann, B., & Williams, R. (1977). Changing pattern of alcoholic liver disease in Great Britain: Relation to sex and signs of autoimmunity. *British Medical Journal, 1,* 1487-1550.

Lawson, G., Ellis, D., & Rivers, C. (1984). *The essentials of chemical dependency counseling.* Rockville, MD: Aspen.

Lieber, C. S. (1988). Biochemical and molecular basis of alcohol-induced injury to liver and other tissues. *New England Journal of Medicine, 319,* 1639-1650.

Martin, B. R. (1986). Cellular effects of cannabinoids. *Pharmacological Reviews, 38,* 45-74.

Maykut, M. O. (1985). Health consequences of acute and chronic marihuana use. *Progress in Neuro-Psychopharmacology and Biological Psychiatry, 9,* 209-238.

McLellan, A. T., Alterman, A. I., Cacciola, J., Metzger, D., & O'Brien, C. (1992). A new measure of substance abuse treatment: Initial studies of the treatment services review. *American Journal of Psychiatry, 180*(2), 101-110.

McLellan, A. T., Luborsky, L., O'Brien, C. P., & Woody, G. E. (1980). An improved evaluation instrument for substance abuse patients: The Addiction Severity Index. *Journal of Nervous and Mental Disease, 168,* 26-33.

Mendelson, J. H., & Mello, N. K. (1979). Biologic concomitants of alcoholism. *New England Journal of Medicine, 301,* 912-921.

Mendelson, J. H., Mello, N. K., Ellingboe, J., Skupny, A. S. T., Lex, B. W., & Griffin, M. (1986). Marihuana smoking suppresses luteinizing hormone in women. *Journal of Pharmacology and Experimental Therapeutics, 237,* 862-866.

Mody, C. K., Miller, B. L., McIntyre, H. B., Cobb, S. K., & Goldberg, M. A. (1988). Neurologic complications of cocaine abuse. *Neurology, 38,* 1189-1193.

Monaghan, D. T., Bridges, R. J., & Cotman, C. W. (1989). The excitatory amino acid receptors: Their classes, pharmacology, and distinct properties in the function of the central nervous system. *Annual Review of Pharmacology and Toxicology, 7,* 283-313.

Ng, S. K. C., Hauser, W. A., Brust, J. C. M., & Susser, M. (1988). Alcohol consumption and withdrawal in new-onset seizures. *New England Journal of Medicine, 319,* 666-673.

Nurco, D. N., Kinlock, T. W., Hanlon, T. E., & Ball, J. C. (1988). Non-narcotic drug use over an addiction career: A study of heroin addicts in Baltimore and New York City. *Comprehensive Psychiatry, 29,* 450-459.

O'Brien, C. P., McLellan, A. T., & Alterman, A. (1993). Effectiveness of treatment for substance abuse. In S. G. Korenman & J. D. Barchas (Eds.), *Biological basis of substance abuse* (pp. 487-510). New York: Oxford University Press.

Perkins, K. A., Epstein, L. H., Marks, B. L., Stiller, R. L., & Jacob, R. G. (1989). The effect of nicotine on energy expenditure during light physical activity. *New England Journal of Medicine, 320,* 898-903.

Rathbone-McCuan, E., & Roberds, L. (1980). Treatment of the older alcoholic. *Focus on Women, 1,* 104-139.

Razdan, R. K. (1986). Structure-activity relationships in cannabinoids. *Pharmacological Reviews, 38*, 75-150.

Reichman, M., Nen, W., & Hokin, L. E. (1988). Tetrahydrocannabinol increases arachidonic acid levels in guinea pig cerebral cortex slices. *Molecular Pharmacology, 34*, 823-828.

Ritz, M. C., Lamb, R. J., Goldberg, S. R., & Kuhar, M. J. (1987). Cocaine receptors on dopamine transporters are related to self administration of cocaine. *Science, 237*, 1219-1223.

Roth, D., Alarcon, F. J., Fernandez, J. A., Preston, R. A., & Bourgoignie, J. J. (1988). Acute rhabdomyolysis associated with cocaine intoxication. *New England Journal of Medicine, 319*, 673-677.

Ryan, L., Ehrlich, S., & Finnegan, L. P. (1987). Cocaine abuse in pregnancy: Effects on the fetus and newborn. *NIDA Research Monographs, 76*, 280.

Saunders, J. B., Davis, M., & Williams, R. (1981). Do women develop alcoholic liver disease more readily than men? *British Medical Journal, 282*, 1141-1143.

Schatzkin, A., Jones, Y., Hoover, R. N., Taylor, P. R., Brinton, L. A., Ziegler, R. G., Harvey, E. B., Carter, C. L., Licitra, L. M., Dufour, M. C., & Larson, D. B. (1987). Alcohol consumption and breast cancer in the epidemiologic follow-up study of the first national health and nutrition examination survey. *New England Journal of Medicine, 316*, 1169-1173.

Schmidt, W., & Popham, R. E. (1980). Sex differences in mortality: A comparison of male and female alcoholics. In O. J. Kalant (Ed.), *Research advances in alcohol and drug problems* (Vol. 5). New York: Plenum.

Sellers, E. M., & Busto, U. (1982). Benzodiazepines and ethanol: Assessment of the effects and consequences of psychotropic drug interactions. *Journal of Clinical Psychopharmacology, 2*, 249-262.

Sherer, M. A., Kumor, K. M., Cone, E. J., & Jaffe, J. H. (1988). Suspiciousness induced by four-hour intravenous infusions of cocaine—Preliminary findings. *Archives of General Psychiatry, 45*, 673-677.

Smith, C. M. (1977). The pharmacology of sedative/hypnotics, alcohol, and anesthetics: Sites and mechanisms of action. In W. R. Martin (Ed.), *Drug addiction I: Morphine, sedative/hypnotic and alcohol dependence* (pp. 413-587). *Handbuch der Experimentellen Pharmakologie* (Vol. 45, Pt. 1). Berlin: Springer-Verlag.

Smith, E., Cloninger, C. R., & Bradford, S. (1983). Predictors of mortality in alcoholic women: A perspective follow-up study. *Alcoholism: Clinical and Experimental Research, 7*, 232-243.

Tarter, R. E., & Schneider, D. V. (1976). Models and theories of alcoholism. In R. E. Tarter & A. A. Sungleman (Eds.), *Alcoholism: Interdisciplinary approaches to an enduring problem* (pp. 202-210). Reading, MA: Addison-Wesley.

Willett, W. C., Green, A., Stampfer, M. J., Speizer, F. E., Colditz, G. A., Rosner, B., Monson, R. R., Stason, W., & Hennekens, C. H. (1987). Relative and absolute excess risks of coronary heart disease among women who smoke cigarettes. *New England Journal of Medicine, 317*, 1303-1310.

Wilsnack, S. C., Klassen, A., & Wilsnack, R. (1984). Drinking and reproductive dysfunction among women in a 1981 national survey. *Alcoholism: Clinical and Experimental Research, 8*, 451-458.

Wise, R. (1988). The neurobiology of craving: Implications for the understanding and treatment of addiction. *Journal of Abnormal Psychology, 97*, 118-132.

Wroblewski, J. T., & Danysz, W. (1989). Modulation of glutamate receptors: Molecular mechanism and functional implications. *Annual Review of Pharmacology and Toxicology, 29,* 441-474.

Wu, T.-C., Tashkin, D. P., Djahed, B., & Rose, J. E. (1988). Pulmonary hazards of smoking marijuana as compared with tobacco. *New England Journal of Medicine, 318,* 347-351.

8. Treating the Adolescent Drug Misuser

Annette U. Rickel
Wayne State University

Evvie Becker-Lausen
Boston Children's Hospital

INTRODUCTION

Alcohol and drug use and abuse among adolescents has been well documented, as have the behavioral, physiological, and social consequences. Yet much less attention has been paid to specific adolescent needs for treatment. There has been little recognition of the differences between the needs of adolescents and those of adults, with much less research in and clinical attention to adolescent alcohol and drug abuse compared to adult addiction. Before we can properly care for these young addicts, we need to develop specific guidelines for the treatment of alcohol and drug abuse in adolescence (Rickel & Allen, 1987; Shedler & Block, 1990).

Large numbers of young people are at risk for substance-related problems—particularly from alcohol and tobacco use. In a 1991 survey of U.S. high school seniors, 54% said they had used alcohol in the past month, 30% reported they had consumed more than five drinks in a row in the past 2 weeks, and 28% said they were current cigarette smokers (Klitzner, Fisher, Stewart, & Gilbert, 1993).

A broader survey of junior and senior high school students (7th through 12th grade) revealed that 51% had at least one drink within the past year; 8 million of these students drink weekly; and more than 5 million students report having binged, 3 million within the past month. Perhaps of greatest concern clinically are reports from those who drink that 31% drink alone, 41% drink to feel better when they're upset, and 25% drink because they are bored (Office of the Inspector General, 1991).

In addition, the National Household Survey on Drug Abuse (National Institute on Drug Abuse [NIDA], 1991) found that among youth aged 12 to 17, 16.8% used an illicit drug within the past year, and 9.2% had used an illicit drug at least once in the past month. For the next age group of older youth (18 to 20), the rates were about twice those of the younger cohort (30.3%, past year; 18.9%, past month).

When parents discover their youngsters are using drugs, they generally are in a quandary, not knowing how to respond to the child or where to turn for help. In an emotionally charged family situation, parents frequently overreact or react inappropriately. Even trained professionals (i.e., doctors, teachers, clergy) often have difficulty counseling these families and steering them to someone who can give them guidance.

Early intervention strategies are not economically feasible for the large numbers of youth who may try drugs or alcohol—nor are they necessary, because most adolescent substance users reduce or discontinue use in adulthood without experiencing clinically significant problems. For most young people, therefore, we simply need to prevent use more effectively. Targeted early intervention strategies are estimated to be needed for about 1 adolescent in 15 or 20 (Klitzner et al., 1993).

Most young people do not perceive their drug use as a problem, probably because they are in the early stages of drug use. For many, drug use is a regular part of their daily lives. Drug use is related to environmental, cultural, and adaptational issues for adolescence such as peer pressure and family influence (Jalali, Jalali, Grocetti, & Turner, 1981; Rickel & Allen, 1987).

Agencies and institutions in this country have not been very successful in attracting and holding adolescent drug abusers in treatment. Traditional drug treatment modalities often do not have the range and/or types of services needed by adolescents. Despite a number of programs developed in recent years, still relatively few adolescent treatment programs are available, particularly for public sector clients, who often have some of the most serious problems.

Numerous factors or barriers make it difficult for adolescents to commit themselves to drug treatment programs, and programs must overcome these barriers if they are to have any success in treating adolescents. Unfortunately, little attempt has been made to look at drug problems from the adolescents' perspective.

The problem is apt to be more complex than it seems on the surface, usually involving the entire family. The young drug user is likely to be confused, at odds with his or her family, and to deny that his or her drug use is a serious problem. The youngster will probably not be motivated to seek help just because others perceive he or she has a drug problem. Unfortunately, too often, community service agencies are reluctant or unable to respond to the family crisis in a timely way. Many counselors view adolescent substance abusers as extremely difficult to treat and do not have the resources required to work with the family.

Little information is available about the effectiveness of programs that treat adolescent substance abusers. No absolute standards are available by which to judge a local program. Adolescent treatment programs tend to operate independently. Rarely do they have the resources or inclination to evaluate how effective they are in treating adolescents (Shapiro, 1985). Too often, these programs also fail to follow up on clients, particularly those who drop out early, to determine which client benefits most and which benefits least from the services provided. As a result, referral sources often lack adequate data to make a sound referral, and decisions are based primarily on word-of-mouth information.

IDENTIFICATION OF SUBSTANCE ABUSE IN ADOLESCENTS

The Psychological Perspective

Most adolescents experiment with drugs of one type or another, but the majority do not end up with serious problems, according to researchers Shedler and Block (1990). Four criteria are key to determining high-risk users:

- Use of substances that are extremely dangerous, such as cocaine or inhalants
- Use in preadolescence
- Use in inappropriate settings, such as while driving or in school
- Use with clear signs of tolerance, withdrawal, or dependence (Klitzner et al., 1993)

For a number of years researchers have recognized a connection between children and adolescents who display antisocial behavior and those who use drugs. For example, a National Institute of Justice study (1993) revealed juvenile males arrested or detained had variable rates by city of positive urine tests for cocaine, opiates, PCP, marijuana, amphetamines, benzodiazepines, and others.

In Washington, D.C., 44% of male youth arrestees/detainees tested positive (the highest rate), whereas 10% of these youth in St. Louis tested positive. Contrary to stereotypic views of the various cities, however, San Diego was second to Washington, D.C., with 43% and had the highest percentage of multiple drug use (19%). Denver, with a positive test rate of 34%, had the second highest rate of multiple drug use (13%). Cocaine was the most prevalent drug for juveniles in only Cleveland and St. Louis; marijuana was the most prevalent drug in all other cities studied (Birmingham, Denver, Indianapolis, Los Angeles, Phoenix, Portland, San Diego, San Jose, and Washington, D.C.).

Many parents of disruptive, law-breaking children and teenagers insist, however, that their youngsters' aggressive behavior is caused by the use of drugs. Which comes first, drug use or antisocial behavior? Preliminary data from a Colorado study suggest that the assumption that drug use typically comes first and is the cause of law-breaking and antisocial behavior may not be accurate (Swan, 1993).

In the study, 51 substance-abusing boys aged 14 to 19, diagnosed with conduct disorder, were asked how and when their antisocial behavior began. The 13 recognized diagnostic symptoms of conduct disorder include stealing, truancy, fighting, arson, property destruction, cruelty to people or animals, lying, and running away, according to the American Psychiatric Association (APA). The APA considers substance abuse to be an "associated feature" of conduct disorder in youths.

Just 25% of the boys said they engaged in the behaviors only while using drugs. With the exception of forced sex between two boys, only 20% engaged in these behaviors for drug-related reasons. The majority engaged in these behaviors both while they were intoxicated and when they were not. According to the boys' own reports, the antisocial behaviors not only begin before the substance abuse but continue to occur independently of the substance abuse.

During the past decade, the number of adolescents identified with and treated for behavioral and psychological disorders has increased dramatically (Babor et al., 1991). Substance abuse is a primary reason for many of these treatment referrals. Epidemiologic and program evaluation studies have provided some insight into the characteristics of adolescent substance abusers (Hubbard et al., 1989; Johnston, O'Malley, & Bachman, 1988; Loney, 1988). Psychological disturbances (anxiety, depression), rebelliousness, poor school performance, delinquency, and personality disorder, especially sociopathy, are common characteristics found in this population.

Marijuana is second only to alcohol as the primary drug used, although polydrug use, often combined with the heavy use of alcohol, is frequently a distinguishing characteristic of the clinical picture (Babor et al., 1991).

Family, social, and personal problems of adolescents, as well as patterns of substance abuse, differ sufficiently from adult's problems and patterns to warrant different treatment approaches for each group (Beschner, 1985). Help-seeking is a complex process for these adolescents and is often precipitated by school, family, or legal problems, not by alcohol or drug abuse itself. Despite methodological limitations and sampling difficulties, treatment evaluation studies suggest that treatment interventions can be effective both in reducing substance use and in improving psychosocial functioning (Hubbard et al., 1989; Rahdert & Grabowski, 1988).

The Sociological Perspective

Sociologists and criminologists have determined that there are common elements, or stages, in the development of new drugs (Chaiken, 1993). From studies of three locales, New York City, Los Angeles, and Oahu, they conclude that identifying these stages early, at the local level, may allow communities to deter the development of epidemic drug use.

Clinicians need to be aware of these factors, particularly the cultural differences in drug use. Clinicians can join forces with other community leaders, including police, school districts, and local government, to prevent new drugs from reaching the most vulnerable members of the community. Several stages are identified.

Stage 1. Drug use is confined to isolated communities or subcultures. This is the lowest level of use that can be realistically achieved. For example, in the early to mid-1970s, cocaine was confined primarily to relatively affluent groups in the entertainment industry. Likewise, endemic methamphetamine use was confined primarily to remnants of groups that had been users during previous periods of the drug's popularity.

Stage 2. Users switch to various types of drugs or preparations. At times, when one drug loses its appeal or accessibility, users will experiment with another drug, usually one in endemic use among people in close proximity. Different forms and modes of administration may be tried. In Manhattan, for instance, opiates, especially heroin, were the drugs of preference in the 1970s.

Stage 3. Local opinion coalesces around a specific drug preparation. Frequent users of drugs discuss and justify to themselves the selection of a particular substance. By 1980, cocaine had emerged as a favored drug in the three sites studied. In inner-city Los Angeles and in North Manhattan, the base form of cocaine rapidly gained popularity. Local lore, a mixture of fact and fantasy, touted base as being less harmful than the acid form. It was said to induce euphoria without unpleasant side effects. On Oahu, the drug was popular among Caucasians but among ethnic groups, such as Filipinos, who traditionally did not use drugs, neither the acid nor the base form of cocaine became popular.

Stage 4. Distribution by enterprising drug dealers accelerates. The organization of local drug dealerships reflects typical free enterprise patterns. The most likely participants are those who seek to move rapidly up the economic ladder but reject or lack the legitimate means, for example, marginally employed residents of the drug-using communities. In Los Angeles and Manhattan the first dealerships were respectively called rock houses and base houses. Perhaps because there were too few users to support this form of enterprise in the early 1980s, such organized houses did not appear on Oahu.

Stage 5. Drug use increases precipitously, with a sharp increase in use when a substance that is widely believed to be desirable becomes readily available at low cost. As stories about the drug spread, demand increases and more suppliers are drawn into the market. In Los Angeles and in Manhattan the number of cocaine users rose sharply between 1983 and 1984, about a year before the term *crack* was coined. Between 1985 and 1986, crystal methamphetamine smoking increased on Oahu.

Stage 6. Drug use reaches epidemic proportions, overloading public agencies and health systems. The number of new users spirals upward, and prior users raise their consumption of the drug. If the drug is physically addictive, emergency rooms and other health services are overwhelmed by users as well as with infants born to addicted mothers. Drug-induced psychosis or violent episodes over-load psychiatric and other emergency facilities with users and victims. Child abuse and neglect resulting from parental drug abuse increases. Rises in drug-related crimes strain criminal justice systems.

Stage 7. The media report on the drug. Articles in newspapers call attention to the drug problem. Media stories may implicitly or explicitly suggest that the drug is new. In the late 1980s, articles on crack and ice created the impression that these were new drugs even though, in Los Angeles, base cocaine and rock had been around for a decade. Employing the term *crack* tended to make the drug seem more desirable to youngsters who wanted to impress their peers.

The stages described represent the worst case; many drugs do not make it past early stages. Endemic use (Stage 1) can last for decades. Progression through the early stages does not necessarily presage an epidemic.

ISSUES IN TREATMENT OF ADOLESCENTS

Focusing solely on the provision of intervention services to adolescents with alcohol or drug-abuse problems is inadequate to address the problem. Traditional categories and levels of care may need to be modified to meet the needs of substance-abusing adolescents. Comprehensive, integrated, and systemic services need to be available so that a specific treatment approach can be tailored to the needs of each youth.

Intervention

Intervention refers to services designed to interrupt the progression of alcohol or drug abuse and to persuade the client to enter treatment. The most commonly used intervention was initially developed by Vernon Johnson and was later popularized by the Johnson Institute (Schonberg, 1993). The process includes strategies to convince individuals that they have an alcohol or drug problem, to help them recognize the need for treatment, and, eventually, to change their substance-abusing behavior. Perhaps the most well-known case is the intervention of the family of former President Gerald Ford with his wife, Betty. Publicity surrounding Betty Ford's recovery and subsequent founding of a treatment facility led to a certain degree of popularity for this technique.

Typically, interventions involve a carefully rehearsed and controlled meeting in which the client is confronted by significant others, usually with a professional in attendance. Interventions that do not include a professional have also been successful (Schonberg, 1993). During these meetings an adolescent listens to information about his or her chemical use along with the concerns and feelings of members of the group. Goals of an intervention are to make the adolescent aware of the perceptions and concerns of the important people in his or her life regarding the alcohol or drug use and to convince the adolescent to submit to a formal screening and assessment by appropriate professionals. Sometimes a plan for entering treatment will be presented to the adolescent at the time of the intervention.

Interventions can be powerful and effective tools. They can motivate adolescents to enter treatment and also help overcome the denial of family members, while strengthening generational boundaries and empowering the adults as parents. In some cases, interventions may include the use of social or institutional leverage. Pressure from the courts, probation officers, and schools can be used to encourage an otherwise resistant adolescent to seek treatment (Schonberg, 1993).

Each intervention program is unique. Defined by the community it serves, an intervention program should incorporate various components of treatment and resolve different program issues so that client needs can be matched with available resources.

Detoxification

Adolescents requiring detoxification may be treated as inpatients or outpatients. Because adolescents are usually in the early stages of substance addiction, it is rare for an adolescent to develop a potentially fatal withdrawal syndrome. Furthermore, many substances popular with adolescents do not have a significant withdrawal effect. An adolescent's particular psychosocial circumstances, personal characteristics, or addictions may, however, require inpatient care. The client's need for detoxification should be assessed to determine the most appropriate site for treatment. Whether as an outpatient or inpatient, the client's detoxification should be monitored by appropriately trained personnel under the direction of a physician with specific expertise in the consequences and management of addiction and withdrawal (Kusnetz, 1985).

Treatment Communities

Only a small number of treatment communities—structured residential programs—specialize in treating adolescents. Despite a long history of treating substance abuse, the treatment community is not for everyone. According to one evaluation study, less than 15% of all admissions graduate from treatment, and more than half leave treatment before 90 days (DeLeon, 1984). Most treatment communities are highly structured, nonpermissive, drug-free residential settings.

The daily regimen of an adolescent treatment community is intense, generally including encounter groups or group therapy, individual counseling, family therapy and/or family support meetings, tutorial learning sessions, remedial and formal education classes, recreational therapy, residential job functioning (e.g., cleaning, painting, cooking), and in the last stages of treatment, regular occupations for clients who may then live outside of the treatment community. Attendance at 12-step meetings, such as Alcoholics Anonymous (AA) or Narcotics Anonymous (NA), and Al-Anon meetings for family members often are an integral part of the program.

In recent years, managed care and the reluctance of insurance companies to pay for extended inpatient treatment has resulted in reductions in the length of stay in treatment communities and has led to the demise of numerous hospital-based programs. Another recent trend in adolescent treatment communities is the wilderness community, with facilities in places such as Colorado or Montana providing a combination of substance-abuse treatment, isolation from family and friends, physical activity designed to challenge the youth's self-image, and structured time-limited therapeutic interactions with family—for example, the family may spend a week at the site in intensive group and family therapy with their adolescent.

In the treatment community, drug abuse is considered deviant behavior that reflects impeded personality development as well as deficits in social, educational, and economic skills. In this perspective, substance abuse is a disorder of the whole person. Addiction is seen as a symptom, not the essence of a disorder. The goal of treatment, then, is a global change in the individual, which includes the integration of conduct, feelings, values, and attitudes with a drug-free lifestyle (DeLeon & Deitch, 1985).

In this paradigm, drug-abuse recovery is always the responsibility of the individual. The structure and process of the treatment community facilitates self-help change through sequenced stages of learning characterized as "growing up" or maturation. The social organization is a family surrogate model, vertically stratified. Primary staff, clinical and custodial, are frequently paraprofessionals, usually ex-offenders or ex-addicts successfully rehabilitated in treatment community programs. Ancillary staff may include educational, mental health, medical, and vocational service professionals as well as fiscal administrators and lawyers.

It has long been held that a physically and psychologically safe environment is critical to the successful treatment of the adolescent in a treatment community. A large majority of these clients have undergone fearful experiences in the streets, in abusive homes, or in jail. Moreover, an intimidating social environment tends to increase belligerence among the more aggressive clients and withdrawal in the more passive or nonviolent adolescents. Safety is particularly important in age-integrated treatment communities, because adolescents can easily feel threatened by older clients.

Physical and psychological safety are related to the concept of trust. Trust is crucial for clients' personal disclosure as well as for their ability to confront negativity, accept the program regimen, and believe in the eventual positive outcome of treatment. Residents who perceive the environment as physically safe will also be more likely to experience the psychological safety necessary to a commitment to the treatment process.

Explicit efforts must be made to sustain the perception that a residential setting is safe. Strong sanctions are invoked against any behavior that threatens the safety of the therapeutic environment. Breaking the treatment community's cardinal rules—especially the rules against violence or the threat of violence, either verbal or physical—can thus bring immediate expulsion. Usually, strong prohibitions against a client engaging in sex or in drug use are also part of the program. Even minor violations of house rules are addressed, such as stealing mundane items (toothbrushes, books, etc.). Once detected, any and all infractions that directly or indirectly threaten the safety of the house must be publicly confessed to reassure the general community of others (DeLeon & Deitch, 1985).

Intensive Confrontation: Straight

Some programs have a different theory about trust and safety, however. An example of a tough, confrontational approach is the "Straight" program, which has sites located across the country. At Straight, youth are allowed to yell at an adolescent who is denying his or her substance abuse, to break down the defenses of the denier. Called a "boot camp for druggies" (Hollandsworth, 1990), the program has met with a great deal of controversy over its harsh methods. Group therapy at times has been conducted by the adolescents themselves, not by counselors, because the staff believe that peers are the best sources of confrontation and support for the teens. Although Straight has been investigated for complaints of physical abuse and violations of civil liberties (and, in one case, fined) in several states, the group had the endorsement of President Bush during his presidency.

Aftercare

Especially important for the adolescent are the issues of aftercare and the return to the primary family. Adult graduates of treatment communities are generally encouraged to live independently, apart from their family. The unemancipated adolescent usually must continue to be a part of his or her family. Family members must be prepared and strengthened so that they can be competent mediators of the positive gains in treatment. Therefore, treatment communities must develop aftercare resources for adolescents that successfully integrate family participation.

One option for aftercare is a preexisting link to specialized agencies in the community. These agencies, however, may not be oriented to the treatment community's perspective. As an alternative, many treatment communities have been expanding their efforts to keep families involved beyond the residential stage of treatment. Through both the provision of outpatient services and the development of family networks, the treatment community's basic self-help perspective can continue to influence the aftercare phase of treatment.

Meeting Multiple Needs:
Covenant House

Programs such as Straight attract middle-income families with private insurance or other means, but the long-standing program at Covenant House in New York City addresses the needs of youth who have no home or who are estranged from their families. Since the departure of founder Father Bruce Ritter, surrounded by controversy and allegations of child abuse, the organization has regrouped and appears to be successfully providing much needed services to inner-city New York youth.

Founded in 1972, Covenant House is the nation's largest non-profit, adolescent care shelter. Although Covenant House New York is the oldest and biggest program, centers have also been established in Anchorage, Atlantic City, Ft. Lauderdale, Houston, Los Angeles, Newark, and New Orleans, as well as Toronto, Canada, and sites in Latin America. Within the United States each year, Covenant House provides food, shelter, and other services to more than 25,000 youth under 21 years of age.

The New York City site is located in midtown Manhattan, where it provides multiple services to about 5,000 youth annually. On a daily basis, about 30 adolescent male substance abusers receive treatment in a short-term residential on-site facility and are then referred as necessary to longer term programs elsewhere. Covenant House is a strong proponent of comprehensive services, especially with this high-risk population for whom multiple services are necessary as a form of both prevention and intervention. Consequently, in New York, Covenant House also *daily* provides up to 190 kids with shelter, food, and crisis counseling in a Crisis Center; 80 pregnant or parenting teens and their babies with shelter, nutritious food, and parenting skills in the Mother/Child Program; 125 youth with independent living skills in a long-term transitional living program; 60 teens with comprehensive health care in the Health Clinic; and more than 50 homeless youth with food, a hot drink, and counseling from Outreach vans.

For the near future at least, this comprehensive prevention and intervention approach is going to be necessary to reach the most high-risk populations in the inner cities. Substance abuse is but one of many issues facing these youth today—soaring rates of violent death, epidemic rates of teen pregnancy, increasing rates of HIV infection, record rates of school dropouts, lack of employment skills, and lack of health care and adequate housing. Therefore, to be successful, any program for this population must address most or all of these related issues.

Day Treatment/Partial Hospitalization

The most intensive form of outpatient treatment is the structured day-treatment program. Frequently used as an aftercare option following a residential or inpatient stay, it provides evaluation and treatment, usually with a specialized school on the premises, for the most dysfunctional adolescents. It allows them to return home in the evenings while continuing a high level of structure and treatment throughout their days.

The strength and creativity of a day-treatment program comes from the milieu—the treatment community. This environment encourages personal growth through models of honest caring, open communication, and responsible concern. Feelings of strength, hope, and trust must be present. The role of staff is key to providing models for students to emulate. Through the active involvement of parents, referral agents, and other concerned persons, the community is designed to be open and cooperative. Each individual must develop a sense of belonging to the treatment community. As the affiliation becomes more binding, the individual's pride and self-respect increases. Although the treatment community is in many respects quite different from the traditional public school environment, the community respects the values and expectations of the outside community (Ottenberg, Olsen, & Schiller, 1985).

Although the primary client in day treatment is the adolescent, a family-based approach is employed throughout the program and strongly in evidence in the treatment milieu. Although parents can be perceived at times as part of the problem, it is important to avoid an adversarial approach in which they feel blamed and scapegoated. Parents who feel this way will be very difficult to involve in the treatment process. From the start, at intake, parents should be told that the program recognizes their responsibility and authority and will support them in their parenting role. In return, the program asks that the parents support the day-treatment community's efforts. Parents need and receive continuing support, guidance, and counseling in the form of weekly parent group meetings, progress review meetings, and weekly phone calls from their child's counselor.

The treatment community augments the parental role in both nurturing and discipline. A partnership between parents and staff will often lead naturally to joint decision making. In a more subtle way, the relationship of parents to their children is strengthened through the parents' relationships with staff. With adequate support, parents who were hostile to school and treatment personnel and who were initially unwilling to participate may gradually join in the program. At times, other parents may help in this process of encouraging reluctant parents.

LEVELS AND TYPES OF CARE

Outpatient Treatment. Outpatient treatment provides a broad range of intensity levels without overnight accommodation. Standard outpatient treatment is a substance-abuse-focused treatment that includes professionally directed evaluation and treatment of less than 9 hours per week in regularly scheduled sessions. Outpatient alcohol and drug treatment may also address related psychiatric, emotional, and social issues. More intensive outpatient treatment involves 9 to 20 hours per week in a structured program that may be after school or in the evening and frequently includes some week-end programming (Shapiro, 1985).

Day Treatment/Partial Hospitalization. Day treatment/partial hospitalization is a substance-abuse-focused, professionally directed evaluation and treatment of more than 20 hours per week in a structured program. This is the most intensive of the outpatient treatment options and can be used for treating those adolescents who demonstrate the greatest degree of dysfunction but do not require inpatient treatment.

Inpatient Treatment. Inpatient treatment can include intensive medical, psychiatric, and psychosocial treatment provided on a 24-hour basis. Medically monitored intensive inpatient treatment involves around-the-clock medical and nursing monitoring, evaluation, and treatment in an inpatient setting.

Residential Care. Although providing overnight accommodations, residential care should not be considered treatment in the same sense as the inpatient levels of care. The level of residential care continuum includes psychosocial care at the most intensive end and group home living without any professional involvement or supervision at the least intensive end.

Individual Therapy. Individual therapy is often a necessary adjunct to group and family therapy. Some adolescents are too withdrawn or socially uncomfortable to benefit from the group process, and others may have issues—such as a history of sexual abuse—that they do not wish to disclose to the group, particularly when it is coed. Individual therapy is particularly effective in helping adolescents (a) confront and cope with obstacles to utilizing group therapy, family therapy, or self-help groups; (b) discuss issues they are not ready to disclose to the group; (c) strengthen the treatment alliance; and (d) work on interpersonal difficulties or weaknesses (Schonberg, 1993).

Group Therapy. For most adolescents, group therapy is one of the most effective processes for change. The involvement of peers in the process encourages youth to confront their substance abuse, to address personal issues, and to deal with the consequences of their substance abuse. Group therapy is usually led by a counselor or therapist, whereas self-help groups are run by peers or adult addicts. Group therapy is designed to solicit the involvement and support of others in the adolescent's recovery while encouraging healthy interactions between peers. Sharing, discussion, and problem solving as a group process teach youth to take responsibility for their substance-abuse problems as well as to recognize denial and other symptoms of addictive behavior.

Family Therapy. Sessions with families may be helpful whether or not the client is present. Sometimes adolescent substance abuse reflects family dysfunction and/or family tolerance of substance abuse. Adolescents who will be remaining with or returning to their family may have difficulty recovering without the family's active involvement and support. Systemic therapy can address the family's patterns of behavior as well as its modes of communication, its values, and its methods of problem solving (Rickel, Gerrard, & Iscoe, 1984; Shapiro, 1985).

TREATMENT MATCHING

As clinicians and researchers have begun to realize the complexity of adolescent drug and alcohol abuse and to understand that substance-abusing youth frequently have a variety of underlying problems that need to be addressed, new concepts for treatment have emerged.

One such program is the Youth Evaluation Services (Y.E.S.) program, based in Greater Bridgeport, Connecticut, where it serves the state's poorest city as well as some of its most affluent suburbs, in Fairfield County. The program grew out of a community-based effort —the Regional Youth Substance Abuse Project (RYSAP)—that attempted to integrate substance-abuse services to provide a continuum of care accessible to youth across urban, suburban, and rural settings. The Y.E.S. program provides both assessment and case management for early identification, referral, and monitoring of youth needing substance-abuse intervention. An independent assessment and case management agency serves as the hub for identifying cases, coordinating treatment, developing new services, and containing service costs (Babor et al., 1991).

Y.E.S. is part of a research demonstration project carried out by the University of Connecticut Alcohol Research Center. Its approach has thus developed out of knowledge of current research, particularly findings indicating that the nature, severity, and course of substance use by youth can be predicted to some degree from an assessment of demographics; personality factors; childhood factors such as hyperactivity, poor school performance, early use of certain substances; emotional distress; peer relations; family history and dysfunction; psychopathology; and early problems with the law (Babor et al., 1991).

Utilizing this knowledge, a treatment-matching procedure was developed specifically for Y.E.S. based in part on Skinner's (1981) problem-oriented approach and the Cleveland Criteria (Hoffman, Halikas, & Mee-Lee, 1987). These two approaches had been designed to match clients to types or intensities of treatment based on client characteristics or behaviors. In addition, a comprehensive survey of regional facilities provided a compendium of services for use by the Y.E.S. program.

Screening of clients occurs in numerous settings, such as courts, schools, and agencies. Referrals also come from a broad spectrum of sources, including families, physicians, or the youth themselves. When a client is referred, the first step is assessment, which involves compiling a diagnostic profile of the client, including interviews, questionnaires, family assessment measures, school records, and urine screens. A treatment team reviews the profile together with the types of services that may be needed for each of the client's problems. The team then devises a treatment plan based on diagnostic information, their clinical judgment, and services available. Costs of treatment and the family's resources are taken into account when recommending services. The team presents the plan to the client and his or her family, along with the evidence that treatment is necessary. The client then is assigned to one of several treatment options whereby the youth continues to be followed by the Y.E.S. case manager.

Treatment recommendations vary widely within the Y.E.S. program, reflecting a wide range of services available in the region. Babor et al. (1991) report that during the first 2 years of operation the Y.E.S. program referred 29.3% of its clients to the more expensive residential programs, and 26.4% were referred to the least expensive programs such as mutual help groups (11.5%) and school programs (14.9%). Most clients, however—41.6%—were referred to some type of outpatient treatment program.

Particularly striking in the data from the Y.E.S. study is the percentage of youth referred for substance-abuse problems who were found to be positive for other problems. For example, 26.7% of the males and 37.3% of the females reported physical abuse; 41.2% of females reported sexual abuse; 29.4% of females reported symptoms of eating disorders (none of the males showed symptoms of eating disorders); 18.5% of males and 29.4% of females showed suicide potential, and 23.5% of females showed overdose potential, compared to 18.5% for the males (Babor et al., 1991).

These data, combined with those cited above related to conduct disorder, suggest that there are substantial differences in substance-abusing populations and thus appear to support the importance of matching treatment modalities to the individual's needs. No one treatment works for everyone.

Babor et al. (1991), on the basis of their evaluation of the first 2 years of the Y.E.S. program, suggest that an improved database is needed in five critical areas: (a) screening and early identification of substance abuse in youth; (b) diagnostic procedures capable of identifying the various interrelated social and psychological problems of these youth; (c) criteria for matching and referring adolescents to treatment; (d) the efficacy of various treatment options; and (e) the use of case management and coordination of services.

Data from the first 2 years of Y.E.S.'s operation indicate that the program has been successfully established, with more than 300 clients referred and subsequently evaluated. The 6-hour assessment battery has performed well. Evaluation data show that 77% of the clients completing the diagnostic evaluation were successfully referred and followed the recommended treatment plan. For the first 100 clients, a 6-month follow-up interview with parents found a high degree of satisfaction with the program. Fully 66.1% reported their child's functioning had improved; only 10.7% reported deteriorated functioning.

SELF-HELP APPROACHES

Self-help meetings appropriate to the age, gender, and culture of an adolescent can be of great benefit. Some exposure to adult meetings may also be helpful, particularly for older adolescents beginning the difficult transition to adulthood. Sometimes these older adults can serve as positive role models and assist older adolescents in their adult passage. Meetings are useful during and after the initial treatment stage, as adjuncts to outpatient care, and often as part of an inpatient, residential, or day-treatment program.

In addition to role models, self-help groups help the adolescent find sober friends, ideas for substance-free recreation, and strategies for coping with stress and with the urge to use substances (Rickel, 1989). Staff can be most useful in helping youth overcome their self-consciousness in speaking up in these meetings so they can obtain the maximum benefit from them. Twelve-step models are the most common self-help programs (Schonberg, 1993).

Twelve-Step Programs. The 12-step model promotes abstinence as well as the medical model of addiction. These programs provide social support, an opportunity to explore spiritual questions, models of the substance-free lifestyle, and guidelines for interpersonal interactions. Their popularity has grown tremendously in recent years, and there are groups representing every manner of addiction, from compulsive eating to dysfunctional sexual behavior.

Support Meetings. Parents of substance-abusing teens can also benefit from 12-step programs such as Al-Anon, where they can learn new behaviors for dealing with their child's behavior from parents who have been down the road ahead of them. The teen whose parents also have substance addictions can sometimes find help in Alateen. Parents may benefit from Adult Children of Alcoholics, because substance-abuse problems often have been part of the parent's own past.

These meetings are particularly important for aftercare planning, because they will be there for the adolescent after the primary treatment has ended. If the youth and the family can become connected to one or two of these groups, they will continue to find support and ongoing help for as long as they need it.

Family Support. Outpatient, inpatient, and residential programs are making greater efforts to include families in adolescent substance-abuse treatment. Family therapy, multifamily groups, and family education programs are part of many treatment programs. Referrals to 12-step programs for families are commonly part of this approach (Snyder & Ooms, 1992).

RELAPSE PREVENTION

Relapse is fairly common in recovery from substance addiction, and it should be incorporated into the treatment planning. Usually it is best to assume that the relapse is a temporary slip rather than a permanent slide back into drug use. Treatment teams should be alert for any significant family or emotional crises that may be occurring so that these can be addressed directly. Sometimes adolescent substance use can serve to distract the family from dealing with underlying interpersonal issues (Todd & Selekman, 1992).

Drug "Craving." A significant issue related to relapse prevention is the so-called craving for drugs. Unfortunately, researchers disagree on what constitutes this popular notion of "craving." Neither a standardized definition of drug craving nor a method of measurement has been successfully developed (Swan, 1993).

Currently, researchers identify and measure craving by client statements, physical symptoms, and continued use of substances. Yet subjects who tried desipramine as a means to control cocaine addiction said their craving decreased, even though they did not decrease their drug use (Swan, 1993).

Kosten (1992) suggests there may be two levels of craving, acute and chronic. Acute craving is elicited by using the drug; chronic craving may be a response to environmental stimuli that trigger associations to drug-using behavior. This would explain sudden relapses after long periods of abstinence, triggered by a new exposure to an old environmental cue.

A number of studies support the notion of environmental cues as powerful stimulants for drug-taking behavior. Researchers have found that these cues can provoke withdrawal symptoms as well as relapse (Swan, 1993). Carroll, Rounsaville, and Keller (1991) explain these findings as an example of classical conditioning. They suggest that distraction is useful in teaching patients to disregard these cues, as well as psychotherapy and pharmacotherapy, as a relapse prevention strategy.

OUTCOME STUDIES

Studies of adolescent substance-abuse treatment outcome are notably scarce. Issues contributing to this paucity of data include the controversy over abstinence versus controlled use as a successful outcome, as well as measurement problems unique to adolescents such as distinguishing successful treatment results from improvement related to developmental maturation (Bailey, 1989).

Adolescent treatment studies suggest results that may be similar to adult findings. For example, social support has been linked to successful abstinence by teens following treatment (Richter, Brown, & Mott, 1991), and treated teen drug users performed better on several measures of school success (grades, absences, citizenship) compared to nontreated adolescent drug users (Kirk, Chapman, & Sadler, 1990).

Brown, Vik, and Creamer (1989) studied adolescents receiving inpatient treatment to determine post-treatment relapse rates and found that adolescents had rates and patterns of relapse similar to those of adults. Two thirds of the teens relapsed during the first 3 months post-treatment. At the end of 6 months, 69.7% reported at least one alcohol or drug-use incident. The findings indicated that two or more relapses within the first 3 months constitute a major risk for returning to alcohol or drug abuse. For adolescents, social pressure was the most critical variable for relapse.

Studies of adult treatment outcomes have suggested that psychopathology and cognitive impairment may mediate successful treatment. McLellan, Luborsky, O'Brien, and Barr (1986) found that pretreatment psychiatric problems were the best predictor of outcome, whereas Fals-Stewart and Schafer (1992a) found a relationship between cognitive impairment and length of stay in a therapeutic treatment community (see also Miller, 1991).

Other research, however, has suggested that these relationships are not so straightforward. For example, studies have shown that a diagnosis of depression may be associated with a successful drug or alcohol treatment outcome (Ries & Ellingson, 1990), particularly for females (Rounsaville, Dolinsky, Babor, & Meyer, 1987). Pharmacological treatment of depression in drug users resulted in decreased usage in a placebo-controlled trial (Ziedonis & Kosten, 1991). In addition, patients diagnosed with obsessive-compulsive disorder (OCD) stayed in a therapeutic treatment community longer and had higher 12-month abstinence rates when they were treated for their OCD as well as their substance abuse (Fals-Stewart & Schafer, 1992b).

These latter studies further support the significance of matching clients to treatments that fit their individual problems, something that is as likely to be as true for adolescents as for adults. Cooney, Kadden, Litt, and Getter (1991) randomly assigned adult alcoholics to aftercare treatment that provided either coping skills training or interactional therapy. Clients scoring high on sociopathy or global psychopathology showed more success with coping skills training, whereas individuals low on these variables had more improvement with interactional therapy. Those with cognitive impairment also improved most with interactional therapy, however, a finding contrary to the predicted results.

This is clearly an area in need of further study, both to determine the efficacy of the various treatments and to continue to determine how best to match treatment modalities to the individual adolescent's needs.

CONCLUSIONS AND THE FUTURE OF DRUG TREATMENT

- Little information is available about effective treatment programs for adolescent substance abusers despite well-documented evidence concerning the behavioral, physiological, and social consequences of alcohol and drug abuse.
- Adolescents' patterns and problems of substance abuse differ sufficiently from adults' to warrant different treatment approaches.

- Clinicians need to be aware of the stages in the development of substance use as well as the cultural differences that exist in order to deter epidemic alcohol and drug abuse.
- Comprehensive, integrated, and systemic services need to be available so that a specific treatment approach can be tailored to the needs of each youth.
- Interventions can be powerful and effective tools to motivate adolescents to enter treatment.
- Adolescents requiring detoxification should be monitored by appropriately trained personnel under the direction of a physician with expertise in management of addiction and withdrawal.
- In the treatment community, the goal of treatment is global change in the individual that includes the integration of conduct, feelings, values, and attitudes with a drug-free lifestyle.
- Aftercare, such as day treatment for the adolescent, is especially important. Staff and family members must be prepared to be competent mediators of treatment gains made by the treatment community.
- Treatment matching is a new concept of adolescent services whereby clients are matched to specific types or intensities of treatment on the basis of particular characteristics and behaviors (e.g., individual, group, or family therapy).
- Self-help approaches such as 12-step programs or family support meetings that are appropriate to the age, gender, and culture of an adolescent are useful as part of an inpatient, residential, or day-treatment program or as adjuncts to outpatient care.
- Relapse is common in recovery from substance addiction, and its prevention should be incorporated into treatment planning.

Many policy makers now admit that the so-called War on Drugs has been a dismal failure. The appointment of Dr. Lee Brown, former New York City Police Commissioner, as "Drug Czar" and Janet Reno as Attorney General signals the dawn of a new era in the United States with regard to our drug control policies. Both Dr. Brown and Attorney General Reno bring to their offices an appreciation for the importance of prevention and treatment. Both are on record in support of such approaches—Dr. Brown with the promotion of community policing and Attorney General Reno with her efforts to secure treatment for convicted substance abusers.

It thus seems unlikely that the need for substance-abuse treatment will drop appreciably in the 1990s. Moreover, as we see the fruits of the major social problems of this era—as a generation of substance-exposed infants grows into their teens, as child abuse and neglect continues unabated (McCurdy & Daro, 1993), as violence affects an ever-widening circle of children and youth, and as age of use decreases—it is likely that the rate of substance abuse by adolescents will remain high (Westermeyer, 1992). Managed care, health care reform, and the concern for the federal deficit will all contribute to how these services are funded as well as what types of services will be available.

The competing forces of mounting societal pressure to address youth problems on the one hand and the desire to limit health costs and government spending on the other suggest that the decade leading into the next century will be an interesting one indeed.

REFERENCES

Babor, T. F., DelBoca, F. K., McLaney, M. A., Jacobi, B., Higgins-Biddle, J., & Hass, W. (1991). Just say Y.E.S.: Matching adolescents to appropriate interventions for alcohol and other drug-related problems. *Alcohol Health & Research World, 15*(1), 77-86.

Bailey, G. W. (1989). Current perspectives on substance abuse in youth. *Journal of the American Academy of Child and Adolescent Psychiatry, 28*(2), 151-162.

Beschner, G. M. (1985). The problem of adolescent drug abuse: An introduction to intervention strategies. In A. S. Friedman & G. M. Beschner (Eds.), *Treatment services for adolescent substance abusers* (pp. 1-12) (DHHS Publication No. ADM 85-1342). Rockville, MD: National Institute on Drug Abuse.

Brown, S. A., Vik, P. W., & Creamer, V. A. (1989). Characteristics of relapse following adolescent substance abuse treatment. *Addictive Behaviors, 14*, 291-300.

Carroll, K. M., Rounsaville, B. J., & Keller, D. S. (1991). Relapse prevention strategies for the treatment of cocaine abuse. *American Journal of Drug and Alcohol Abuse, 17*(3), 249-265.

Chaiken, M. R. (1993, April). Can drug epidemics be anticipated? *National Institute of Justice Journal*, pp. 23-30.

Cooney, N. L., Kadden, R. M., Litt, M. D., & Getter, H. (1991). Matching alcoholics to coping skills or interactional therapies: Two-year follow-up results. *Journal of Consulting and Clinical Psychology, 59*(4), 598-601.

DeLeon, G. (1984). *The therapeutic community: Study of effectiveness* (DHHS Publication No. ADM 84-1286). Rockville, MD: National Institute on Drug Abuse.

DeLeon, G., & Deitch, D. (1985). Treatment of the adolescent substance abuser in a therapeutic community. In A. S. Friedman & G. M. Beschner (Eds.), *Treatment services for adolescent substance abusers* (pp. 216-230) (DHHS Publication No. ADM 85-1342). Rockville, MD: National Institute on Drug Abuse.

Fals-Stewart, W., & Schafer, J. (1992a). The relationship between length of stay in drug-free therapeutic communities and neurocognitive functioning. *Journal of Clinical Psychology, 48*(4), 539-543.

Fals-Stewart, W., & Schafer, J. (1992b). The treatment of substance abusers diagnosed with obsessive-compulsive disorder: An outcome study. *Journal of Substance Abuse Treatment, 9*(4), 365-370.

Hoffman, N. G., Halikas, J. A., & Mee-Lee, D. (1987). *The Cleveland admission, discharge, and transfer criteria: Model for chemical dependency treatment program.* Cleveland, OH: The Greater Cleveland Hospital Association.

Hollandsworth, S. (1990, June). Can kids on drugs be saved? *Texas Monthly,* pp. 107-111, 153, 155, 158-162.

Hubbard, R. L., Marsden, M. E., Rachal, J. V., Harwood, H. J., Cavanaugh, E. R., & Ginzburg, H. M. (1989). *Drug abuse treatment: A national survey of effectiveness.* Chapel Hill: University of North Carolina Press.

Jalali, B., Jalali, M., Grocetti, G., & Turner, F. (1981). Adolescents and drug use: Toward a more comprehensive approach. *American Journal of Orthopsychiatry, 51*(1), 120-129.

Johnston, L. D., O'Malley, P. M., & Bachman, J. (1988). *Illicit drug use, smoking, and drinking by America's high school students and young adults: 1975-1987.* Rockville, MD: National Institute on Drug Abuse.

Kirk, D. L., Chapman, T., & Sadler, O. W. (1990). Documenting the effectiveness of adolescent substance abuse treatment using public school archival records. *High School Journal, 74*(1), 16-21.

Klitzner, M., Fisher, D., Stewart, K., & Gilbert, S. (1993). *Substance abuse: Early intervention for adolescents.* Princeton, NJ: Robert Wood Johnson Foundation.

Kosten, T. R. (1992). Can cocaine craving be a medication development outcome? Drug craving and relapse in opioid and cocaine dependence. *American Journal on Addictions, 1*(3), 230-239.

Kusnetz, S. (1985). An overview of selected adolescent substance abuse treatment programs. In A. S. Friedman & G. M. Beschner (Eds.), *Treatment services for adolescent substance abusers* (pp. 31-48) (DHHS Publication No. ADM 85-1342). Rockville, MD: National Institute on Drug Abuse.

Loney, J. (1988). Substance abuse in adolescents: Diagnostic issues derived from studies of attention deficit disorder with hyperactivity. In E. R. Rahdert & J. Grabrowski (Eds.), *Adolescent drug abuse: Analyses of treatment research* (pp. 19-26) (DHHS Publication No. ADM 88-1523). Rockville, MD: National Institute on Drug Abuse.

McCurdy, K., & Daro, D. (1993). *Current trends in child abuse reporting and fatalities: The results of the 1992 Annual Fifty State Survey.* Chicago: National Committee for Prevention of Child Abuse.

McLellan, A. T., Luborsky, L., O'Brien, C. P., & Barr, H. L. (1986). Alcohol and drug abuse treatment in three different populations: Is there improvement and is it predictable? *American Journal of Drug and Alcohol Abuse, 12*(1-2), 101-120.

Miller, L. (1991). Predicting relapse and recovery in alcoholism and addiction: Neuropsychology, personality, and cognitive style. *Journal of Substance Abuse Treatment, 8*(4), 277-291.

National Institute of Justice. (1993, May). *Drug use forecasting quarterly report* (Third quarter 1992). Washington, DC: U.S. Department of Justice.

National Institute on Drug Abuse. (1991). *Drug use among youth: Findings from the 1988 National Household Survey on Drug Abuse* (DHHS Publication No. ADM 91-1765). Rockville, MD: U.S. Department of Health and Human Services.

Office of the Inspector General. (1991). *Youth and alcohol: A national survey* (Document No. OEI-09-91-00652). Washington, DC: U.S. Department of Health and Human Services.

Ottenberg, D. J., Olsen, G. R., & Schiller, B. D. (1985). The day treatment center: An alternative for adolescent substance abusers. In A. S. Friedman & G. M. Beschner (Eds.), *Treatment services for adolescent substance abusers* (pp. 195-203) (DHHS Publication No. ADM 85-1342). Rockville, MD: National Institute on Drug Abuse.

Rahdert, E. R., & Grabowski, J. (Eds.). (1988). *Adolescent drug abuse: Analysis of treatment research* (DHHS Publication No. ADM 88-1523). Rockville, MD: National Institute on Drug Abuse.

Richter, S. S., Brown, S. A., & Mott, M. A. (1991). The impact of social support and self-esteem on adolescent substance abuse treatment outcome. *Journal of Substance Abuse, 3*(4), 371-385.

Rickel, A. U. (1989). *Teenage Pregnancy and Parenting*. New York: Taylor & Francis/Hemisphere.

Rickel, A. U., & Allen, L. (1987). *Preventing maladjustment from infancy through adolescence*. Beverly Hills, CA: Sage.

Rickel, A. U., Gerrard, M., & Iscoe, I. (Eds.). (1984). *Social and psychological problems of women: Prevention and crisis intervention*. New York: Harper & Row/Hemisphere.

Ries, R. K., & Ellingson, T. (1990). A pilot assessment at one month of 17 dual diagnosis patients. *Hospital and Community Psychiatry, 41*(11), 1230-1233.

Rounsaville, B. J., Dolinsky, Z. G., Babor, T. F., & Meyer, R. E. (1987). Psychopathology as a predictor of treatment outcome in alcoholics. *Archives of General Psychiatry, 44*(6), 505-513.

Schonberg, S. K. (1993). *Treatment of alcohol-and-other-drug (AOD)-abusing adolescents* (SAMHSA Contract No. ADM 270-91- 0007). Rockville, MD: Substance Abuse and Mental Health Services Administration, Center for Substance Abuse Treatment.

Shapiro, D. (1985). Many doorways: A comprehensive approach to intervention and treatment of youthful drug users. In A. S. Friedman & G. M. Beschner (Eds.), *Treatment services for adolescent substance abusers* (pp. 164-177) (DHHS Publication No. ADM 85-1342). Rockville, MD: NIDA, U.S. Department of Health and Human Services.

Shedler, J., & Block, J. (1990). Adolescent drug use and psychological health, a longitudinal inquiry. *American Psychologist, 45*(5), 612-630.

Skinner, H. A. (1981). Different strokes for different folks: Differential treatment for alcohol abuse. In R. E. Meyer, T. F. Babor, B. C. Glueck, J. H. Jaffe, J. E. O'Brien, & J. R. Stabenau (Eds.), *Evaluation of the alcoholic: Implications for research, theory and treatment* (pp. 349-367). Washington, DC: Government Printing Office.

Snyder, W., & Ooms, T. (Eds.). (1992). *Empowering families, helping adolescents: Family-centered treatment of adolescents with alcohol, drug abuse, & mental health problems* (DHHS Publication No. ADM 92-1745). Rockville, MD: U.S. Department of Health and Human Services.

Swan, N. (1993, May/June). Researchers probe which comes first: Drug abuse or antisocial behavior? *NIDA Notes* (NIH Publication No. 93-3478), pp. 6-7.

Todd, T. C., & Selekman, M. (1992). A structural-strategic model for treating the adolescent who is abusing alcohol and other drugs. In W. Snyder & T. Ooms (Eds.), *Empowering families, helping adolescents: Family-centered treatment of adolescents with alcohol, drug abuse, & mental health problems* (pp. 79-89). (DHHS Publication No. ADM 92-1745). Rockville, MD: U.S. Department of Health and Human Services.

Westermeyer, J. (1992). Substance use disorders: Predictions for the 1990s. *American Journal of Drug and Alcohol Abuse, 18*(1), 1-11.

Ziedonis, D. M., & Kosten, T. R. (1991). Pharmacotherapy improves treatment outcome in depressed cocaine addicts. *Journal of Psychoactive Drugs, 23*(4), 417-425.

9. Minimization of Substance Use: What Can Be Said at This Point?

Aleta L. Meyer
Virginia Commonwealth University

Because of the cost to society in loss of human potential whenever an individual has a substance-use problem, an overall reduction in the number of people who develop such problems is a desirable target. Such a focus calls for primary prevention programs. The goal of primary prevention, in general, is to (a) anticipate problems (Goldston, 1977); (b) reduce the number of new cases; (c) promote competencies that protect against the development of problems (Felner, Jason, Moritsugu, & Farber, 1983); and (d) encourage optimal health (Goldston, 1977). Therefore, the goals of primary preventions in the substance-use field are to (a) determine who is at risk for substance abuse; (b) reduce the number of people who abuse substances; (c) promote behaviors that protect against the abuse of substances; and (d) encourage healthy behavior that is inconsistent with substance abuse.

The developmental period many substance-use prevention programs target is early adolescence (e.g., Ellickson, Bell, & Harrison, 1991; Flay et al., 1985). Targeting early adolescence is important because the onset of using "gateway substances" (tobacco, alcohol, and marijuana) often occurs during these years (Crockett & Petersen, 1993; Kandel, 1980; Kandel & Logan, 1984). Moreover, if initiation of use leads a youth to choose to consume drugs and/or alcohol in order to cope with personal problems, such behavior is likely to interfere with "essential maturational processes and development" that optimally occur in this developmental period (Newcomb & Bentler, 1989, p. 248). Therefore, the perspective of many in the substance-use field is that *any* use of substances by youth is undesirable (Johnson et al., 1990).

LACK OF SOLID
EVIDENCE FOR LONG-TERM CHANGE

The task of establishing substance-use prevention programs alter the *long-term* substance-use behavior patterns of youth has been a difficult one (e.g., Cook, Anson, & Walchli, 1993; Flay et al., 1989). For example, many programs have successfully delayed the onset of smoking in treatment groups (Botvin, Baker, Renick, Filazzola, & Botvin, 1984; Ellickson & Bell, 1990; Flay et al., 1985; Johnson et al., 1990; Perry, 1987) and, with booster sessions, maintained group differences over time (Botvin et al., 1984; Flay et al., 1985; Johnson et al., 1990), yet few have examined the smoking behavior of youth in the years following program boosters. Much to the credit of the Waterloo Smoking Prevention Program evaluation, a 6-year follow-up was conducted to see if treatment effects continued into late adolescence, even after the cessation of booster sessions (Flay et al., 1989). The three primary findings of this study were (a) the overall effect of the treatment had dissipated; (b) those at low risk because of their social environment were the least likely to be smoking after 6 years, whether or not they were in the treatment group; and (c) youth who dropped out of school but remained in the sample were much more likely to be smokers after 6 years (68%) than were those who remained in school (28%). Apparently, the initial reduction in smoking behavior that was related to the program did not manifest in less smoking behavior later on in the lives of the youth.

The case for substance-use prevention programs that focus on other "gateway substances" is even less convincing. In terms of marijuana use, programs have had success in delaying onset (Ellickson & Bell, 1990; Johnson et al., 1990), yet enduring measurable differences between groups have yet to be documented. By far the most difficult area of substance-use behavior to alter has been alcohol use. For example, although Johnson et al. (1990) found support for their program's delaying of marijuana and tobacco use, alcohol use was unaffected. In contrast, however, even though Caplan et al. (1992) found no overall difference in self-reported frequency of substance use, they did find that excessive use of alcohol increased significantly in the control group compared to program students. In this study, excessive use referred to having three or more drinks on a single occasion. Had Johnson et al. measured *excessive* alcohol use in addition to asking whether or not a youth had used alcohol at all, they may have had results similar to those of Caplan et al.; however, that remains an empirical question. (A more thorough review of substance-use prevention programs will be presented later in this chapter.)

Despite the lack of solid statistical evidence that substance-use prevention programs have their intended impact, the tone of the conclusions of those who have written thorough reviews of the effectiveness of such programs remains optimistic. Consider the following examples:

Remarkable progress has been made in an important area of health psychology and public health [smoking prevention]. The tested programs have been improved and strengthened dramatically; difficult research design issues have been resolved or their seriousness reduced; and recent findings provide some confidence that psychosocial approaches to smoking prevention may be worthwhile. (Flay, 1985, p. 481)

The social influence models do provide some optimism for primary prevention efforts. Prevention programs appear most effective when 1) the target behavior of the intervention has received increasing societal disapproval (such as cigarette smoking), 2) multiple years of behavioral health education are planned, and 3) community-wide involvement or mass media complement a school-based peer-led program. (Perry & Kelder, 1992, p. 360)

Social influence and comprehensive programs are most consistently effective at reducing substance abuse among students exposed to these programs. The effectiveness of programs, however, cannot be guaranteed. Numerous intervening characteristics must be considered, including training and background of teachers, fidelity of presentation, and target population. This review found little research on these issues. Nonetheless, social influence and comprehensive programs clearly appear superior in their potential to have an impact on substance abuse behaviors [compared to other modalities for substance-use prevention]. (Hansen, 1992, p. 427)

CONTINUING SUBSTANCE-USE PREVENTION IN THE FACE OF PESSIMISTIC INFORMATION

Given the disappointing information about the long-term efficacy of substance-use prevention programs, why is it that people (e.g., program developers, evaluators, school staff, and community members) continue to direct energy and resources toward these programs? Three intriguing possible explanations are (a) many program developers and evaluators are committed to the "experimenting society" model for social reform (Campbell, 1971, p. 1, in Heller, 1984); (b) despite the lack of statistically significant evidence, many program developers, evaluators, school staff, and community members have tacit knowledge that certain programs are working; and (c) when substance-use prevention programs are evaluated for measurable change, the *multiple goals* of primary prevention are often not considered.

The *experimenting society* Campbell (1971) described is one in which prevention efforts are viewed as social experiments to be fully evaluated and then modified or eliminated if the effort is found to be ineffective and/or harmful. Such a perspective sees humans as complex beings within varying ecosystems (Heller, 1984) where efforts to change behavior will be undoubtedly flawed and in constant need of revision. Therefore, efforts that do not meet expectations are viewed as guideposts for future directions in prevention, *not* as failures.

Tacit knowledge refers to what individuals know but cannot articulate clearly (Guba & Lincoln, 1989). This type of knowledge, often called *hunches* or *intuition,* is perhaps undervalued by the world of quantitative research. The significance of tacit knowledge cannot be denied, however, even if the knowledge itself is not readily verifiable or valued by all. Consider the widespread use of grassroots programs such as MADD and DARE in the United States and Quest-International across the globe: To date, none of these programs has been evaluated in a manner that would establish its impact. Even so, society continues to support their implementation.

The *multiple goals* of primary prevention include both efforts to reduce the number of new cases and efforts to promote optimal health (e.g., Felner et al., 1983; Goldston, 1977). Attempts at evaluation, however, have often looked solely at the reduction-of-new-cases side of the equation. According to Albee (1985), there are seven ways in which the goals of prevention can be met. The first three methods are reduction efforts aimed at decreasing the degree of organic risk factors, stress, and/or exploitation. The next four methods are promotion efforts aimed at improving coping skills, competency, self-esteem, and/or social support. In other words, there are multiple ways in which substance-abuse problems can be reduced. Hence, there are multiple variables that should be assessed when evaluating substance-use prevention programs. These include the variables of social competence, peer pressure, peer support, stress, self-esteem, and coping skills.

In fact, the tacit knowledge of society members who continue to support substance-use prevention programs may be the awareness of changes in these additional variables, variables that more traditional evaluation may not measure. In other words, the salient issue may be the *combination* of (a) reduced substance use with (b) decreased exploitation and stress and (c) increased coping skills, competence, social support, and self-esteem. From this perspective, information from studies such as the one by Flay et al. (1989), in which the onset of experimentation with cigarettes was delayed (even though long-term differences were not maintained), is much more encouraging. Perhaps the delay in experimentation gave students opportunities to learn alternative coping mechanisms that protect them from the more severe consequences of cigarette use. In this light, their program should be viewed as a success.

Together, these explanations for continuing in the face of inconclusive evidence pose a significant challenge to the methodology of prevention research and the development of future substance-use prevention programs. That challenge is: How do we know when substance-use prevention is working, with whom and in what settings it is working, and how do we improve prevention efforts over time? Moreover, what is meant by the term *working*? According to Bloom (1993), it is the ethical imperative of prevention specialists to answer these questions.

A METHOD FOR MEETING THE CHALLENGE

The most effective tool at our disposal for answering these questions is a feedback process that connects program realities to program theories (i.e., Chen & Rossi, 1987; Dodge, 1991; Linney, 1989; Patterson, 1986; Weissberg, Caplan, & Sivo, 1989). Weissberg et al. (1989) call this process the "Five Phases of Program Development." In these five phases, program developers can improve their overall prevention programs by utilizing research results (from their own evaluations and others' research) (a) to inform the operating theory of change, (b) to redesign the program, (c) to rethink program implementation, (d) to increase the probability of establishing a program within a school, and (e) to improve the maintenance of positive outcomes within youth over time. Chen and Rossi (1987) label a process similar to this the "Theory-Driven Approach to Validity," and many program evaluation specialists have responded quite favorably to their suggestions (e.g., Palumbo & Oliverio, 1989; Patton, 1989; Trochim, 1989). At the Oregon Social Learning Center, where the etiology and treatment of aggressive behavior have been studied through the use of applied research for the past 15 years, this process is called "Bootstrapping" (Patterson, 1986). The successes of their center in helping families with aggressive children and in identifying key causal processes in the development of aggressive behavior are testimony to this approach. Another way to view these processes is as reformulations of Lewin's (1951) action research model in which there is a cyclical relationship between fact-finding, action, and evaluation.

According to Cook et al. (1993), many evaluations of health promotion programs that have examined short- and long-term outcomes have omitted the middle part of this feedback loop and could easily have been improved by including a focus on program implementation and mediating processes (p. 22). Their definitions of program implementation and mediating processes are as follows:

> All conceptualizations of implementation are predicated on a description of program activities, particularly to check on whether those activities built into the original program design actually occurred at local sites. (Cook et al., 1993, p. 340)

> We call this the *mediational* approach to explanation because it depends so heavily on determining which factors are responsible for the demonstrated link between a global intervention and an out come (Cook et al., 1993, p. 343)

In other words, the examination of program implementation gives insight into such things as the type of program the average person received, whereas examination of causal mediating processes helps in understanding the ways in which changes in important relationships affect substance use. Therefore, when the effectiveness of prevention efforts is discussed in this chapter, program implementation and causal mediating processes will be addressed as well as program outcomes.

THE ROLE OF THE RESEARCHER AT THE COMMUNITY LEVEL

What seems to be missing from these current models of a feedback process between program reality and theory is an explicit statement of the important and involved role of the evaluator in community change. Because findings of social science are being used to inform public policy, this role of the evaluator, as being responsible to the community, is more important now than ever before. If social science researchers use models of explanation that are not complex enough to explain how processes and mechanisms could produce effects over a long period of time, social science risks (a) reinforcing political preference for single strategies and inexpensive solutions; (b) perpetuating the concept that the impact of an intervention can be understood separately from its context; (c) ignoring the fact that experimental projects may not be replicable in new settings; and (d) encouraging advocates of such programs to overstate the possible effects of their programs (Woodhead, 1988, p. 446).

THE DANGER OF SIMPLISTIC PREVENTION MODELS: THE EXAMPLE OF HEADSTART

As Woodhead (1988) illustrates, a simplistic model of cause and effect between an increase in cognitive ability immediately following participation in Headstart and later higher employment has encouraged policy members to continue investing in preschool programs with the assumption that similar outcomes will result in new settings. Such a model ignores the issues of generalizability from an experimental program to new implementation sites, not to mention the fact that the cognitive ability of Headstart participants returned to a level equal to the control group soon after leaving Headstart.

Woodhead (1988) offers a transactional model as an alternative explanation for the long-term effects whereby the initial difference in participation resulted in a changed environment where the teachers were less likely to place participants in remedial programs in first grade—often the initial site of a cycle of failure. Woodhead suggests, therefore, that perhaps a better target for intervention is the tracking process of remediation. If a school has taken such a perspective and changed its policy for remediation tracking, the presumed positive effects of Headstart per se may not be found *if* that causal pathway was the crucial one. As Woodhead acknowledges, this pathway is suggested mainly because of the extent of assessment that has been done on cognitive factors; possibilities exist for other processes such as improved self-concept, relationships, and expectations for school success.

OVERLY SIMPLISTIC MODELS
IN SUBSTANCE-USE PREVENTION

An example of an overly simplistic model in substance-use prevention is one in which it is assumed that knowledge *alone* about the dangers of drugs and alcohol will empower individuals to make personal choices not to use substances. In the past, this model was heavily relied upon; it has been found to be deficient and *harmful* in some cases (Heller, 1984; Tobler, 1986). The national "Just Say No" campaign was a simple model as well. Both of these models failed to acknowledge many important factors (e.g., that the short-term effects of substance use can be pleasurable, or that substance use is often a "prerequisite for socialization and peer acceptance" [Heller, 1984, p. 197]). As Woodhead (1988) suggests, although simple and inexpensive strategies may have initial appeal, their oversimplicity makes them inadequate solutions to a complex social problem.

OVERSIGHTS OF TRANSFERRING
A SUBSTANCE-USE PREVENTION
PROGRAM TO A NEW COMMUNITY

As with the case of Headstart, if there is not a fit between the program and the community from the onset, what might make a program "click" in one community may make the program "thud" with the heavy weight of disappointment in another. Gullotta (1987) addressed the importance of this fit when he described the five tools of prevention and how these tools are best utilized when they are coordinated within a community. The five tools he described are education, competency promotion, natural caregiving, collaboration/consultation, and community organization/systems intervention.

In order to illustrate this point, assume that in one community there is a school-based, psychosocial prevention program called LIFE; this program performs as the education and competency promotion tools. The other tools in place in that community are (a) a student assistance program whereby community mental health workers provide training in listening and crisis counseling skills to selected middle school teachers and principals (consultation and organization intervention tools); (b) an active local church youth group that offers meaningful activities and fun to all interested youth after school and on weekend nights (a natural caregiving tool); and (c) national speakers who are brought into the schools every year to address large assemblies about topics of concern (another educational tool). Through some form of evaluation the community has decided that their school-based program is successful. The community then publicizes its success and requests are made about transferring the LIFE program to a school in a new community. If the relationship between those tools in the first community is not acknowledged *prior* to the transfer of the LIFE program, it is not likely the same results will occur in the next. This will be especially true if there is already a competence-focused program in the schools that the LIFE program can complement and/or replace. In such a situation, animosity may be provoked between advocates of the old program and advocates of the new. In addition, resources may be spent on training and new materials that could have been utilized to develop other tools within that community. Another example of mismatched tools would be a "quick fix" solution of bringing in a provocative and moving speaker (such as David Toma in the early 1980s) to give a heartwrenching documentary *without* having created a local, supportive context (e.g., student assistance and peer counseling programs) in which students can process the experience and place it in perspective.

A SNAPSHOT OF THE EFFECTIVENESS OF WELL-DOCUMENTED PREVENTIONS

In order to address the challenge of answering the three questions posed earlier (How do we know when substance-use prevention is working, with whom and in what settings it is working, and how do we improve prevention efforts over time?), the conceptualization, design, implementation, mediating processes (mediators and moderators), and short- and long-term outcomes of selected prevention programs will be described (for additional reviews, see Flay, 1985; Hansen, 1992; Tobler, 1986, 1992). In general, the programs chosen for discussion are those that have published extensively about their evaluation, which limits the focus primarily to school-based programs. It is hoped that this examination of school-based programs will (a) provide a framework of what to look for when examining *any* substance-use prevention program, (b) aid in identifying future directions for substance-use prevention, and (c) assist in clarifying the role of the evaluator in substance-use prevention.

Life Skills Training

The Life Skills Training program is based on Bandura's (1977) social learning theory and the Jessors' problem behavior theory (Jessor & Jessor, 1977): "Substance use behavior, like other types of behavior, is learned through a process of modeling and reinforcement which is mediated by personal factors such as cognitions, attitudes, and beliefs" (Botvin & Tortu, 1988, p. 100). In many ways, this theoretical basis calls for the creation of barriers to substance use. Even so, the program developers acknowledge that youth who are not motivated to utilize barriers will *not* use them even though they may be skilled in resistance and other areas. Therefore, in an effort to reduce the motivation to use substances, Life Skills Training supplements the idea of increasing an individual's ability to resist with that of improving her or his general personal and social competence to the desired end of reducing motivation to use drugs.

The Life Skills Training core program is made up of five major components that span 18 sessions in 7th grade (Botvin & Tortu, 1988). Boosters in 8th and 9th grade serve to strengthen the intervention by emphasizing practice of the social and personal skills presented in the 7th grade (10 booster sessions taught in 8th grade; 5 taught in 9th grade). A unique feature of the Life Skills Training curriculum is an 8-week self-improvement project in which each student selects a skill or behavior and sets short-term and longterm goals for achieving it. Weekly progress reports help the students "learn to shape their own behavior" (p. 102). The 15 booster sessions over the following

2 years provide increased opportunity for the students to generalize skills across settings and across problem areas in their lives.

In terms of implementing innovative curricula in schools, Botvin and Tortu (1988) described the process as being "fraught with psychological, sociological, political, and economic concerns" (p. 106). They suggest a pattern of entry into individual school districts that gradually incorporates all concerned into the decision-making process.

Over the years Life Skills Training has usually been implemented as part of a health or a science course. Certain teacher qualities (student rapport, commitment to the program, and motivation to teach Life Skills Training), however, appear to be more important to successful implementation of Life Skills Training than the subject the teacher has been trained to teach. To attract teachers with such qualities Botvin and Tortu suggest that school officials provide "professional recognition, release time, or other suitable incentives" to those who teach their program (1988, p. 107).

Using the definitions of program implementation and mediating processes described earlier (see "A Method for Meeting the Challenge," above) as the standard against which they analyzed three exemplary evaluations of health promotion programs (including the Midwestern Prevention Project and Life Skills Training), Cook et al. (1993) asked how each program dealt with implementation issues and how the evaluators went about explaining descriptive causal relationships. To answer these questions, Cook et al. accessed all available literature about each program, including not-yet-published references obtained directly from the program developers. This complete literature review resulted in an extremely comprehensive overview of exactly where each program was at the time Cook et al.'s chapter was written.

In the literature about Life Skills Training, Cook et al. (1993) comment that Botvin makes no explicit mention of implementation in his published papers before 1989. A study done in 1989, however, utilized observers to document the number of curriculum points and objectives from the teachers' manual that were actually covered in class (p. 354). By observing each teacher at least three times, they determined that "65 percent of the program content was covered in the average class" (p. 354). Unfortunately, this figure cannot be understood in comparison to other programs or to past implementations of Life Skills Training because this type of information is rarely gathered in other program evaluations.

One reason observations are not usually conducted is the expense; yet self-report questionnaires completed by teachers would be relatively inexpensive and would provide valuable implementation information. Cook et al. (1993) express dismay at this oversight, and they criticize Botvin for explaining differences in treatment outcome as differences in program implementation without having measured implementation processes while they were occurring. For example, differences between peer-led and teacher-led groups were attributed to peers implementing the treatment more faithfully than teachers (p. 354). Cook et al. label this conclusion as "an *ex post facto* conjecture based on a few unsystematic and incidental reports from members of the field staff" (p. 354). Aside from this conclusion being made without clear documentation, the whole idea that peers can be more effective role models than adults (which would explain their superior results) was ignored. Because implementation will invariably differ across settings, Cook et al. assert that program evaluations must always include extensive implementation assessment and that the time has passed for repeating that deficiency in evaluation.

Cook et al. (1993) report that because Botvin has kept a record of treatment dosage, including booster sessions, possibilities exist to "systematically explore the number of Life Skills Training sessions or the amount of curriculum coverage that are necessary for observing effects" (p. 354). If such analyses are conducted in the future, the analyses would be invaluable toward determining how much treatment is necessary for which populations.

In terms of mediators, the very title of Life Skills Training includes the term *life skills*, which are assumed to be the key mechanisms through which individual change in substance use occurs. Cook et al. (1993) pointed out, however, that these skills have never been made the only component of the intervention. In fact, when Botvin and others have attempted to assess mediating variables, (a) they found disappointing results when direct measures of social skills were gathered; (b) they realized there was an alternative interpretation of the program, in terms of revised norms about substance use; and (c) they found it difficult to move from distal results to any single mediating process because the program was so multidimensional. Moreover, measures of self-esteem and other personality attributes, key components of Botvin's theory, have not been analyzed or reported in ways that were meant to shed light on the original theory). The measures that have been shown to be linked more closely to outcomes than skills acquisition in the Life Skills Training analyses are those that speak to changed perceptions of norms.

The focus of *outcome* evaluations on the Life Skills Training program has been on program efficacy in reducing substance use behaviors (Botvin & Tortu, 1988). In a study of the effectiveness of peer leaders compared to school teachers, the only effects found immediately after the initial 7th-grade program were for those in the peer-led groups. Compared to the control groups, there were 40% fewer experimental cigarette smokers in the peer-led groups. In addition, 71% fewer students in the peer-led group reported marijuana use in comparison to the control group. One year later, still "fewer students in the peer-led booster Life Skills Training group than controls were smoking and using marijuana" (p. 105). Two years later, Botvin and Tortu claimed that cigarette smoking reported the strongest results. Unfortunately, the magnitude of this effect is not reported. In addition, there are no evaluations of these students beyond 2 years, and any data that was collected was gathered during the 8th- and 9th-grade years when the 15-session booster series was being implemented.

Evaluations of Life Skills Training that are currently under way will provide information on the efficacy of Life Skills Training with urban minority students and will illuminate the efficacy of various training procedures for Life Skills Training implementation (Botvin & Tortu, 1988). These evaluations are moving in exciting directions. First, given that Life Skills Training has generally been implemented only with white, upper-middle- to middle-class youth, issues of generalizability (external validity) can be addressed. Second, research has not previously been gathered on the efficacy of training programs. In general, it has been assumed that quality training has been essential to treatment fidelity and that schools need to invest in this process in order to implement Life Skills Training—however, this hypothesis has not been directly tested. The current evaluation will compare the following three conditions: a formal teacher-training workshop, a packaged (written and video) training program in Life Skills Training, and a no-contact control. The findings of this study will serve either to reinforce or refute previous beliefs about treatment fidelity, helping schools make informed decisions about how to allocate their money.

In summary, the long-term effects of Life Skills Training have not been assessed beyond the implementation of booster sessions (Botvin & Tortu, 1988). Therefore, all that can be said from what Botvin and

Tortu report about how to maintain positive outcomes within youth is that booster sessions appear to contribute to the fact that program effects lasted for 2 years. When Cook et al. (1993) reinterpreted Life Skills Training analyses, however, they gleaned from the results that changes in social norms about substance use may be the source of change within the youth. If norms had actually changed and the youth were assessed after the cessation of booster sessions it could be asserted that changes in social norms maintain change within youth. At this time, however, this cannot be claimed.

Project ALERT

Project ALERT is based on Janz and Becker's (1984) health belief model and Bandura's (1977) self-efficacy theory of behavior change. Ellickson et al. (1991) believe there are barriers to effectively resisting pressures to use drugs. Their efforts are therefore aimed at creating new barriers—barriers that serve to protect youth from these influences. The three susceptibilities they believe youth have include:

> 1) insufficient resistance skills (inability to identify self-imposed pressures to use drugs, to counter pro-drug arguments, and to withstand pressures to use); 2) a corresponding perception that one is unable to resist pro-drug pressures; and 3) normative beliefs that drug use is widespread and acceptable behavior. (p. 6)

The authors briefly state that they also focus on helping adolescents to "recognize the serious negative consequences of drug use, to understand their own susceptibility to those consequences, and to identify the benefits of not using" (p. 7).

Project ALERT's eight sessions were taught to the students in their 7th-grade year using two different methods of delivery at the treatment schools. In half of these schools the classroom teachers taught the classes unassisted; in the other half the teachers were assisted by older teens drawn from neighboring high schools (Ellickson et al., 1991). Three booster sessions were given to both treatment groups when the students were in 8th grade.

Ellickson et al. (1991) chose to utilize peer leaders in response to Tobler's (1986) review of substance use prevention programs, which found better results when peer leaders were included in classroom delivery. Ellickson et al. explain that older peers were chosen because they have more experience in coping with social pressure than their younger counterparts, which makes them "more credible communicators" (Ellickson et al., 1991, p. 10). In addition, they viewed older peers as role models for successful nonuse in which their "primary function was to provide personal examples of effective resistance and to help students believe that they, too, could successfully resist drugs" (p. 10). Project ALERT thus served as a test of previous findings and beliefs about social influence.

Both methods of delivery—teacher alone and teacher with peer leaders—utilized various social learning techniques to build "resistance self-efficacy" (Ellickson, 1991, p. 7). The desired resistance skills were modeled, practiced, and reinforced through demonstrations on video and through actual "live" role-playing. In the groups in which older peer leaders were assistants, it was hoped that a social climate of nonuse might be fostered.

The program also hoped to challenge the students' beliefs about substance use in their community by comparing beliefs about use with actual use. Students were also asked to think of immediate consequences of substance use and to write down the benefits of resisting substance use.

Out of concern for the possible inability to make conclusions about the effects of the program if there is no information about the degree to which Project ALERT was implemented according to plan, Ellickson and Bell (1992) made a priority of assessing and ensuring program fidelity. Their means for doing this were to allocate the necessary staffing resources to monitor 41% of the 2,300 classroom sessions that were planned for 7th and 8th grade. The standardized observation forms the monitors used measured such things as the degree to which (a) the key components of the session were completed and (b) the intended classroom environment was established. From these assessments Ellickson and Bell (1992) concluded that "all curriculum activities were presented in the vast majority of classes" (p. 89), and that the intended classroom environment was established in 90% or more of the classes that were observed. For these reasons Ellickson and Bell (1992) can be relatively confident that, in the case that the expected changes in behavior do not occur, they will know that the conceptual model needs to be reexamined, instead of being in a position where they cannot discriminate between an inadequate model and poor implementation.

Because Project ALERT was designed to reduce substance use by changing certain cognitive risk factors, the evaluators expected the program to change the following mediators: (a) to increase the students' agreement with statements about the negative consequences of drugs and to decrease agreement with positive consequences; (b) to lower the students' estimates of peer drug use and perceived peer tolerance of use, while increasing perceptions that resistance gains respect; (c) to increase the students' resistance self-efficacy; and (d) to lower the proportion who expected to use drugs in the future (Ellickson et al., 1991, p. 15). In addition to assessing these cognitive mediating factors Ellickson et al. categorized youth at baseline into different risk groups that they thought would moderate the effect of the program: nonusers, experimenters, and users. Data were collected until 15 months after program initiation, immediately following the completion of the booster sessions. Students who were not assessed by follow-up surveys were "significantly more likely to have before-treatment characteristics often cited as risk factors for drug use (for example, family disruption and early drug use)" (p. 16). There were no differences in attrition across the experimental conditions.

In terms of the cognitive mediating factors, Ellickson et al. conclude that Project ALERT was effective in dampening cognitive risk factors for cigarette and marijuana use over time. It was not effective in altering these factors around the topic of alcohol use. They partially attribute this to the ways in which societal attitudes do not support the program's message for not using alcohol in the same ways societal attitudes support the nonuse of cigarettes and marijuana.

This is exemplified in the difficulty the program had in modifying the students' beliefs about peer use of alcohol. The hope was that students would recognize that fewer peers used alcohol than was believed. The technique used was a comparison of perceived use by peers to the peers' actual use. If 50% of one's peers are using alcohol, however, there is "little potential for dampening their motivations to drink" (Ellickson et al., 1991, p. 26). In other words, there is little chance that the students will overestimate use to such an extent that dissonance between perceived use and actual use will be created. In fact, the possibility of a boomerang effect is highly likely, whereby students who are *not* drinking may feel that they are unusual and should start drinking. Across the schools the use of alcohol by 7th graders was about 49%, making this technique relatively useless.

The groups led by adults who utilized teen leaders were somewhat more effective, though not substantially. The cognitive factors most differentially affected by groups with teen leaders were that the students were more likely to take on antidrug attitudes, to feel increased self-efficacy, to believe friends did not tolerate use, and to believe friends respected resistance. These remained after 15 months.

Over all groups, Project ALERT had a greater impact on beliefs about the social and addictive consequences of drug use than on normative perceptions, expected use, and resistance self-efficacy (Ellickson et al., 1991). The extent of these outcomes varied by the baseline risk status of the students. This was most significant for students who had used alcohol prior to program implementation. Most students had tried alcohol before implementation and their experiences had "already shaped perceptions about their own ability to resist alcohol, as well as its likely effects and its acceptability to others" (p. 26). These experiences in conjunction with societal norms about alcohol consumption made it very difficult to change the cognitive risk factors of normative perceptions, expected use, and resistance self-efficacy surrounding alcohol.

In a fashion similar to the evaluation of Life Skills Training, Project ALERT was also assessed immediately after the cessation of the booster sessions and not beyond (Ellickson et al., 1991), making it difficult to understand if program effects outlast the time period within which the program is implemented. Project ALERT's efficacy in altering cognitive risk factors was highest for marijuana and tobacco. With alcohol, the program was not able to show changes in risky cognitions, especially for youth who had experimented with alcohol already. In fact, it appears that the program was effective only in changing cognitions about substances that were not supported by norms in our society at the same time that boosters were being implemented (i.e., marijuana and tobacco). Therefore, in terms of how to maintain changes within youth, boosters may affect risk factors for smoking behavior, yet factors that place youth at risk for experimenting with alcohol are unlikely to be altered, with or without boosters.

Midwestern Prevention Project

The Midwestern Prevention Project's use of research findings and current theory is much more comprehensive than any of the aforementioned programs (Johnson et al., 1990). For example, they make a specific attempt to affect youth at high risk for substance use because current studies show that (a) these youth seem to have the least amount of access to prevention programs and community services for early intervention, (b) a lack of change in drug-abuse treatment rates among high-risk populations suggests that "current community prevention/education efforts may not be affecting these groups" (Johnson et al., 1990, p. 449), and (c) these youth are often at high risk for other problem behaviors, such as delinquency and school failure (Johnson et al., 1990). In other words, they believe that if high-risk youth are not affected by prevention efforts, the prevention efforts have come to naught. This reasoning is in line with Newcomb and Bentler's (1989) interpretation of the findings of Tobler's (1986) meta-analysis of drug and alcohol prevention programs:

> It is misleading to bask in the success of some peer programs that have reduced the number of youngsters who experiment with drugs (but would probably never have become regular users, let alone abusers) and ignore the tougher problems of those youngsters who are at high risk for drug abuse as well as other serious difficulties. (Newcomb & Bentler, 1989, p. 246)

The prevention program itself is based on previous, relatively effective programs that have utilized concepts such as youth peer pressure resistance; inoculation against mass media messages; perceptions of social norms; social comparison; person perception, attributional, and social learning processes; "the special vulnerability of young adolescents to social influences"; adolescent drug use as a sign of independence because it represents adult behavior; self-esteem and self-image enhancement; affective education; and an emphasis on healthy living behaviors (Johnson et al., 1990, p. 448).

Because programs that utilize only one channel for affecting youth (e.g., school education programs for prevention) have not been effective in producing long-term changes in adolescent substance-use behavior, the Midwestern Prevention Project is comprehensive. Their comprehensive community intervention consists of four components. The program is implemented during the middle school years when attendance is still mandatory. The four components of the program are:

a) a 10-session school program emphasizing drug use resistance skills training, delivered at Grade 6 or 7, with homework sessions involving active interviews and role plays with parents and family members;

b) a parent organization program for reviewing school prevention policy and training parents in positive parent-child communication skills;

c) initial training of community leaders in the organization of a drug abuse prevention task force; and

d) mass media coverage. (Johnson et al., 1990, p. 451)

Because the control and treatment schools are within the same communities, the control groups receive components (c) and (d). The treatment groups receive all four. The Midwestern Prevention Project also receives extensive media coverage, with all schools having the same access to the coverage. When discussing the Midwestern Prevention Project's adequacy of implementation evaluation, the first thing Cook et al. (1993) point out is that two different research groups conducted the evaluation. One group was primarily interested in the program's impact on substance use (researchers at the University of Southern California [USC]); the other was primarily interested in managing and studying program implementation (program developers in Kansas City). The USC team, however, did not leave the implementation evaluation entirely up to the program developers. Some implementation data were collected directly from the teachers in addition to the "less systematical data from program developers" (Cook et al., 1993, p. 360). Cook et al. suggested that the Midwestern Prevention Project evaluators "conduct a multi-method description of implementation quality" with these two sets of information. Analyses of the teacher data alone indicated a high level of implementation (i.e., some of the material was taught in all the treatment groups, "an average of 8.76 sessions lasting 40 minutes was devoted to the curriculum," and deviations from the curriculum were additions to the curriculum, not substitutions) (pp. 361-362). Cook et al. stated that the small number of treatment schools prevented a comparison of outcomes between schools that were high or low implementers.

The fact that nothing is known about what is occurring in the control schools in the Midwestern Prevention Project was brought up by Cook et al. (1993). Apparently, by not assessing the level of "program relevant activities" at each control school, the Midwestern

Prevention Project is assuming that each of these schools is the same and that none of them are implementing any programs slightly similar to the Midwestern Prevention Project's curriculum. Without accurate information the experimental process cannot "assess the consequences of treatment *contrasts*" (p. 361), thus leaving the evaluators with insufficient information about how to interpret outcomes at the different schools. In fact, Cook et al. made this same observation about Life Skills Training.

Cook et al. (1993) also discussed that individual curriculum components were not measured. They view such measurement as desirable because they are interested in seeing which components are taught most often, how well they are taught, and if there is a relationship between these implementation variables and program efficacy.

As stated earlier, the Midwestern Prevention Project extends beyond the school setting to the community through its mass media components. Because all who are in the community are potential recipients of this component, however, the mass media component is really "part of the context in which the intervention is embedded" and not *part* of the intervention itself (Cook et al., 1993, p. 361). Although part of the context that the Midwestern Prevention Project attends to is the amount and content of the media presentations, none of the outcome variables have been connected directly to the media delivery—for example: "no awareness or attitude surveys have been carried out to determine the saliency of the media or their impact on general community knowledge or attitudes (norms) about drug use" (p. 361). The same types of assessments are missing for the parent, community, and policy components.

Analyses of causal mediation are more elusive for the Midwestern Prevention Project than for Life Skills Training because the program is not only based in several different theories but implemented across numerous settings and is implemented one component after/ before another. Therefore, Cook et al. (1993) claimed that "it will be very difficult to determine which set of program components is responsible for any global effects achieved" (p. 362).

An analysis of mediating variables that *was* conducted revealed that reduction in cigarette use was caused by changes in students' perceptions of how their friends would react if they smoked (Cook et al., 1993). Cook et al. concluded this supported a social norm change explanation. The evaluator challenged this model with the opposing theory that drug use might have changed prior to a change in students' perceptions of their peers' reactions. This model did not fit the data as well. Cook et al. commend this particular Midwestern Prevention Project evaluation for utilizing opposing models of change.

A problem in mediating variables that Cook et al. (1993) pointed out was that, once again, resistance skills do not appear to have the primary role in changing behavior that their eclectic model credits to such skills. Cook et al. admitted that these skills may not have been measured by reliable instruments and that that might have made "better" measured variables appear superior. Interestingly, they connected this effect to the Life Skills Training program by stating that resistance skills have not yet been demonstrated to play the crucial mediating role and that knowing more about social norms might help uncover a major mediator. In summary, Cook et al. view the Midwestern Prevention Project as fully equipped to answer questions that other program developers may not be as skilled at answering (i.e., efforts at prevention that are not funded by research institutes). Aside from the social norm possibility, Cook et al. posited that certain key mediating variables that may play important roles (e.g., self-efficacy to resist peer pressure) have yet to be measured.

The Midwestern Prevention Project *outcome* evaluation focused on assessing the moderating influence of prior drug use, social environment (use by parents and friends), gender, age, and experimental condition on current drug use (Johnson et al., 1990). Data were collected 3 years following the implementation of the school program, whether it was implemented in 6th or 7th grade. The substance-use measure was a self-report questionnaire on the use of tobacco, alcohol, and marijuana in the past 30 days. This was a dichotomous variable, coded as either *yes* or *no*. Johnson et al. did not categorize more specifically by level of use because they argued that *any* use in youth, especially in terms of cigarette use, "is abusive because amount of exposure to tobacco smoke is related linearly to heart disease and lung cancer" (p. 454). Finally, "each student was measured for CO [carbon monoxide] level at each measurement wave" in order to "increase the accuracy of subsequent student self-reported drug use" (p. 452). Program effects corresponded highly between self-reported use and CO expiration when either was used as the dependent variable.

At the 3-year follow-up, two major findings emerged. First, even though "prevalence rates for all three substances increased over time, . . . the rate of increase for tobacco and marijuana was less for adolescents in the program schools than for those in the control schools" (Johnson et al., 1990, p. 453). Thus it appears that the 2-year ceiling on program effects has been altered. There were still no effects for alcohol use, however. Second, the program did *not* have a differential impact on youth dependent on their risk status at baseline. This finding is especially exciting given that high-risk youth have not been affected by the same programs that affect youth at other risk levels. In other words, it appears that the multicomponent community-based structure of the Midwestern Prevention Project has somehow reached these elusive youth, while maintaining efficacy with lower risk youth.

Therefore, what stands out about the Midwestern Prevention Project is that changes were maintained within individuals over time—3 years—*without* booster sessions (Johnson et al., 1990). Perhaps what served as booster sessions for this program was the media component. This can only be speculation, however, because no assessments were done on the media component. Even so, because this program stands out for maintaining change over time without boosters and because what makes this program different from the others is the multicomponent nature of the program, *not* some new conceptualization in the school-based intervention, one can argue that there is compelling evidence that change within individuals over time can be fostered through utilizing the multiple tools of prevention (Gullotta, 1987).

Unfortunately, these effects did not exist for alcohol-related behavior, only for marijuana and tobacco use. This once again indicates that changes at the societal level may be needed if real improvements are to occur for youth. Johnson et al. (1990) conclude that "community support of drug prevention practices and a social norm for nondrug use" is necessary to change adolescent substance use behavior (pp. 449-450).

The initial conceptual model for the Midwestern Prevention Project (Pentz et al., 1989) included intervention in the local government that would specifically address community systems change through rethinking billboard advertisements and other community messages about drug and alcohol use. At this time it is not clear from the current literature whether efforts for this desired change have begun. Lack of information about this could be due to (a) the qualitative nature of measuring such change; (b) the length of time it takes for community support to be garnered for such reorganization;

and/or (c) some prevention tools may be easier to implement (e.g., education: changes and/or additions in school curriculum) than others (e.g., community organization: changes in community support for alcohol use). Unfortunately, when some tools of prevention are easier to implement than others, only a portion of preventions goals are addressed.

Adolescent Alcohol Prevention Trial

The Adolescent Alcohol Prevention Trial compared the effects of two conceptually different prevention programs: Resistance Training and Normative Training (Hansen, Graham, Wolkenstein, & Rohrbach, 1991). Resistance Training is a skills training program focused on teaching how to resist "overt social pressures" for using substances; Normative Training is focused on creating "conservative normative beliefs about the prevalence and acceptability of alcohol and drug use" (p. 570). These two programs were combined with Information about Consequences of Use (ICU), a knowledge-focused component that identifies the social and health consequences of substance use, to create four comparison groups: Normative Training with ICU (NORM); Resistance Training with ICU (RT); a combination of Normative Training, Resistance Training, and ICU; and ICU alone.

These programs were delivered to 3,500 fifth-grade students in 44 schools over the course of nine weekly sessions (ICU alone was only four sessions long) (Hansen et al., 1991). In order to assess implementation, those who conducted the sessions rated the degree to which they had "maintained program integrity, including assessments of their own performance and of students' responses to the program" (p. 572). In addition, trained observers used the same rating scales and rated at least one session per class of students.

In order to see if there were differential outcomes depending on the mediating processes the program targeted, Hansen et al. (1991) measured a wide range of mediating variables. What they found was that participants in RT had greater knowledge of the effects of substance use, ability to refuse substances, and intent to refuse substances than those in the ICU alone group. In contrast, those in NORM had higher self-efficacy and lowered perceptions about the acceptability and prevalence of substance use in the school. Those in the combined program had lower scores on peer pressure knowledge than did those in RT.

In another study done on the same sample (Graham, Collins, Wugalter, Chung, & Hansen, 1991), previous substance-use patterns moderated the impact of NORM on participants. For students who had tried only tobacco prior to the 7th grade, the program was ineffective, compared to those who had either not used any substances or tried only alcohol.

In addition to assessing the varying impact of these programs, Hansen et al. looked at the integrity of program delivery to see how different levels of integrity moderated the effects of the programs. Classrooms were categorized according to high and low integrity, where *high* was the upper two thirds of the range and *low* was the bottom third. In RT classrooms in which program integrity was high, there was an increased level of self-efficacy, resistance knowledge, and ability to resist peer pressure. Similarly, there were increased levels of knowledge and skill in refusing peer pressure in NORM groups with high integrity. Given these results from the Alcohol Prevention Trial it is clear that there is important information to be gained when evaluations rise to the challenge of addressing the important links between theory, program implementation, mediating processes, and outcomes.

ADDITIONAL
CONCEPTUAL CONCERNS

In addition to utilizing the results of program evaluation, evaluators need to use findings of developmental research to improve their programs. Summaries of some very insightful criticisms of prevention programs are now discussed from a developmental perspective.

The criticism that Levanthal and Keeshan (1993) most strongly assert against current prevention programs is that they ignore the "adolescent and drug interaction" (p. 26). Their self-regulation model predicts that experimentation and continued use of substances will occur when the rewards of drug use exceed the punishments:

> The experience with use will include emotional reactions and moods that are direct effects of the drug and of the bodily sensations and *interpretations* given the somatic sensations the drugs create. The expe-

rience during use will be further affected by beliefs and expectations
respecting future benefits and losses from continued substance use.
(p. 26)

In other words, if youth are having fun drinking alcohol and/or
using drugs and are forming friendships around substance use,
programs that do not help the students have *more* fun, feel good, and
have *better* friendships will not be effective.

Levanthal and Keeshan argue that this dynamic is compounded
by the fact that many high-risk youth do not see alternatives in
adulthood (that do not involve substance use) as personally appli-
cable to them. In other words, a program that assumes that all youth
perceive rewarding adult roles as real options for them is disregard-
ing the possibility that substance use is much more rewarding to
some youth than the other options they perceive as available to
them. Levanthal and Keeshan believe that discussing drug use as
something that closes off the number of options a youth has available makes more sense than attempting to get a youth to visualize
a specific career goal at this age.

The second lesson Levanthal and Keeshan (1993) claim has been
learned is that "methodological improvements alone will not lead
to improved outcomes" (p. 17). This lesson was learned in response
to the hope that improved research methods would show that
existing programs reduce substance use. Because well-designed, carefully executed, and thoroughly evaluated programs have *not* produced results that persist beyond 9th grade (2 years after 7th grade,
when most programs are implemented), Levanthal and Keeshan
assert, doing more of the same, even with improvements, will not
lead to superior outcomes for youth.

Therefore, Levanthal and Keeshan suggest that program developers consider using the following factors when developing new
programs:

1. Attach concrete personal risk perceptions to the target behavior to
   generate motivation to avoid the behavior;
2. Undermine the motivation to use substances in order to satisfy certain
   basic needs (e.g., need for affiliation and regulation of affect);
3. Increase the salience and desirability of alternative behaviors that satisfy
   the same needs that substance use is perceived as fulfilling; and

4. Establish and promote goals incompatible with use that are consistent with the adolescent's needs and aspirations (adapted from Levanthal & Keeshan, 1993, pp. 18-19).

In other words, substance-use prevention programs must promote social competence: (a) a sense that the youth belongs; (b) a sense that the youth is valued; and (c) opportunities for the youth to contribute meaningfully (Gullotta, 1989).

Moreover, Shedler and Block (1990) argue that most preventive education efforts pathologize "normative adolescent experimentation" by viewing abstinence as the desirable outcome of intervention efforts and they *"trivialize* the factors underlying drug *abuse,* implicitly denying their depth and pervasiveness," by seeing substance use in adolescents as a result of a lack of education or ability to resist peer pressure (p. 628).

Shedler and Block (1990) conclude that prevention efforts should be aimed much more at reducing individual susceptibility to substance abuse *instead* of being aimed at preventing experimentation, a behavior that may be impossible, if not undesirable, to eliminate. Their strong feelings about focusing on susceptibility are based in research that has shown that there is a select population for whom experimentation with drugs is highly destructive. They are *not* arguing, therefore, that efforts to prevent substance use should be curtailed. Instead, they argue that the focus of prevention programs must shift from a focus on preventing experimentation to a focus that more closely matches the reality of youth who are at high risk for developing long-term problems with substance abuse.

This argument is supported by the results of Tobler's (1986) meta-analysis, in which she found that what works for low-risk youth is ineffective with high-risk youth. From Tobler's meta-analysis it appears that Peer Programs, which focus on resistance skills training, are effective in the short term for average students. For at-risk youth, Alternatives (utilizing adventure programming and community service, without a specific focus on substance use) appear effective. Perhaps this success is a result of how "this type of program helps to put a child in the special population in *control* of some part of his life for the first time" (Tobler, 1986, p. 561). As stated before, note that at-risk youth are being separated from the general youth population as a group that needs an approach that is different from the rest. This is consistent with the conceptual arguments of

Shedler and Block (1990), Johnson et al. (1990), and Levanthal and Keeshan (1993), who agree that substance-use prevention must specifically address the needs of those at risk. The ideal prevention will therefore need (a) to stay conscious of the complete definition of prevention and (b) to utilize all of the tools of prevention (Gullotta, 1987), because problematic developmental outcomes arise from transactions *between* individuals and their environments (Felner & Felner, 1989), not from a singular cause within each youth.

CONCLUSIONS

Given what has been presented in this chapter, knowledge of where to go next with substance-use prevention's experimenting society is readily available. It is hoped that evaluators will respond to this accessibility of ways for improving substance-use prevention with evaluation research that avoids known pitfalls and difficulties —which may be difficult, given limited resources. Because of concerns about how best to allocate resources, evaluators need to engage the challenge with their eyes open to the complexities of substance-use prevention. The following points summarize the suggestions made in this chapter.

1. Those who design substance-use prevention programs and those who evaluate them need to stay cognizant of the multiple goals of primary prevention: (a) to anticipate problems (Goldston, 1977); (b) to reduce the number of new cases; (c) to promote competencies that protect against the development of problems (Felner et al., 1983); and (d) to encourage optimal health (Goldston, 1977).

2. Intervening at the level of the individual is not enough. Not only do programs need to consider multiple levels of intervention, but when decisions are made to work at different levels there must be assurance that those programs are actually occurring. Therefore, thorough assessments of the large social context can and should be conducted.

3. In order to be effective, programs need to reach both high-risk and normal-risk youth. Programs that include community-level components seem to be most effective for high-risk youth, and programs based in skills training and social norm changing seem to work

with normal-risk youth. These two types of programs can be implemented simultaneously.

4. Social norms about substance use may be more salient than the ability to resist pressure to use substances. This is indicated by the fact that (a) the majority of the programs have not been able to affect alcohol use; (b) when skills have been measured for how they affect substance use, there has been no impact for resistance skills (this may be due to poor measurement); (c) there is a large amount of interschool variability in initial substance-use levels; and (d) booster sessions seem to prolong the effects of interventions. Therefore, creative means (e.g., qualitative methods) for examining these norms can be utilized in order to create an empirical base for future quantitative assessment.

5. Conceptualizations about the relationship between youth and drugs need to be expanded beyond models that assume that the reasons youth use drugs are because they do not have enough information and they are pressured to use drugs. Future programs need to explore the rewarding role that drugs may play in the lives of youth and think of ways to make incompatible alternatives desirable. Programs also need to explore the factors that make certain youth at risk for substance-use problems (e.g., inability to enjoy personal relationships, lack of meaningful goals, lack of parental warmth) (Shedler & Block, 1990) and include them in their programs. Once again, substance-use prevention programs must promote competencies and reduce risk.

6. Implementation evaluation can be improved through steps such as thoroughly assessing comparison groups and gathering information about how programs are implemented at various sites. As described before, the implementation phase is one of the most important information links between treatment and outcome. In my opinion it would greatly benefit the prevention field if a journal existed solely for the purpose of reporting treatment fidelity. The standards for submission to this journal would not be to document perfect implementation but to report the level of implementation, whether "poor" or "excellent." Such information would aid in our understanding of the degree to which programs are followed and how much they *need* to be followed. Ideally, being accepted for publication in this journal would be a requirement *prior* to reporting about any outcomes.

7. Causal mediating variables should be assessed. If such information could be gathered about how well specific techniques work for specific outcomes, those individuals who make choices about prevention programming within schools would be served much more adequately than they have been so far. At this point, information is not available about how well different programs work with different populations. Such information could be invaluable to decision makers.

8. Evaluators have the responsibility of going beyond simplistic models of change to complex models that address the realities of substance use by adolescents.

CLOSING COMMENTS

The people who are involved in the creation, promotion, and evaluation of programs to prevent substance-use problems in youth are some of the most energetic, enthusiastic, and hopeful in the helping professions. They aspire to prevent unnecessary human suffering and to promote the highest quality of living for all. If their energy to improve the human condition can be partially channeled in the service of the comments above, our understanding of how to prevent substance use will be greatly enhanced. This will spill over into an increasing array of informed and effective programs for youth.

REFERENCES

Albee, G. (1985). The argument for primary prevention. *Journal of Primary Prevention,* 5(4), 238-241.

Bandura, A. (1977). Self-efficacy: Toward a unifying theory of behavioral change. *Psychological Review, 84,* 191-215.

Bloom, M. (1993). Toward a code of ethics for primary prevention. *The Journal of Primary Prevention, 13*(3), 173-182.

Botvin, G., Baker, E., Renick, N., Filazzola, A., & Botvin, E. (1984). A cognitive-behavioral approach to substance abuse prevention. *Addictive Behaviors, 9,* 137-147.

Botvin, G., & Tortu, S. (1988). Preventing adolescent substance abuse through life skills training. In R. Price (Ed.), *Fourteen ounces of prevention: A casebook for practitioners* (pp. 98-110). Washington, DC: American Psychological Association.

Campbell, D. (1971, April). *Methods for the experimenting society.* Paper presented at the meetings of the Eastern Psychological Association, Washington, DC.

Caplan, M., Weissberg, R., Grober, J., Sivo, P., Grady, K., & Jacoby, C. (1992). Social competence promotion with inner-city and suburban young adolescents: Effects on social adjustment and alcohol use. *Journal of Consulting and Clinical Psychology, 60*(1), 56-63.

Chen, H., & Rossi, P. (1987). The theory-driven approach to validity. *Evaluation and Program Planning, 10*, 95-103.

Cook, T. D., Anson, A. R., & Walchli, S. B. (1993). From causal description to causal explanation: Improving three already good evaluations of adolescent health programs. In S. G. Millstein, A. C. Petersen, & E. O. Nightingale (Eds.), *Promoting the health of adolescents: New directions for the twenty-first century* (pp. 339-374). New York: Oxford University Press.

Crockett, L. J., & Petersen, A. C. (1993). Adolescent development: Health risks and opportunities for health promotion. In S. G. Millstein, A. C. Petersen, & E. O. Nightingale (Eds.), *Promoting the health of adolescents: New directions for the twenty-first century* (pp. 13-37). New York: Oxford University Press.

Dodge, K. (1991, April). *On the empirical basis for preventive intervention.* Paper presented at the biennial meeting of the Society for Research in Child Development, Seattle, WA.

Ellickson, P., & Bell, R. (1990). Drug prevention in junior high: A multi-site longitudinal test. *Science, 247*, 1265-1372.

Ellickson, P., & Bell, R. (1992). *Challenges to social experiments: A drug prevention example.* Santa Monica, CA: RAND.

Ellickson, P., Bell, R., & Harrison, E. (1991, August). *Changing adolescent motivations to use drugs: Results from Project ALERT.* Paper presented at the 99th Annual Convention of the American Psychological Association, San Francisco, CA.

Felner, R., & Felner, T. (1989). Primary prevention programs in the educational context: A transactional-ecological framework and analysis. In L. Bond & B. Compas (Eds.), *Primary prevention and promotion in the schools* (pp. 13-49). Newbury Park, CA: Sage.

Felner, R., Jason, L., Moritsugu, J., & Farber, S. (1983). Prevention psychology: Evaluation and current status. In R. Felner, L. Jason, J. Moritsugu, & S. Farber (Eds.), *Prevention psychology: Theory, research, and practice* (pp. 3-10). Elmsford, NY: Pergamon.

Flay, B. (1985). Psychosocial approaches to smoking prevention: A review of findings. *Health Psychology, 4*(5), 449-488.

Flay, B., Koepke, D., Thomson, S., Santi, S., Best, J. A., & Brown, K. S. (1989). Six-year follow-up of the first Waterloo school smoking prevention trial. *American Journal of Public Health, 79*(10), 1371-1376.

Flay, B., Ryan, K., Best, J. A., Brown, K. S., Kersell, M., d'Avernas, J., & Zanna, M. (1985). Are social-psychological smoking prevention programs effective? The Waterloo study. *Journal of Behavioral Medicine, 8*(1), 37-59.

Goldston, S. (1977). Defining primary prevention. In G. Albee and J. Joffee (Eds.), *Primary prevention psychopathology: Vol. 1. The issues.* Hanover, NH: University Press of New England.

Graham, J., Collins, L., Wugalter, S., Chung, N., & Hansen, W. (1991). Modeling transitions in latent stage-sequential processes: A substance use prevention example. *Journal of Consulting and Clinical Psychology, 59*(1), 48-57.

Guba, E., & Lincoln, Y. (1989). *Fourth generation evaluation.* Newbury Park, CA: Sage.

Gullotta, T. P. (1989). Preface. In T. P. Gulllotta, G. R. Adams, R. Montemayer (Eds.), *Developing social competency in adolescence*. Newbury Park, CA: Sage.

Hansen, W. (1992). School-based substance abuse prevention: A review of the state of the art in curriculum, 1980-1990. *Health Education Research, 7*, 403-430.

Hansen, W., Graham, J., Wolkenstein, B., & Rohrbach, L. (1991). Program integrity as a moderator of prevention program effectiveness: Results for fifth-grade students in the Adolescent Alcohol Prevention Trial. *Journal of Studies on Alcohol, 52*(6), 568-579.

Heller, K. (1984). Introduction. In K. Heller, R. Price, S. Reinharz, S. Riger, A. Wandersman, & T. D'Aunno (Eds.), *Psychology and community change: Challenges of the future* (pp. 172-226). Pacific Grove, CA: Brooks/Cole.

Janz, N., & Becker, M. (1984). The health belief model: A decade later. *Health Education Quarterly, 11*(1), 1-47.

Jessor, R., & Jessor, S. (1977). *Problem behavior and psychosocial development: A longitudinal study of youth*. New York: Academic Press.

Johnson, C. A., Pentz, M., Weber, M., Dwyer, J., Baer, N., MacKinnon, D., & Hansen, W. (1990). Relative effectiveness of comprehensive community programming for drug abuse prevention with high-risk and low-risk adolescents. *Journal of Consulting and Clinical Psychology, 58*(4), 447-456.

Kandel, D. (1980). Drug and drinking behavior among youth. *Annual Review of Sociology, 6*, 235-285.

Kandel, D., & Logan, R. (1984). Patterns of drug use from adolescence to young adulthood: I. Periods of risk for initiation, continued use, and discontinuation. *American Journal of Public Health, 74*, 660-666.

Levanthal, H., & Keeshan, P. (1993). Promoting healthy alternatives to substance abuse. In S. G. Millstein, A. C. Petersen, & E. O. Nightingale (Eds.), *Promoting the health of adolescents: New directions for the twenty-first century* (pp. 260-284). New York: Oxford University Press.

Lewin, K. (1951). *Field theory in social science*. New York: Harper & Row.

Linney, J. (1989). Optimizing research strategies in the schools. In L. Bond & B. Compas (Eds.), *Primary prevention and promotion in the schools* (pp. 50-76). Newbury Park, CA: Sage.

Newcomb, M., & Bentler, P. (1989). Substance use and abuse among children and teenagers. *American Psychologist, 44*(2), 242-248.

Palumbo, D., & Oliverio, A. (1989). Implementation theory and the theory-driven approach to validity. *Evaluation and Program Planning, 12*, 337-344.

Patterson, G. (1986). Performance models for antisocial boys. *American Psychologist, 41*(4), 432-444.

Patton, M. (1989). A context and boundaries for a theory-driven approach to validity. *Evaluation and Program Planning, 12*, 375-377.

Pentz, M., Dwyer, J., MacKinnon, D., Flay, B., Hansen, W., Wang, E., & Johnson, C. A. (1989). A multicommunity trial for primary prevention of adolescent drug abuse. *Journal of the American Medical Association, 261*(22), 3259-3266.

Perry, C. (1987). Results of prevention programs with adolescents. *Drug and Alcohol Dependence, 20*, 13-19.

Perry, C., & Kelder, S. (1992). Models for effective prevention. *Journal of Adolescent Health, 13*, 355-363.

Shedler, J., & Block, J. (1990). Adolescent drug use and psychological health: A longitudinal inquiry. *American Psychologist, 45*(5), 612-630.

Tobler, N. (1986). Meta-analysis of 143 adolescent drug prevention programs: Quantitative outcome results of program participants compared to a control or comparison group. *Journal of Drug Issues, 16*(4), 537-567.

Tobler, N. (1992). Drug prevention programs can work: Research findings. *Journal of Addictive Diseases, 11*(3), 1-28.

Trochim, W. (1989). Outcome pattern matching and program theory. *Evaluation and Program Planning, 12,* 355-366.

Weissberg, R., Caplan, M., & Sivo, P. (1989). A new conceptual framework for establishing school-based social competence promotion programs. In L. Bond & B. Compas (Eds.), *Primary prevention and promotion in the schools* (pp. 255-296). Newbury Park, CA: Sage.

Woodhead, M. (1988). When psychology informs public policy: The case of early childhood intervention. *American Psychologist, 43*(6), 443-454.

10. Social Policy and Adolescent Drug Consumption: The Legalization Option

Thomas Nicholson
Western Kentucky University

INTRODUCTION

Progress toward the amelioration of adolescent drug problems will require a rational, comprehensive U.S. drug policy. Strategies should have a sound scientific base and emphasize primary prevention. Wherever possible, the goal of our activities should be the prevention of drug abuse rather than the criminalization of behavior. Because much of the abusive drug behavior in adults begins in adolescence the additional benefits of such a policy should be an overall reduction in drug abuse within the United States.

The development of drug policy during the 20th century has been a gradual progression toward stronger criminalization efforts. Prior to this time, most commerce in and use of psychoactive substances were uncontrolled by the federal government. In 1906, Congress passed the Pure Food and Drug Act to prohibit the interstate commerce of adulterated or misbranded foods and drugs. A plethora of later laws—including the Harrison Act of 1914, the Jones-Miller Act of 1922, the 1937 Marijuana Tax Act, the 1951 Boggs Amendment to the Harrison Act, the 1956 Narcotic Drug Control Act, the Comprehensive Drug Abuse Prevention and Control Act of 1970, and the 1988 Omnibus Drug Act—focused increasingly harsher and more restrictive controls on psychoactive drugs (Ray & Ksir, 1990). Since 1980, during the War on Drugs an estimated $35 billion were spent combating illegal drugs, with more than 70% of this money being spent on interdiction and law enforcement efforts. This has contributed to more than one million people being incarcerated; twice the prison population in 1980. The majority of this increase is due to nonviolent drug offenders (American Public Health Association [APHA], 1992). Antidrug laws are based on three key assumptions: (a) the consumption of recreational, psychoactive drugs (excluding alcohol and tobacco) is always harmful to the individual, (b) society suffers an inordinate burden from the use of these substances, and (c) laws and law enforcement programs can effectively eliminate their production, distribution, and consumption. The validity of these notions has been *assumed* or based on emotions and unsubstantiated opinions but never actually verified by historical reality or research.

The majority of Americans have accepted these approaches as commonsense ideas. Surely if drugs are illegal, law abiding citizens will avoid them—and those people who break the law will be arrested and removed from society. Thus fear of both the often alluded to hazards of drug consumption and the threat of going to jail is expected to protect society. As we shall discuss later, these results have not come to pass. More Americans use and abuse drugs than ever before; many individuals from government, law enforcement, and the health professions are becoming keenly aware of the invalidity of the aforementioned assumptions and expectations about drugs, laws, and individual behavior.

As we approach the 21st century it is apparent that drug consumption has occurred throughout the history of humankind. An assortment of drugs have been consumed for recreational, therapeutic, and religious reasons. In America today most, if not all, Americans consume psychoactive drugs (Duncan & Gold, 1982). Legal products such as alcohol, tobacco, coffee, tea, chocolate, and certain prescription drugs are widely consumed. Less widely used are the predominantly illegal drugs such as heroin, cocaine, and marijuana. These drugs have been *used* with no or minimal ill effects and *abused* with tragic human consequences. It also is apparent that myriad factors contribute to psychoactive drug consumption. As Schlaadt and Shannon (1990) state:

> The reasons individuals use psychoactive substances vary as much as the individuals themselves: to find sexual fulfillment, to seek spiritual enlightenment, to have fun, to produce mood fluctuations, to enhance athletic performance, to reduce inhibitions in bar settings, to fight boredom, to satisfy curiosity, to be "in" opposed to "left out." (p. 16)

Ray and Ksir (1990) state that people consume drugs either to reduce the pain or increase the pleasure in their lives. Recent research has begun to illuminate basic biological and genetic factors that relate to consuming drugs (Cloninger, Bohman, & Sigvardsson, 1981; Collins & deFiebre, 1990; Goodwin, 1971; Huber & Omenn, 1981). Human drug consumption is thus of multifactorial origin. Any attempt to mitigate drug abuse, such as eliminating or controlling adolescent drug consumption, must take into consideration these factors.

It is important to remember that not all drug consumption is harmful. Most psychoactive drugs are used with no or minimal health consequences by 90% of the people who consume them, whereas 10% of consumers are abusers. The major exceptions to this are tobacco consumers, 90% of whom are abusers. *Drug use* is defined as taking a drug in such a manner that the sought for effects are attained with minimal hazard. *Drug misuse* occurs when a drug is taken or administered under circumstances and at doses that significantly increase the hazard to the individual or to others. *Drug abuse* is defined as taking a drug to such an extent that it greatly increases the danger or impairs the ability of an individual to function or cope with his or her circumstances adequately (Irwin, 1973).

It must also be remembered that the legal status of drugs (i.e., licit or illicit) is not based on their potential for abuse. For example, in the United States in 1988 the illegal drug cocaine was directly responsible for about 1,600 deaths, whereas the legal drug tobacco killed 390,000 people (U.S. Department of Health and Human Services, 1989).

With regard to adolescents, I take the view that most consumption of tobacco, alcohol, or illegal drugs is misuse, but more practically it is transient experimentation. Most drug consumption should fall into the category of "adult behavior" (e.g., voting, marriage, military service, etc.). As will be discussed later, however, eliminating adolescent drug use/misuse may not be feasible given the very real motivations behind human, including adolescent, drug consumption. It may also not be necessary from the public health standpoint of disease prevention and health promotion. Of the millions of U.S. high school students who experiment with or use drugs, the majority exercise restraints and/or obey social controls in their drug-taking behavior. Most importantly, the majority will go on to adulthood without a drug-abuse problem (The Drug Abuse Council, 1980). In fact, the overwhelming majority of all U.S. adolescents grow into adulthood without a drug problem. The question is, then, how can we affect the minority of adolescents who do develop a drug problem?

Unfortunately, programs and policies of recent decades have not significantly impacted on adolescents who have developed drug problems. Usage rates fluctuate over time, and the popularity of specific drugs varies, but drug use and abuse continues to occur. It can be argued that U.S. drug laws, policies, and attitudes have been ineffective in preventing this abuse and have also been maladaptive. Illicit drugs are widely available despite decades of intense law enforcement efforts to limit their availability. Approximately 10% of regular users of these drugs are dependent on them in some fashion and suffer substantial negative consequences. More than 50 million Americans are addicted to alcohol and/or tobacco. The costs of these abuses are staggering. Cocaine is now the most profitable article of trade in the world and a $100 billion a year business in the United States alone ("It Doesn't Have," 1989). Significant negative drug-related consequences are also felt in the areas of health, family relations, legal systems, and economic productivity (APHA, 1989).

Attempts to eliminate drug consumption through legal approaches have obviously failed. In a free society such as the United States, prohibition is a fundamentally flawed approach. For example, during alcohol prohibition alcohol use was discouraged for only some people, changes in use/abuse levels were modest, and consumption remained pervasive in society (Burnham, 1968; Duncan & Gold, 1982; Emerson, 1932; Gusfield, 1976). Lemert (1967) and Marshall and Marshall (1990) note that alcohol prohibition has been tried in Finland, Norway, and the United States, but that it always fails to prevent some people from drinking. Lemert (1967) argues that alcohol prohibition failed historically (a) because it costs too much, (b) because of the instability of power bases that support it, (c) because pockets of societal resistance grow, and (d) because of the inherent limitations of power and societal control. In other words, it is impossible for a diverse society such as the United States, with its strong passion for individual freedom and privacy, to prohibit drug consumption legally. There are simply not enough police to monitor and prisons to hold all of the people who consume drugs. Considering that the majority of these users are otherwise law-abiding, tax paying, functional citizens, do we really want to put them in jail? We already have the world's highest rate of incarceration: 1 out of 25 American males is currently in jail or on probation (Smart, 1992).

It is also becoming apparent that many of our drug problems are the result of our drug policies rather than drug consumption itself (Table 10.1). These problems are the direct result of our legalistic

TABLE 10.1 Societal Effects of Drug Control Activities

Crime, violence, and loss of life
Corruption
Disruption to economic development and increase in national debt
Emergence of black/counterfeit markets
Disruption of agricultural development
Damage to ecosystems
Increase in health problems
Loss or repression of cultural traditions
Militarization and attacks on civilians
Straining of international relations
Loss of civil liberties and personal rights
Conflicts between races, classes, and nationalities (countries)
Infringement of sovereignty and territoriality
Disruption and destabilization of social, political, and judicial institutions

SOURCE: From "Societal Consequences of International Illicit Drug Trafficking and Supply-Reduction Efforts" by M. Montagne, in *Strategies for Change: New Directions for Drug Policy*, Drug Policy Foundation Press, Washington, DC, 1992. Used with permission.

approach to drugs, not of the drug consumption per se. Such was also the case with alcohol prohibition, which nurtured the development of organized crime, created widespread disrespect for the law, reduced tax revenue, made millions of otherwise law-abiding citizens criminals, eliminated the positive aspects of moderate consumption, and hurt the economic interests of those who had been involved in the production and distribution of alcohol (Lemert, 1967).

Supply reduction approaches have been at the heart of present and past efforts. The main thrust of these has been deterrence, defined and implemented via legislation with the intent of disruption of distribution networks. At best, however, the U.S. government estimates that enforcement agencies intercept only 15% of illicit drugs that enter this country. The decline in marijuana production in South America in recent years has been concomitant with increased production of marijuana in the United States and of coca in South America (Montagne, 1992). As Montagne (1992) notes, "It appears that all phases of illicit drug trafficking have expanded greatly since the early 1980s . . . and this illicit industry shows no signs of diminishing" (p. 339). We have thus relied on an approach that encourages the production of illicit drugs. In discussing government drug activities, Smart (1992) argues:

The effect of all these activities on the prices of illegal drugs is the same as for agricultural commodities. . . . The effect upon the bottom line (profit) of drug traffickers within the United States is spectacular. Indeed, there is no entrepreneurial activity in the capitalist world which our society rewards with comparable generosity. The war on drugs therefore functions, in practical fact, as a price support program for the enrichment of drug industrialists. (p. 4)

Smart (1992) also notes that years of market activity have demonstrated that drug demand is inelastic to price, and the quantity of a commodity that suppliers put on a market varies concomitantly with price. Thus, increased prices have not reduced the use or demand for illegal drugs. High prices have, however, meant huge profits for the illegal drug industry. Smart (1992) succinctly states, "The essential fact that explains the failure of the war on drugs . . . is that the economic function of the war on drugs is to stimulate and energize production at all levels of the illicit drug industry" (p. 3). Given these realities, future policy must change in substantial ways. The very real motivations behind human drug consumption and free marketplace economics must be fully considered. Consideration must be given to both decriminalization and legalization options.

ADOLESCENT DRUG CONSUMPTION

Any national drug policy must consider levels of consumption. As noted earlier, millions of American youth have experimented with alcohol or some other psychoactive drug—evidence indicates that young Americans use more drugs than adolescents in all of the more developed countries in the world (National Institute on Drug Abuse [NIDA], 1987). Table 10.2 presents data from a survey of 15,000 high school seniors in the United States in 1991. Note that the percentages of students who "ever used," "used in the last 30 days," and "used daily for last 30 days" for certain drugs are reported. "Ever used" is an attempt to measure any exposure to or experimentation with a drug. "Used in the last 30 days" is an attempt to pick up ongoing consumption. "Used daily for last 30 days" is an attempt to pick up abusive behavior. It is obvious from Table 10.2 that the most commonly consumed drugs by adolescents are alcohol and

TABLE 10.2 Percentage of High School Seniors (Class of 1991) Reporting
Use of Seven Types of Drugs

Drug	Ever Used	Used in Last 30 Days	Used Daily for Last 30 Days
Alcohol	88	54	3.6
Cigarettes	63	28	18.5
Marijuana/hashish	37	14	2.0
Inhalants	18	2	0.2
Stimulants	15	3	0.2
Hallucinogens	10	2	0.1
Cocaine (all)	8	1	0.1
"Crack"	3	1	0.1

SOURCE: From "Summary of 1991 Drug Study Results" by L. Johnston, J. Bachman, & P. O'Malley. Press release from Institute for Social Research, University of Michigan, 1992.

tobacco, both of which are "legal" drugs, at least for adults. Almost 90% of seniors have tried alcohol and 63% have tried cigarettes. No illicit drug even comes close to these drugs in frequency of use. Marijuana, the most widely used illicit drug, had been tried by 37% of seniors, but only 14% had used it in the past 30 days. For the remaining illicit drugs, consumption was much less frequent. For all the media attention applied to it, crack (i.e., a smokable form of cocaine) was tried by only 3% of these students. These data indicate that ongoing illicit drug consumption is *not* the norm for high school seniors.

Another notable pattern emerges from these data. There are dramatic reductions in the percentage of usage as you move from ever used to used in the past 30 days to daily use. For example, though 88% had tried alcohol, 54% had used it in the past month, and only 3.6% had drunk it daily. For the illicit drugs, excluding marijuana, 3% or less had used any category of these in the past 30 days; and daily use of these drugs was much less common. Daily use of hallucinogens and cocaine, for example, was one tenth of one percent, and it was two tenths of one percent for inhalants and stimulants. As the Drug Abuse Council (1980) has noted, "A failure to distinguish between the misuse and the use of drugs creates the impression that all use is misuse or 'drug abuse' . . . the number of young Americans who are in serious personal difficulties because of the misuse of drugs is relatively small" (pp. 5-6). As young people grow into late adolescence and early adulthood (i.e., 18 to 25 years) monthly consumption of these drugs increases a small amount (NIDA, 1991). As individuals continue to age and progress through adulthood, consumption of drugs continually declines. These realities of drug consumption should be reassuring. Although experimentation among adolescents is relatively common, abuse is rare. Most youth will experiment briefly, if at all, then stop. Those who continue to use will do so "occasionally" and most will not suffer negative consequences.

Some risk taking is generally considered normal for adolescents: a developmental behavior individuals go through prior to the onset of adulthood. If drug use is viewed as a risk-taking behavior, its occurrence among adolescents should not be surprising, and for some adolescents it may indeed be a normal, transitional behavior. Shedler and Block's (1990) longitudinal study found that adolescents who experiment with drugs are, on the average, more mentally healthy than those who do not. In such a context, punishing such behavior with severe, criminal sanctions seems inappropriate.

The real priority for our society should be how to affect the relatively small number of adolescents who do go on to develop drug-abuse behavior. Unfortunately, recent policies have primarily targeted casual/recreational users (APHA, 1992). The stated federal government policy of "zero tolerance" during the 1980s targeted the wrong people, thereby committing a double mistake. It harmed individuals (i.e., drug users) who were not hurting themselves or society while at the same time it largely avoided the much more difficult but appropriate task of preventing and treating abuse.

SOCIAL POLICY EXPERIMENTS
IN CONTROLLING DRUG CONSUMPTION

Given the failure of past and present national prohibition policies and their negative side effects, are there other options of dealing with drug issues? A number of alternative approaches have been proposed and attempted within the United States and other countries.

During the 1970s numerous states decriminalized the possession of small amounts of marijuana for personal use. Monitoring of consumption patterns detected no appreciable increase in marijuana use in these areas. In Oregon, for example, during the 4 years after decriminalization the percentage of adults classified as current users went from 9% to 10%. Also, the percentage of adults older than 18 who had "ever used" marijuana went from 19% to 25% (Ray & Ksir, 1990). It should be noted that marijuana use went up during the same period all across America, including states that did not decriminalize. Additional surveys also indicated the primary reason people chose either not to begin use or to stop using marijuana was a lack of interest, not criminal sanctions. This behavioral phenomenon is consistent with the experience of New York during the 1960s, where a get-tough policy on drugs was implemented. Research indicated little change in consumption rates of illicit drugs following these new, harsher laws. Criminal sanctions apparently are not the main reason many people do not use drugs (Drug Abuse Council, 1980). Passage of laws such as decriminalization, however, appears to reduce law enforcement and judicial costs to governments. For example, it is estimated that California saved $95 million a year between 1976 and 1985 due to its decriminalization efforts (Aldrich & Mikuriya, 1988).

To date, the Netherlands is the only country to have decriminalized cannabis products through its policy of normalization. Possession of up to 30 grams of a cannabis product is a misdemeanor and prosecution policy allows for considerable discretion. Studies show these policies have not encouraged more use. Only 4.2% of 10- to 18-year-olds have "ever tried" cannabis, less than 2% use it occasionally, and only 1 in 1,000 is a daily user (Engelsman, 1989). As Engelsman (1989) states, "The Dutch have been pragmatic and have tried to avoid a situation in which consumers of cannabis products suffer more damage from criminal proceedings than from the use of the drug itself" (p. 45). In addition, the policy has effectively kept cannabis distribution out of the hands of hardened criminals. Trebach (1989) makes the following comparison:

> Amsterdam has a population of roughly 670,000. In Washington, DC, the population is roughly 622,000. Amsterdam has a lot of drug trade in the street. In 1988, the city had approximately 40 murders, one third of them connected with the drug trade. Last year Washington, DC had 372—60 to 80 percent connected with the drug trade. (p. 225)

It is also notable that between 1981 and 1987 the average age of heroin and cocaine users in the Netherlands rose from 26 to 36 years.

It would appear their policy does not encourage youth to consume drugs and may in fact do the opposite.

Data for Amsterdam and New York City are available on cocaine consumption. According to Sandwijk, Westerterp, and Musterd (1988), lifetime "ever use" of cocaine in Amsterdam was 6.1% in 1987 and usage within the past year was 1.7%. In New York, lifetime prevalence was 13% in 1986 and usage within the past 6 months was 6% (Frank, Marel, Schmeidler, & Maranda, 1988). As Cohen (1989) notes: "A low level of policing does not necessarily provoke high levels of life time prevalence. . . . These data support a view that increased law enforcement does not necessarily go hand in hand with decreasing prevalence" (pp. 15-16).

In many counties in several states in the United States another social experiment has been going on for decades, namely, local alcohol prohibition. Currently, alcohol sales are prohibited in 406 counties in 15 states (Distilled Spirits Council of the United States, 1985). Research on these regions shows varying results but does not lend strong support to the efficacy of local prohibition in reducing negative consequences of alcohol abuse (Colon, 1981, 1983; Hoadley, Fuchs, & Holder, 1984). Wilson and Nicholson (1989) studied teenage alcohol consumption in wet versus dry counties in Kentucky. Data were collected on 38,964 students (i.e., grades 7 through 12) in all 77 dry and 41 wet counties in the state. Results showed 69.3% of students in wet counties and 61.7% in dry counties had "ever drank," indicating a small reduction in experimentation within dry counties. No difference was found between the two populations, however, in terms of age at first onset for drinking, the percentage who were daily drinkers, and the occurrence of personal and social problems due to alcohol consumption. These results suggest that county-level alcohol prohibition has little value in discouraging adolescent drinking.

In 1980 the Drug Abuse Council argued, "We propose a major research effort to analyze the actual effects of drug laws and drug law enforcement on personal decisions to use or not use illicit drugs" (p. 17). Although, as the aforementioned review indicates, research has progressed since then, more knowledge is still needed. As previously discussed, current policies are largely ineffective and maladaptive. The United States should thus implement a dramatically different drug policy along with substantial, ongoing research and monitoring efforts.

The primary goal of this new policy should be to minimize the harm and dysfunction that occurs out of the misuse and abuse of psychoactive drugs, both licit and illicit. Programs and policies should also respect the delicate balance between individuals' responsibilities to society and citizens' constitutional rights to freedom and happiness.

A PROACTIVE LEGALIZATION
APPROACH TO DRUG POLICY

As Duncan (1992) states, "Truly effective primary prevention of drug abuse must begin with a clear recognition of the distinction between use and abuse of drugs" (p. 319). Drug abuse, instead of describing a category of unhealthy behaviors, has been society's method of differentiating between illicit and licit drug consumption (Drug Abuse Council, 1980). Real "drug abuse" is the result of not only what drug is taken but who takes it, how much is taken, by what route, and in what setting it is taken. A handful of aspirin taken by a person with a peptic ulcer is misuse or abuse. Heroin, regardless of its status as illegal, is used occasionally by a large number of people without addiction developing (Duncan, 1992; Zinberg, 1979).

Given the failure of drug prohibition, the very real motivations behind human drug consumption, and the distinction between the majority of people who use drugs and the minority who abuse them, the decriminalization and eventual legalization of drugs for adults is warranted. For adolescents, drugs should be decriminalized. Numerous authors have described variations of nonprohibitionistic policies and the reader is referred to them for a broad societal look at these alternatives (Nadleman, 1992; Nicholson, 1992; Smart, 1992).

In the postlegalization United States the negative sequelae of drug laws (see Table 10.1) should be greatly reduced or eliminated. Dramatic reductions in drug-related law enforcement costs concomitant with increased tax revenues from the sale of previously illicit drugs should produce a large net economic gain to all levels of government. Not only would revised laws save money, as noted earlier, but, for example, the taxation of cannabis alone could yield billions of dollars a year. This would provide a large pool of new money for drug education, drug-abuse prevention, and drug treatment.

What would these programs be like in this new environment? As Duncan (1992) states, "I . . . see legalization as a liberating opportunity for drug abuse prevention. I see it lifting the dead hand of legalism from drug education " (p. 137). Programs would be more effectively targeted toward "Harm Reduction" (Clements, Cohen, & Kay, 1990; Duncan & Gold, 1982; Engs, 1979; Vogler & Bartz, 1982). Duncan (1992) further elaborates:

> The key to such a strategy is to focus on strengths rather than weaknesses. In the context of legalization, the twin goals of drug education will be to enhance the student's [sic] ability to make their own choices about drug taking and to enhance their abilities to act wisely and well on those choices. Some of them will choose to take the currently illegal drugs . . . but the important thing is whether they use or abuse the drug. If they don't abuse it, then they aren't hurt—no one is hurt. It will be our task to help them keep their drug taking healthy, to help them keep it within limits, and to help them avoid the adverse consequences which can arise from uninformed use. (pp. 321-322)

Such a strategy is not a hands-off approach to our drug problems. Rather than a "Get Tough" policy, however, it is a "Get Smart" one. It says, let's focus on abuse and get serious about eliminating it. Although drug abusers, including adolescent ones, are in the minority they still represent millions of people living very painful existences. Added to these are the tens of millions of family members, friends, co-workers, and so forth who are also hurt by this abuse.

Within this postlegalization environment, laws, strong regulations, and law enforcement would still have key roles. Law enforcement agencies, in lieu of current programs of national/international interception, interdiction, and eradication could focus efforts on *public safety* and the prevention of violent crime. For example, we could dramatically increase the number of "cops on the beat." Strategies toward tobacco, the only major drug *abused* by the majority who consume it, could be toughened, particularly as they relate to children and adolescents. Each of the following proposals offers the possibility of reducing teenage smoking: (a) banning vending machines, (b) substantially raising sales taxes, (c) banning all advertising, and (d) making schools "tobacco-free" environments.

Concomitant with the above strategies, ongoing monitoring of adolescent drug consumption should continue and be expanded. As with any new public policy, not all outcomes and possible side effects are predictable. Because the major reasons why people choose to use or not use drugs are not related to laws, I do not expect a significant increase in adolescent drug use. Alcohol will remain the drug of choice as it has been across the planet and throughout human history. Alcohol's social lubrication qualities along with its connection with eating will keep it popular with humans because we are very social beings. Shooting up heroin, whether at dinner or at a party, is not going to be a realistic option for most people. Although adolescent experimentation may initially increase due to easier access, there is no need to assume abuse will increase, especially if students are receiving drug education, as described earlier, along with comprehensive mental health education. Duncan (1992) states: "We also need to recognize the importance of self-esteem, affectionate relations and stress coping skills in the avoidance of drug abuse by those who choose to take drugs. . . . Prevention of drug abuse is inextricably tied to the promotion of mental health" (p. 321).

We may in fact realize a reduction in both recreational use and abuse. Effective education can provide individuals with adaptive short- and long-term coping skills for managing stress and life issues in lieu of taking drugs to deal with personal pain. As the "risk-taking" status of taking certain drugs is reduced (i.e., they are no longer illegal and thus not taboo), their attractiveness may diminish for some adolescents.

In conclusion, hundreds of years of drug prohibition have revealed its bankruptcy as social policy. It is time we as a society honestly face the realities of our drug consumption and the inevitable availability of psychoactive substances. Primary prevention and education strategies offer the real possibility of impacting on drug abuse in ways that laws and prisons have been unable to do. At some time in the future, drug consumption will fall into its proper and rather small, inconsequential place among the broad array of human behaviors: namely, the occasional or momentary lapse of reason in a lifetime of predominately rational living.

REFERENCES

Aldrich, M., & Mikuriya, T. (1988). Savings on California marijuana law enforcement cost attributable to the Moscone Act of 1976—a summary. *Journal of Psychoactive Drugs, 20,* 75.

American Public Health Association. (1989). *A public health response to the war on drugs: Reducing alcohol, tobacco and other drug problems among the nation's youth* (Policy Statement No. 8817). Washington, DC: Author.

American Public Health Association. (1992). *The war on drugs: Failure and fantasy* (Policy statement). Washington, DC: Author.

Burnham, J. (1968). New perspectives on the prohibition "experiment" of the 1920s. *Journal of Social History, 2,* 51-68.

Clements, I., Cohen, J., & Kay, J. (1990). *Taking drugs seriously: A manual of harm reduction education on drugs.* Liverpool: Healthwise Helpline.

Cloninger, C., Bohman, M., & Sigvardsson, S. (1981). Inheritance of alcohol abuse. *Archives of General Psychology, 38,* 861-868.

Cohen, P. (1989). *Cocaine use in Amsterdam in nondeviant subcultures.* Amsterdam: University of Amsterdam.

Collins, A., & deFiebre, R. (1990). *A review of genetic influences on psychoactive substance use and abuse in treatment choices for alcoholism and substance abuse.* Lexington, MA: Lexington Books.

Colon, I. (1981). Alcohol availability and cirrhosis mortality rates by gender and race. *American Journal of Public Health, 71,* 1325-1328.

Colon, I. (1983). County-level prohibition and alcohol related fatal motor vehicle accidents. *Journal of Safety Research, 14,* 101-104.

Distilled Spirits Council of the United States. (1985). *Annual statistical review 1984/85.* Washington, DC: Author.

The Drug Abuse Council. (1980). *The facts about drug abuse.* New York: Free Press.

Duncan, D. (1992). Drug abuse prevention in post-legalization America: What could it be like? *The Journal of Primary Prevention, 12,* 317-322.

Duncan, D., & Gold, R. (1982). *Drugs and the whole person.* New York: John Wiley.

Emerson, H. (1932). *Alcohol and man.* New York: Arno Press.

Engelsman, E. (1989, Summer). *The Dutch model. New Perspectives Quarterly,* pp. 44-45.

Engs, R. (1979). *Responsible drug and alcohol use.* New York: Macmillan.

Frank, B., Marel, R., Schmeidler, J., & Maranda, M. (1988). *Statewide household survey of substance abuse among adults in New York state.* New York: NY State Division of Substance Abuse Services.

Goodwin, D. (1971). Is alcoholism hereditary: A review and critique. *Archives of General Psychology, 25,* 545-549.

Gusfield, J. (1976). The prevention of drinking problems. In W. Fulstead, J. Rossi, & M. Keller (Eds.), *Alcohol and alcoholic problems: New thinking and new directions* (pp. 267-291). Cambridge, MA: Ballinger.

Hoadley, J., Fuchs, B., & Holder, H. (1984). The effect of alcohol beverage restriction on consumption: A 25 year longitudinal analysis. *American Journal of Alcohol and Drug Abuse, 10,* 375-401.

Huber, E., & Omenn, G. (1981). Evidence of genetic predisposition to alcoholic cirrhosis and psychosis: Twin concordance for alcoholism and its end points by zygosity among male veterans. *Alcoholism, 5,* 207-215.

Irwin, S. (1973). A rational approach to drug abuse prevention. *Contemporary Drug Problems, 2,* 3-46.

It doesn't have to be like this. (1989, September). *The Economist,* pp. 21-24.

Johnston, L., Bachman, J., & O'Malley, P. (1992). Summary of 1991 drug study results [Press release from Institute for Social Research, University of Michigan].

Lemert, E. M. (1967). *Social problems and social control*. Englewood Cliffs, NJ: Prentice Hall.

Marshall, M., & Marshall, L. (1990). *Silent voices speak: Women and prohibition in Truk*. Belmont, CA: Wadsworth.

Montagne, M. (1992). Societal consequences of international illicit drug trafficking and supply-reduction efforts. In A. S. Trebach & K. B. Zeese (Eds.), *Strategies for change: New directions in drug policy* (pp. 337-343). Washington, DC: Drug Policy Foundation Press.

Nadelmann, E. (1992, Summer). Thinking seriously about alternatives to drug prohibition. *Daedalus, 121*, 85-132.

National Institute on Drug Abuse. (1987). *National trends in drug use and related factors among American high school students and young adults, 1975-1986* (DHHS Publication No. AMD-87-1535). Washington, DC: Government Printing Office.

National Institute on Drug Abuse. (1991). *National household survey on drug abuse: Population estimates 1990* (DHHS Publication No. ADM-91-1732). Washington, DC: Government Printing Office.

Nicholson, T. (1992). The primary prevention of illicit drug problems: An argument for decriminalization and legalization. *The Journal of Primary Prevention, 12*, 275-288.

Ray, O., & Ksir, C. (1990). *Drugs, society and human behavior*. Boston: Times Mirror/ Mosby College Publisher.

Sandwijk, J., Westerterp, S., & Musterd, S. (1988). Het gebruik van legale en illegale drugs in Amsterdam; verslag van een prevalentie-onderzoek onder de bevolking van 12 jaan en ouder. In P. Cohen (Ed.), *Cocaine use in Amsterdam* (p. 15). Amsterdam: University of Amsterdam.

Schlaadt, R., & Shannon, P. (1990). *Drugs* (3rd ed.). Englewood Cliffs, NJ: Prentice Hall.

Shedler, J., & Block, J. (1990). Adolescent drug use and psychological health: A longitudinal inquiry. *American Psychologist, 45*, 612-630.

Smart, D. (1992). *An appeal for federal government interposition in the U.S. drug market*. [Available from Donald Smart, 1405 Glendale Ave., Berkeley, CA, 94708]

Trebach, A. (1989). Why not decriminalize? In C. Ladley (Ed.), *Drugs, society and behavior* (pp. 222-225). Guilford, CT: Dushkin Publishing.

U.S. Department of Health and Human Services. (1989). *Smoking tobacco and health* (DHHS Publication No. CDC 87-8397). Washington, DC: Government Printing Office.

Vogler, R., & Bartz, W. (1982). *The better way to drink*. Oakland, CA: New Harbinger Publications.

Wilson, R., & Nicholson, T. (1989). Teenage drinking in wet vs. dry counties. *Southern Health Update, 10*, 9-10.

Zinberg, N. (1979). Nonaddictive opiate use. In R. Dupont, A. Goldstein, & J. O'Donnell (Eds.), *Handbook on drug abuse*. Washington, DC: Government Printing Office.

11. Adolescent Substance Misuse: Personal Reflections on a Theme

Thomas P. Gullotta

Child and Family Agency
of Southeastern Connecticut

In the 10 chapters leading to this conclusion, the authors of this volume have striven to present the reader with a comprehensive overview of substance misuse in adolescence. In this epilogue I will share with the reader personal themes that emerged for me as I reviewed and edited the work of this group of very talented scholars. An *epilogue* is commonly understood to mean a short speech spoken directly to the audience at the end of a play or literary work. The brevity of my remarks certainly will meet that qualification. And although neither I nor the authors of this volume believe that this volume will ever be performed, still, this volume is a play.

How so? Consider the themes that emerged. We learned that concerns over substance misuse are not unique to our times. We learned also that factors other than harmfulness often influence regulatory actions concerning substances. Economic factors, racism, and ethnic hatreds have shaped American drug policy as much as the real—or is that perceived—harm of illicit substances.

In the chapter by Elaine Norman (Chapter 2) other themes developed. A pattern of reoccurring risk factors emerged. Numbered among these were a difficult childhood temperament, low frustration tolerance, impulsive and aggressive behavior, inability to delay gratification, sensation-seeking, and high risk-taking. Other risk factors included childhood depression, school failure, and low religiosity. Norman discussed the developing literature seeking to identify protective factors that shield youth from substance misuse. Resiliency factors included an easygoing disposition, intelligence, an internal locus of control, positive self-esteem, social problem-solving skills, empathy, humor, adaptive distancing skills, and a future-oriented focus.

In Chapter 3 by Sandra Turner, family factors were examined. The onerous influences of poverty, community decay, and familial discord were discussed as powerful contributing factors for adolescent substance misuse. Parents who demonstrate little warmth, exercised limited parental supervision, are abusive, or engage in dysfunctional patterns of behavior increase the probability of adolescent substance misuse. The death of a parent before a child reaches age 11 was also identified as a contributing factor. Turner described the protective family factors that help shield youth from substance misuse. Elements enhancing adolescent resiliency included an ongoing emphatic relationship with an adult and a supportive home environment with parental expectations that included good behavior, family involvement, family participation, and nondrug use. The importance of parental role modeling was also stressed.

David F. Duncan and Rick Petosa in Chapter 4 approached the subject by examining social and community factors. They pointed out that substance use is a normative behavior for adolescents that is socially learned and developmentally functional. Contrary to popular belief, the purchase of substances other than alcohol is most often from a friend, older sibling, or parent to the adolescent. Alcohol is most commonly acquired from parents, with or without their knowledge. They observed that youth live in a society that promotes chemical solutions to problems and misleads youth as to the dangers of substance use. Finally, they noted that although many substance-abusing youth can control their use of substances, other deeply involved youth cannot.

In Chapter 5 Patricia Sivo Cole and Roger P. Weissberg applied this body of knowledge to the ill-defined population of urban adolescents. Their review noted the encouraging decade-long decline in the use of substances—with the exception of tobacco and alcohol—by most youth. Of disturbing concern, they detailed the existing methodological difficulties with present research and observed that those youth most likely to misuse substances are not likely to be counted in these national surveys. Furthermore, these uncounted youth disproportionately are likely to be both poor and belong to ethnic or racial minority groups.

Focusing on rural youth, Fay E. Reilly and her colleagues identified the high levels of substance misuse that occur in rural communities. Peer and family influences were recognized as powerful influences contributing to substance misuse. Methodological shortcomings with research on this population were also identified.

Paul V. Trad's contribution (Chapter 7) and that of Annette U. Rickel and Evvie Becker-Lausen (Chapter 8) not only detailed the pharmacologic aspects of selected substances but discussed the current state of knowledge regarding the effectiveness of therapeutic interventions. Trad's discussion is a striking reminder of the deleterious consequences of nicotine and alcohol abuse. These are two legal substances that yearly cost society billions of dollars in health care expenses, criminal and civil judicial actions, and lost productivity. Rickel and Becker-Lausen discussed the growing acknowledgment of the failure of the War on Drugs and described the factors that are unique to intervening with adolescents. The authors also identified the paucity of evaluation effectiveness research in this area.

In Chapter 9, Aleta L. Meyer reviewed the prevention literature for clues on how to reduce the incidence of substance misuse in adolescence. Her search largely proved futile for one underlying reason: the failure of most programs to intervene in a comprehensive and integrated fashion using all of prevention's available technology.

In Chapter 10, Thomas Nicholson challenged current public opinion to offer legalization as an alternative to the current patchwork of policies in existence. Reiterating many of the themes discussed in other chapters, Nicholson used them to argue for informed and intelligent decision making in a society in which harm reduction would replace prohibition and the illegal and profitable black market that accompanies prohibition.

Collectively, the authors of this volume cry out in different voices for readers to listen to the needs of youth and their families. Like the voices of a Greek chorus, they say do not penalize youth and families for their ethnic and racial differences. Strive to minimize their weaknesses and to nourish the opportunities for their growth. Encourage the development of individual responsibility. Support families, for healthy families nurture healthy youth. Provide opportunities for youth to belong, to be valued, and to be able to make a meaningful contribution to the multiple communities (school, family, peer group, neighborhood) in which they live.

From their observations, I am reminded that youth live in families and that families live in communities. Where those communities do not meet the basic needs of life—*and hope and opportunity are two of those most important needs*—young people and their families surely will suffer. And just as surely, they will seek the means to relieve that suffering.

Much has been written recently about "social capital." That is the glue that binds children to their families, families to their neighborhoods, and neighborhoods to their village, town, or city (see, e.g., Coleman, 1988). The substance of this glue—whether it is called resiliency or social competency or described by its individual ingredients of self-esteem, an internal locus of control, or emotionally nurturing, involved, and invested parents—is increasingly absent among the economically disadvantaged whether locked into the inner city or the rural hamlet.

Emotionally prosperous youth and families live in healthy communities. These are societies in which residents live as a part of and not apart from the community. These are societies in which work can be found and wages earned that provide food and housing and offer hope for an improved tomorrow.

Finally, I heard some authors urging an openness to considering new understandings of the problem. They ask us to be intellectually and empirically willing to weigh the cost of current substance-abuse strategies against the benefits and costs of different paradigms. They and Joycelyn Elders (1993), Surgeon General of the U.S. Public Health Service, are correct in raising the question of whether current substance-abuse policies are the best practice.

These are the voices—the words—this volume speaks to me. May others hear them as well.

REFERENCES

Coleman, J. S. (1988). Social capital in the creation of human capital. *American Journal of Sociology, 94* (Suppl.), S95-S120.

Elders, J. (1993, December 8). Elders says legalizing drug use would reduce U.S. crime rate. *The Day*, p. A14.

Index

About the Editors

Thomas P. Gullotta is CEO of one of the nation's oldest children's service agencies, the Child and Family Agency of Southeastern Connecticut. A nationally recognized authority in the fields of primary prevention and adolescence, he holds an academic appointment at Eastern Connecticut State University in the psychology and education departments. He is the founding editor of the *Journal of Primary Prevention*, serves as a general series book editor for *Advances in Adolescent Development*, and is the senior book series editor for *Issues in Children's and Families' Lives*. He currently serves on the editorial boards of the *Journal of Early Adolescence* and *Adolescence*.

Gerald R. Adams is a Professor in the Department of Family Studies at the University of Guelph. He is a Fellow of the American Psychological Association and has been awarded the James D. Moran Research Award from the American Home Economics Association. He currently has editorial assignments with the *Journal of Adolescence*, *Journal of Primary Prevention*, *Journal of Early Adolescence*, and *Social Psychology Quarterly*.

Raymond Montemayor is Associate Professor of Psychology at The Ohio State University. His research interests include parent-adolescent relations, conduct disorders, behavioral approaches to the study of adolescence, peer relations during adolescence, and adolescent substance abuse. He is Associate Editor for the *Journal of Early Adolescence* and is an editorial board member for the *Journal of Adolescent Research*.

About the Contributors

Sheila Allen was the Project Director for the Regional Action Partnership, a drug and alcohol prevention demonstration project funded by the Center for Substance Abuse Prevention (CSAP) (Grant #1-H86 SP 04009) when Chapter 6 was written.

Evvie Becker-Lausen, Ph.D., currently with Boston Children's Hospital and Harvard Medical School, was a 1992-1993 Congressional Fellow sponsored by the American Psychological Association, working for the U.S. Senate Labor Subcommittee on Children, chaired by Senator Christopher J. Dodd. A member of APA's Committee on Legal Issues, she also serves on the Advisory Board for Connecticut's Children's Law Center. Prior to receiving her doctorate in Clinical Psychology (University of Connecticut, 1991), she was a Public Information Officer for the National Aeronautics and Space Administration and received a NASA Special Achievement Award in 1985. She was a 1991-1992 postdoctoral fellow at Harbor-UCLA Medical Center.

Gary M. Blau (Ph.D., Clinical Psychology) is currently the Director of Mental Health for the Connecticut Department of Children and Families. He was formerly the Director of Clinical Services for the Child and Family Agency of Southeastern Connecticut. Since receiving his Ph.D. from Auburn University (Auburn, Alabama) in 1988, he has worked in children's mental health with a primary emphasis on issues of victimization, child custody, permanency planning, and innovative service models. In his capacity as Director of Mental Health he is committed to developing comprehensive systems of care that focus on the individualized needs of children and families. He serves on the editorial board of the *Journal of Primary Prevention* and has numerous publications and presentations in the areas of child custody, primary prevention, and clinical service delivery.

Patricia Sivo Cole is currently on the staff of the Newington Children's Hospital School, where she works with socially and emotionally disturbed children and adolescents and their families. She received her doctorate in Clinical Psychology from Yale University in 1992. Her dissertation explored the relationships between stress, coping, and adolescent substance use and delinquency. Her current interests include the prevention and treatment of substance use in children and adolescents and group therapy with young children.

David F. Duncan is currently a Research Fellow at the Brown University Center for Alcohol and Addiction Studies. He is the author of more than 100 papers published in scientific journals, of *Epidemiology: Basis for Disease Prevention and Health Promotion*, and of *Drugs and the Whole Person*. He has been Associate Professor of Health Science at the State University of New York at Brockport, Professor of Health Education at Southern Illinois University, and Visiting Professor of Health and Environmental Research at the University of Cologne in West Germany. He has extensive clinical experience with delinquent and drug-abusing youth and adults.

Jingwei Gao was the Evaluator for the Regional Action Partnership, a drug and alcohol prevention demonstration project funded by the Center for Substance Abuse Prevention (CSAP) (Grant #1-H86 SP 04009). She obtained her master's degree in Sociology from the University of Kentucky.

Carl G. Leukefeld is Professor of Psychiatry and Behavioral Science as well as Director of the Center on Drug and Alcohol Abuse Research and a Co-Investigator of the Center for Prevention Research at the University of Kentucky in Lexington. He was with the National Institute on Drug Abuse and the U.S. Public Health Service for more than 23 years. He has coedited several books and monographs, is currently working on one, and has written and made presentations on AIDS, criminal justice, prevention, and treatment.

Aleta L. Meyer recently compled her doctoral work at The Pennsylvania State University, with a specialization in Human Development Intervention Research. She received her B.S. in Human Ecology in 1986 from the University of Tennessee and her M.S. in Human

Development and Family Studies from Penn State in 1991. She is both Director of Training and Co-Director of Evaluation for GOAL as well as Co-Investigator at Virginia Commonwealth University on a Center for Disease Control grant developed to evaluate a primary prevention program for violence. Her future interests are in developing empowering evaluation methods for school-based life skills programs; evaluating the impact of outdoor adventure programs on goal-directed behavior; and developing a violence prevention program, utilizing life skills simultaneously at personal, global, and environmental levels.

Thomas Nicholson is a Professor of Community Health at Western Kentucky University. He received his Ph.D. from Southern Illinois University in Health Education and his M.P.H. from the University of Texas School of Public Health. At WKU he has primary responsibility for Epidemiology and Biostatistics education at the graduate level. He provides consultation to local and regional agencies on health promotion activities. His areas of research interest include drug abuse, drug education, and mental health.

Elaine Norman, Ph.D., has been a Professor at Fordham University Graduate School of Social Work for 20 years. Her publications include coauthorship of books on foster care, teenage pregnancy, and women's issues in social work and articles related to adolescent substance-abuse prevention and the profession of social work.

Rick Petosa is currently Associate Professor of Health Promotion and Education at The Ohio State University. His research interests include theory-based explanations of health behavior acquisition and change, particularly among adolescents.

Fay E. Reilly, Ph.D., was a postdoctoral fellow in the Department of Behavioral Science, College of Medicine, University of Kentucky, Lexington, when Chapter 6 was written. She was supported by training grant MH 15730 from the National Institute of Mental Health to the Department of Behavioral Science. She is currently Assistant Professor in the School of Nursing and Health Sciences, University of Alaska, Anchorage. She earned her doctorate in Nursing from the University of Kentucky, College of Nursing, in 1991.

Annette U. Rickel is Professor and Director of the Community Psychology Program at Wayne State University. She received her Ph.D. from the University of Michigan and is a Fellow and Past President of the American Psychological Association's Society for Community Research and Action. A recent American Council on Education Fellow, she is currently a Senior Congressional Fellow and has served on the President's Task Force for National Health Care Reform. She has published three books and more than 55 articles and chapters.

Paul V. Trad, M.D., is Director of the Child and Adolescent Outpatient Department of the New York Hospital-Cornell Medical Center and an Assistant Professor of Psychiatry at the Cornell University Medical College. Vice-President of the Association for the Advancement of Psychotherapy, he is the Editor-in-Chief of the *American Journal of Psychotherapy* and the *Child and Adolescent Multi-Disciplinary Series.* He also serves on the editorial boards of the *Journal of the American Academy of Child and Adolescent Psychiatry, Journal of Contemporary Psychoanalysis, Journal of Child Psychology and Psychiatry, Infant-Toddler Intervention, Journal of Child and Family Studies,* and the *Journal of Substance Abuse Treatment.* A prolific writer, his most recent book is *Short-Term Parent-Infant Psychotherapy.*

Sandra Turner teaches first- and second-year clinical practice as well as courses on substance abuse at Fordham University School of Social Work. For the past 4 years she has been working with Elaine Norman on a grant funded by New York State Office of Alcoholism and Substance Abuse Services investigating "Adolescent Substance Abuse Prevention." Before joining the faculty at Fordham University she worked for 15 years as an administrator and clinician at an alcoholism treatment facility in New York City.

Roger P. Weissberg is Professor of Psychology at the University of Illinois at Chicago. He has published more than 60 research articles and chapters focusing on issues related to preventive interventions with children and adolescents. He has also cowritten nine curricula on school-based programs to promote social competence and prevent high-risk, antisocial problem behaviors. Formerly, he was director of Yale University's NIMH-funded Prevention Research Training Program for Predoctoral and Postdoctoral Trainees (1989-1993). He is a recipient of the William T. Grant Foundation's 5-year Faculty Scholars Award in Children's Mental Health, the Connecticut Psychological Association's 1992 Award for Distinguished Psychological Contribution in the Public Interest, and the National Mental Health Association's 1992 Lela Rowland Prevention Award.

What factors contribute to the misuse of drugs and alcohol among teens? Do teen's economic background or ethnicity play a role in their avoidance or involvement in substance misuse? **Substance Misuse in Adolescence** explores these questions and untangles widely held beliefs about substance abuse issues using historical, clinical, and research data. This volume begins with an introduction to the social history of tobacco, alcohol, marijuana, cocaine, and heroin. It then examines individual, family, peer, and community variables that may contribute to substance misuse as well as resiliency factors that enable some teens to avoid such problems. It also discusses substance misuse in rural and urban settings, the pharmacological effects of specific substances, and current treatment approaches for substance misusing youth. It also includes coverage of drug legalization issues and a lucid discussion of the current effectiveness of various prevention programs.

Researchers, graduate students, and practitioners who want the latest synthesis and view on adolescent substance misuse will find this volume a useful addition to their libraries and classrooms.